Guide to Denver Second Edition

Architecture

The Denver Architectural Foundation

Guide to Denver Architecture

Second Edition

Mary Voelz Chandler

FULCRUM
Golden, Colorado

Welcome

Welcome to the second edition of the *Guide to Denver Architecture*. The Denver Architectural Foundation is excited that you are about to embark upon a wonderful journey of inspirational discovery and delight. The first edition of the guide was published to celebrate the convening of the 2001 National Convention of the American Institute of Architects (AIA) in Denver, the first national gathering of the organization in Colorado since the late 1960s. This second edition was created to commemorate the AIA's 2013 National Convention, also held in Denver.

There are numerous reasons why a convocation of the world's foremost architects has occurred in the "Queen City on the Plains" twice in such a short timeframe. Denver has quietly evolved as one of the truly great American cities, a place to live, work, and play. The iconic backdrop of the Rocky Mountains to Denver's articulated skyline is also a very compelling setting. Within the confines of that skyline one will uncover the results of highly visionary and skillfully responsive design solutions, orchestrated by a group of talented architects who have chosen to practice their skills in Denver.

The Denver Architectural Foundation is a non-profit, tax-exempt 501(c)(3) organization, established in 1991 by AIA Denver. The DAF has subsequently developed independent of the AIA, with a specific mission to increase public awareness and appreciation for architecture and its influence on our quality of life through education, participation, and advocacy for excellence. The DAF believes an informed public will encourage and, in fact, ensure that, as the city continues to develop, newly constructed and restored buildings will exhibit designs superior to what might have been without the foundation's continuing influence. To learn more about the Denver Architectural Foundation, please access our website at www.denverarchitecture.org.

I am confident you will enjoy and be truly inspired as you discover more about the history and composition of our wonderful city as told by its buildings, landscape, and vistas.

Dennis R. Humphries, AIA
Past President, Denver Architectural Foundation

International Standard Book Number: 978-1-938486-47-0

Designer: Craig Rouse, R Design LLC, Denver, CO

Published by:
Fulcrum Publishing
4690 Table Mountain Drive, Suite 100
Golden, Colorado 80403
(800) 992-2908
www.fulcrumbooks.com

Printed in the United States of America

Library of Congress Cataloging-in-Publication Data
Chandler, Mary Voelz.
    Guide to Denver architecture / Mary Voelz Chandler. — Second Edition.
       pages cm
    Includes index.
    ISBN 978-1-938486-47-0
    1. Architecture—Colorado—Denver—Guidebooks. 2. Denver (Colo.)—Buildings, structures, etc.—Guidebooks. 3. Denver (Colo.)—Guidebooks. I. Title.
    NA735.D38C49 2013
    720'.9788'83--dc23
                                            2013006989

For more information about other fine books from Fulcrum Publishing, please contact your local bookstore, call us at 1(800) 992-2908, write for our catalog, or visit us online at www.fulcrumbooks.com.

Please Note: The author and publisher disclaim any liability for injury or other damage caused by using this book. Numerous buildings in this book are privately owned, and investigation of any building features not visible from streets or other public spaces might constitute trespassing.

Acknowledgments

The design and production of the second edition of the *Guide to Denver Architecture* would not have been possible without the dedication of a committed volunteer committee from the Denver Architectural Foundation. The book's Editorial Committee, chaired by Dennis Humphries, AIA, principal of Humphries Poli Architects, included Jim Bershof, FAIA, principal of OZ Architecture; Sharon Elfenbein, Historic Preservation Consultant; Alan Gass, FAIA, principal of Alan Gass Architecture and Urban Design; Craig Rouse of R Design LLC; and Mary Voelz Chandler of GH Phipps Construction. It should be noted that our book greatly benefited from the efforts on the first edition, created by many of the same individuals in 2001.

Thanks must also be given to the Board and Executive Committee of the Denver Architectural Foundation, specifically Ted Halsey, AIA, president; Britt Probst, AIA, vice president; Ed Naylor, Esq., secretary; and Bill Tracy, AIA, treasurer. A very special thanks to Ed Naylor, who provided legal input in the negotiations of all the various contracts required to create a book of this nature.

The Denver-based graphic design firm of R Design was selected over several quality teams to design the guide. Craig Rouse's graphic touch has been exemplary. Photographs of the featured buildings were typically submitted by the architects of record. However, Alan Gass, FAIA, must be specifically acknowledged for his sharing of his personal collection of photos documenting more recent historic buildings in addition to his highly accomplished skills to record current contemporary buildings included in the book. Jim Bershof, FAIA, was also critical in the editing of photos and contributed many outstanding images to the book.

Mary Voelz Chandler, formerly the art and architecture critic of the *Rocky Mountain News* was highly instrumental in the success of the second edition of this guide, having conducted countless hours of extensive library research, supplemented by driving or walking nearly every square foot of the city in order to carefully craft written narratives for each of the book's entries. As we said twelve years ago, Mary, thanks for hanging in with us once again!

Finally, we want to thank all the wonderful folks at Fulcrum Publishing, in particular Bob Baron, for pulling this book together and for their ongoing marketing and fulfillment of the book. Another round of thanks goes to Jim Bershof, FAIA, and Alan Gass, FAIA, for their individual contributions describing their respective lifelong careers in the architectural community of Denver.

Author's Acknowledgments

It is impossible to thank everyone who has helped in the research and writing of both editions of this guidebook, but I'll try.

For the 2013 book, which began in late 2010, the World Wide Web made a huge difference – if approached with a certain skepticism. Some basic facts were easy to find, newspaper searches could be done at home, and email was a lifesaver.

My thanks go to many people, including the research geniuses at the Denver Public Library's Department of Western History and Genealogy, Gerhardt Petri, Brit Probst, Rich von Luhrte, Seth Rosenman, Brad Buchanan, Brenda Tierney, the Facilities Department – the Auraria Higher Education Center, Savannah Jameson in the city's Planning Department – and more who helped me secure information.

Research for the 2001 Guide to Denver Architecture began in 1990, and was much more intensive than the 2013 edition.

I'll begin with those veterans who came before, whose books and historic inventories have preserved facts about this city's buildings and evolution. founders of the former Modern Architecture Preservation League, who worked mightily to help Denver residents appreciate the city's wealth of mid-century modern structures – beleaguered though they continue to be. Denver: The Modern City, by Michael Paglia, Diane Wray, and Rodd Wheaton, should be in every library. The same is true of The Mid-Century Modern Home in Denver by Michael Paglia and Diane Wray Tomasso, whose legwork and discernment are unparalleled.

I also must credit Colorado historian Thomas J. Noel, whose prolific solo work, as well as texts in conjunction with Barbara Norgren and Stephen J. Leonard, serve as ground zero for many researchers. Noel's Denver's Larimer Street is a treasure chest of lost buildings and souls.

Of great help was on-the-street research and many shelves worth of publications related to architecture here. They include works by Alice Millett Bakemeier, Allen D. Breck, Sandra Dallas, Carolyn and Don D. Etter, Kenneth R. Fuller, Barbara Gibson, Phil Goodstein, Francine Haber, Edith Eudora Kohl, Jack A. Murphy, Dr. Robert Shikes, Annette L. Student, Millie Van Wyke, Ruth Eloise Wiberg, Nancy L. Widmann, Diane Wilk, and Carter Wiseman. Then there are the dozens of people who have toiled on historic inventories over the decades. You are saints, trying to save a history too often sloughed aside in a place ready to reinvent itself every 30 years.

Along with the numerous architects who spoke with passion and precision about their projects, from Donald Roark and Charles Sink to Richard Crowther and James H. Johnson, I must note others who went the extra mile in research assistance. They include Laird Wendt of the Denver Public Schools, John Thompson of the Denver Health Medical Center, lower downtown historian Barbara Gibson, Noel Copeland of the University of Colorado Health Sciences Center, Greg Kale of the Archdiocese of Denver, and Jane Earle of Denver Water. For the first round, DPL historians and researchers, plus the then-Colorado Historical Society and Historic Denver, Inc., were extremely helpful.

ix

For the first book, I gladly credited my employer, the *Rocky Mountain News*, for its support in this project, as well as giving me the opportunity almost 25 years ago to write about the topics of architecture, planning, preservation, and art. It was a rewarding way to make a living and construct a life. I say "was" because the *News* ceased publication in 2009, shuttered by a newspaper chain based out of town and unaware of the *News's* relationship with Denver and Colorado. After that, however, I had a chance to see the business of design and construction from the inside, first as a writer at Fentress Architects, and now as a writer at GH Phipps Construction Companies. There I have learned how some of the area's most complex buildings actually made it out of the ground – and stayed there. I thank them for what they have taught me about the magic they perform.

Finally, to friends and family who offered encouragement and listened to me complain: without you, there would be no book. This edition put more than 2,000 miles on my car. For the first edition, the numbers ratcheted up to about 40,000 miles. I feel as if I have traveled most of the streets in Denver and many in the metro area. In the end, these have been trips filled with the beauty of discovery, the disappointment of loss, and one flat tire. But it's never been dull.

Mary Voelz Chandler

Contents

Guide to the Guide

The second edition of the *Guide to Denver Architecture* is arguably the most comprehensive portable source of information on Denver's built environment. Information available in other books – biographical, theoretical, leisure oriented, and critical – is deliberately minimized, while details concerning functional requirements, client tastes, and materials are often included. It is intended that this guide will be an educational resource about design and the building of a great city. By singling out examples of well-designed buildings and problematic ones, the guide strives to help people see what is good – and sometimes not so good. It also teaches the public about architecture and its larger context, offering a better understanding of how individual structures combine to create a total environment that may have an even greater impact than single buildings. Our hope is that this book will be not only a guide for the neophyte but also a source for the architecturally aware who are seeking to expand their knowledge. Simply, the purpose of the guide is to encourage the reader to discover, look, at and appreciate the influence of architecture and design in Denver.

About The Denver Architectural Foundation: The Denver Architectural Foundation (DAF) is a nonprofit, tax-exempt 501c3 organization founded in 1991 to support the public programs of the American Institute of Architects (AIA) Denver. In subsequent years the DAF developed more broadly based programs with a specific mission to increase public awareness and appreciation for architecture and its influence on our quality of life through education, participation, and advocacy for excellence. A Board of Directors consisting of architects, contractors, attorneys, historians, educators, politicians, and members of the business community oversee the activities of the DAF. Current programs sponsored by the DAF included the acclaimed CAL (Cleworth Architectural Legacy), intended to bring a curriculum about the importance of design to elementary students in Denver; Doors Open Denver, which opens the doors to buildings for a weekend every April free of charge to the general public to learn more about their city; and Doors Open Hard Hat Tours offering expert tours of buildings currently under construction or recently opened. The Denver Architectural Foundation is a Tier III component of the Scientific and Cultural Facilities District. To learn more about the Denver Architectural Foundation we would direct you to, please visit our website at www.denverarchitecture.org.

The Dawning of the book: The guide was created for, and intended as a legacy of the 2013 National Convention of the American Institute of Architects held in June 2013. This second edition is an updated version of the first edition that also served as a legacy to the 2001 National Convention of the AIA. It is difficult to believe it has already been twelve years since that gathering of the world's greatest architects in our city. The first edition was a similar guide to the region's architectural treasurers, which provided the foundation for this version. The Denver Architectural Foundation provided the support for the book's preparation. Many of the photographs complementing the buildings' descriptions came from the respective architectural firms, their clients, public libraries, and other archives. We have taken every reasonable measure to assure proper credit. A number of photos from the First Edition were skillfully photographed by Charles Cordina AIA and are also included in the second edition. A significant number of new entries were taken by Alan Gass FAIA and Jim Bershof FAIA, working as volunteers traveling tirelessly throughout the metropolitan area to document Denver's architecture.

Criteria for inclusion: The guide is illustrative rather than exhaustive, presenting a representative selection of buildings in addition to the essential landmarks. The highlighted neighborhoods are those recognized by the City and County of Denver.

As a beginning point for selection, the committee reviewed buildings included on the National Register of Historic Places and those designated as Denver Landmarks. The committee also reviewed lists of significant buildings from the Colorado Historical Society, Historic Denver, AIA Denver, AIA Colorado, AIA Western Mountain Region, and AIA National Honor Awards programs, in addition to noted books on local architecture and history. The Editorial Committee reviewed each entry in the first edition, eliminating those buildings that have not weathered well over the past years or for which we found the style of the architect might be better illustrated through the selection of other of their works. In order to pare the size of the book, we also consolidated numerous entries in the first edition into mini-districts.

The criteria for selecting entries to the book included not only the quality of their design but also the degree to which they exemplified a style, a trend, or a functional type, or just stood out as unusual. Other important factors included visibility, historical significance, and the "I like that" factor. Practical considerations included geographical fit within the neighborhoods: Good examples of common building types, or projects by significant architects, that were centrally located were often chosen over those in more remote locations. The Committee's likes and dislikes were also significant factors, and no pretense is made of objectivity. Due to limited space, many of the city's prominent but dull buildings have been omitted or only briefly noted in order to include a greater range and number of structures. Few buildings of pure historic nature rather than architectural interest are included.

Organization of the guide: The guide is organized into chapters by city neighborhoods; there are also chapters on outlying areas in order to include significant buildings within the entire metropolitan region. At the beginning of every chapter a map keyed to each building's name and entry number is included. Organization within chapters is arranged so that buildings near each other are consecutively numbered, thus providing a potential tour route. Chapter introductions outline the respective historical development and prominent demarcations of the neighborhood. A final chapter titled "Rest in Peace" serves as a reminder of those buildings that were significant in the evolution of the city yet are no longer standing, often the result of shortsightedness by those responsible as their stewards. Unfortunately, this chapter has grown at an alarming rate since the first edition.

Information on the entries: The heading for each entry begins with the building's reference number on the neighborhood map, current name (or names) of the building, the address of the building, the architect of record (if known), those responsible for subsequent additions or renovations, and the year of the work. The listing of a building's architect is reflective of the name of the firm at the time of the commission and not necessarily the firm's contemporary title. Interiors are generally described only if they are open to the public or are especially noteworthy. Religious buildings are typically open only during services. The listing of parkways and parks includes the generally recognized extent of the space as defined by major public streets. Buildings within parks are typically included as separate entries.

A final word: The opinions expressed in the guide are those of Mary Voelz Chandler and do not represent views or opinions of the Denver Architectural Foundation or any other sponsoring organization. We have made every effort reasonably possible to ensure the accuracy of the documentation in the guide. However, we invite readers who are aware of any inaccuracies to report these to the Denver Architectural Foundation so that we may correct them in our next edition. Information is current as of 2013 – in a city as dynamic as Denver, changes and additions will have likely occurred even prior to publication. Numerous buildings are privately owned and not open to the public; investigation of anything not visible from the street or public property might constitute trespassing. We request your sensitivity to these issues, but, most important, we hope you enjoy the architecture of Denver!

Dennis R. Humphries, AIA

Sponsors

The support of the following financial contributors made possible a book from which we hope many will benefit. Please accept our deep appreciation for your generosity in being our partners in this effort.

Benefactors
AIA Denver
AIA Colorado
Davis Partnership Architects, PC
Dennis Humphries, AIA
Education Fund of the Colorado Society of Architects/Ken Fuller, AIA
Humphries Poli Architects, PC
Scientific and Cultural Facilities District

Patrons
OZ Architecture
Anderson Mason Dale Architects
Tryba Architects

Sponsors
DLR Group
Jim Bershof, FAIA
klipp-gkkworks
Roth Sheppard Architects
Ted Halsey, AIA

Photography, the Siren, Lures Denver Native to Architecture

Alan Golin Gass, FAIA, 22 January 2013

As a fourth-generation Denverite, I have taken many photographs of Denver architecture over the years, some of which I am pleased to share with the readers of this guide. Those images, as well as a number that I have taken specifically for this purpose, are referenced in the appendix.

My fascination with that old folding Kodak in my grandmother's house in Park Hill apparently brought me full circle. My aspiring middle-class family, with immigrant grandparents, somehow shielded me from the exigencies of the Depression. When I was two years old, my father lost his job; however, by the time I was aware, he had a new, stable job that he would pursue the rest of his life. Because my parents recognized that their education had not prepared them to achieve, they urged me to achieve academically. Additionally, they exposed me to the performing arts from an early age. While I developed a lifelong love of theater, I found I had no talent there. I was left to learn about the visual arts through an art history book that one of my aunts had used in college. Later, I explored the meager offerings of the Denver Art Museum. In the 1940s, the collection was located in the City and County Building, and later at Chappell House.

A chemistry set I received as a result of visiting a family friend doing science experiments led to my looking into science as a career. I continued to learn about chemistry with an ever-expanding basement lab. I somehow I realized that taking pictures was related to chemistry. I was able to start experimenting with a series of not very good hand-me-down cameras in different formats, and cobbled together an enlarger from spare parts. Using my chemical knowledge, I mixed my own film and print processing solutions. I had made the leap from pure science to the beginnings of art. At Smiley Junior High School, I manifested my interest in photography and became the protégé of my typing teacher, who did most of the school's photography. Further, I forged a lifelong relationship with four friends, together organizing

the Rocky Mountain Camera Club. I won the school's photo awards in 9th grade with two photos taken of Denver's Civic Center.

I continued to pursue my dual hobbies in school. During my senior year at Denver's East High School, I received an honorable mention in the Westinghouse Science Talent awards. Several of my photos were recognized in the *Rocky Mountain News* photo awards and the National High School Photographic awards, sponsored locally by the *Denver Post*. In addition, two of my photos were hung in local and international photo salons. I was a photographer and assistant editor doing all of the page layouts for the high school yearbook as well.

Fortunately for the continuity of this story, Harvard College admitted me. It was at Harvard, where many new ideas challenged me each day that my career track changed. My innate curiosity took me into the architecture building one day. As I entered, I came upon a design review of student projects for a modern designed cathedral, presided over by an older man. Denver architecture, previous to the 1950s, being primarily in the Beaux Arts style, with a smattering of Arte Moderne, I had never seen architecture like that, except by a couple of architects that local standards adjudged to be "radical." It occurred to me that architecture may actually be the field I was looking for, since it was a synthesis of art and science.

The older man, it turned out, was Walter Gropius, founder of the Bauhaus. While I was still trying to get my head around a life-changing decision, I attended Gropius's introduction to the new basic design course he initiated. During that lecture he described his experience as a member of the site selection committee for the new Air Force Academy. He described the disastrous street that was the main road to Colorado Springs at the time – a ghastly mix of gas stations, bars, and cheap motels, with no sidewalks – very primitive. He was describing South Santa Fe Drive. That moment really drove my decision that I should contribute something to my own city by studying architecture and taking those skills back to Denver.

While in college, I was a photographer for the yearbook and, in my senior year, used my accumulated ability to organize images to good effect as art and layout editor, as I had done in high school.

From that time until now, I have continued to use photography as a medium for information gathering and expression. During my years in active architectural practice, I used photography to record images for reference and presentation. I photographed most of my own work and that of the offices in which I worked. I used those photos to illustrate presentations and marketing pieces that I assembled. On occasion, I sent a few images to the photo competition of the St. Louis Chapter of AIA. I had two of my photos accepted for the annual calendar that they published.

Over the years, I have continued to record architecture, the natural environment, my own professional work and that of the distinguished firms I have worked in, as well as family events and travel experiences. I have accumulated numerous black-and-white and color negatives and thousands of color slides and digital images. I have used my images in many lectures and presentations on subjects such as the development of my firm's solar energy projects in the 1970s to audiences as diverse as the University of Chicago's Energy Policy Group and the vice-governor of Hunan Province, People's Republic of China. Other similarly illustrated lectures included one called "Who was William Zeckendorf?" for Historic Denver, and courses in historic preservation, transit-oriented development, and mid-20th century architecture for the Osher Lifelong Learning Institute senior enrichment program at the University of Denver.

I am delighted to be able to contribute some of my images of Denver architecture for the benefit of the 2013 guide.

My Unspoken Mentors: Denver's Mid-Century Modern Architects

Jim Bershof, FAIA, OZ Architecture

Like many architects, I'm an architectural guidebook enthusiast. When I travel, one of the first things I do is find the guidebook. Denver, my hometown, didn't have one to speak of until 2001, when the *Guide to Denver Architecture* was published, just in advance of that year's National AIA Convention held there. A remarkably compatible group of us persisted for more than a dozen years, off and on, to get it done. After an intervening decade, the core of that group (Dennis Humphries, Mary Chandler, Sharon Elfenbein, Craig Rouse, and I) has reconvened, joined by a very important newcomer, Alan Gass, to create this updated version for the 2013 Convention.

That Denver is hosting the National Convention again after only 12 years says a lot about how far the city and its architecture have come. Before 2001, Denver had not hosted the AIA convention for 36 years, an indication that it did not register much on the national architectural consciousness. For me, the historic and vernacular buildings of the Denver I grew up in, as well as the ubiquitous postwar ranch houses, were like the air itself, hardly noticeable.

This changed for me in the mid-1950s when I had my first encounter with Modern architecture: I. M. Pei's Mile High Center, designed for the developer William Zeckendorf. Pei carved out of Denver's downtown masonry precincts an oasis composed of plazas, shallow pools filled with goldfish, and gravity-defying buildings made variously of steel, glass, and thin-shell concrete. I vividly remember my first reaction to this new kind of architecture: It was a revelation, and it was followed by a similar response to Pei's next project in Denver, the nearby Zeckendorf Plaza. Pei's buildings were simple, light, and highly transparent, suggesting to me new possibilities for our built environment. Unfortunately, over time, both projects have been significantly altered and no longer convey the creativity, energy, and imagination that originally so captivated me.

As I became aware of Modern architecture, I realized that right in my Denver neighborhood, Hilltop, talented architects were creating daring new Modern structures within blocks of our house. Joseph and Louise Marlow created three exquisite houses, looking like no others I had seen. Thankfully, two of them – the Sandler and Joshel Houses – still exist. However, perhaps the most daring design, the Hobart Residence (image above), a glass box floating above a hillside and anchored with pipe columns and retaining walls, has long since been destroyed.

Victor Hornbein, a Denver native who had studied at Taliesin with Frank Lloyd Wright, designed the nearby Touff Residence, now owned by my brother John. This house faces the street with nothing more than brick walls and floating horizontal eaves forming a carport, with the residential uses concealed behind: a daring structure and one that would make a strong impression on me. Years later, I would have the opportunity to design a renovation and expansion of this home.

I became aware of other Denver Modernists. Raymond Harry Ervin had designed the exotic Shangri-La, a large Deco-style home that rose above the southwest corner of Hilltop. However, it was his First National Bank Building tower, one of Denver's first downtown skyscrapers, that captured my imagination. I drew perspectives of that building over and over.

By the mid- to late-fifties, Temple Emanuel, our family's synagogue, had moved from its long-standing downtown location (now the Temple Events Center) to its new home in Hilltop. Designed by New York architect Percival Goodman, its combination of Miesian-inspired straightforward education wings coupled with a Wrightian-inspired rich sanctuary showed me that Modernism did not have to be pure to be beautiful. The new complex almost made me want to attend Saturday and Sunday school!

Finally, there was the work of William Muchow, perhaps Denver's finest mid-century Modern architect. His early experiments in thin-edged A-frame glass structures were as startling in their own way as the Marlows' glass boxes. His work, and the work of his firm, Muchow and Associates, ranged from single family houses to schools to large commercial and institutional structures, such as the Denver Public Schools Administration Building. Muchow's work taught me that such a range was possible in one's architectural career, and it is the path I have followed.

Later, as I advanced in my career, I came to appreciate Denver's historic buildings and the work of earlier Denver architects. Of those, one who stands out for me is Jacques J.B. Benedict. This guide has many fine examples of his work, but in my opinion the best is his Divine Science Church, essentially a Modern building in Classical clothing, and one that inspired our design for the Blair-Caldwell African American Research Library.

Looking back from the vantage point of a 40-year career, it was the impact of Denver's mid-century Modern architecture that set me on my course as an architect and has engendered within me a strong sense of responsibility for the preservation of Denver's architectural heritage, both modern and historic. Serving on Denver's Landmark Preservation Commission for almost eight years has been one way I have attempted to honor this responsibility, as has working on both the original *Guide to Denver Architecture* and on this new edition. It is important that those in the future who grow up in, live in, or visit Denver can benefit from the city's architectural heritage as I did, and I am extremely grateful for the opportunity to have served the Denver community in this manner.

Foreword

Much like the iconic mountains that rise to the west, the architecture of Denver has become a landmark in its own right and created a visual sense of place that highlights the city as a hub for the 21st century. With the expansion of the light rail into the downtown area, along with the continued preservation of Lower Downtown and the Platte River, the city continues a long history of visionary development.

When Denver was first founded in 1858, the result of a gold boom, settlements along the Platte River were primitive and makeshift. By the end of the 19th century, however, spurred by Mayor Robert Speer's vision, Denver began to take shape, not only through its buildings but also through the surrounding public parks and open spaces. These public areas, great democratic spaces to be shared by all people, continue to be a hallmark of the city.

The hard work and dreams of 20th century mayors such as Quigg Newton, Federico Pena, and Wellington Webb, along with visionaries like Jennifer Moulton, director of the City's Planning and Development Agency, and Dana Crawford, the grand dame of LoDo and one of the great developers of the latter 20th century, among countless others, ensured that the dream of a City Beautiful continued. New neighborhoods were developed and integrated into the city plan. Landmark buildings such as a new central library, performing arts complex, convention center, and art museum were built, providing visitors to the city with memorable places to visit. This work continues, with the recent opening of the new Colorado History Museum and the Ralph Carr Justice Center, along with the recent restoration of historic Union Station. Businesses have invested throughout the city to ensure that the urban plan continued to flourish. All the while, recreational spaces were emphasized along the urban corridors, playing a central role in the city's growth.

After arriving in Denver in 1981, I was fortunate to be a part of the growth and development in Lower Downtown, watching first-hand as an area previously known for urban blight and abandoned warehouses was transformed to a thriving destination and residential community. When I was mayor, we took a major step forward in the city's planning through the Greenprint Denver program, focusing on sustainable buildings and infrastructure to ensure Denver's place at the forefront of the new energy economy. Now, as the governor of our great state, I have the opportunity to share the treasures of our great city with people across the globe.

The hard work and vision for a great city, marked by buildings, parks, and vibrant neighborhoods, is an ongoing task. We have created the foundation for a great city, and it is up to the leaders and people of the future to ensure its continued, balanced growth. As you "visit" the architectural icons of Denver in this book, try to appreciate the dreams of those that walked before you in creating the City Beautiful, and imagine a place that will serve as a focal point for urban areas well into the future.

John Hickenlooper
Governor of Colorado

Introduction

Study a city's architecture, and you learn about its people. About its growth and progress, its challenges and travails, foibles and dreams.

That's how I began the introduction to the first edition of *A Guide to Denver Architecture* in 2001, and I see no reason to change it in 2013. Still, looking back over the past twelve years, while researching and writing the second edition, many things have changed. And the severe economic downturn in 2008, which hit all aspects of architecture and construction particularly hard, delayed or killed numerous building projects in Denver.

But between 2001 and 2012, the Denver area took major steps forward. Denver blossomed culturally, adding four new museums (including a beautiful building that houses a Funplex, not a cultural storehouse). Some neighborhoods close to downtown became rejuvenated, while others were created out of sites that once served industry, military bases, an airport, or a tangle of rail lines. Public transportation became a serious topic of discussion, as Union Station began redevelopment as a regional hub for all types of public transit. In contrast, some of Denver's most beloved neighborhoods lost beautiful homes to out-of-scale projects or, worse, empty lots when the economy went sour. And the preservation movement faced continual challenges from those elected or employed to serve its residents' best interests.

As expected, many new buildings are now in these pages, and several have been removed because, unfortunately, they no longer exist. Some buildings are new to these pages because, after landing on the cutting-room floor in 2001, it was decided that several mid-century modern structures should be included.

In the end, though, Denver has grown and, in some ways, matured. It can claim a history rich in evolution, failures, and successes. Begun in 1858 on the banks of Cherry Creek, Denver fits into the category of "an instant city." There really was no reason for this place to exist except as a center to serve those heading west to get rich or get away. And there was no reason for it to grow except for the commitment of its residents to a better life.

Scarce water and drastic climatic shifts made early existence difficult, just as development today is dependent on limited resources. It's a city overlaid on an older culture, since Plains Indians lived, traveled, and traded here long before the first trapper ventured in to hunt down wealth. It's a city – and a region – that has solicited economic infusions from outside, while watching extractive industries, from precious metals to oil, make millions for those far from Colorado.

And it's a city that often has looked for design inspiration elsewhere. Brick – not the stucco or adobe of the Southwest vernacular – made this city. At the end of the 19th century, the source was architectural incubators such as Chicago; from mid-20th century on, big national firms ventured in to stamp their mark on the state.

In turn, area architects have had another struggle on their hands: how to compete with a natural beauty impossible to ignore. Denver style? There's no such thing, much as people might try to find one.

Yet there are remarkable things about this city. Early on, residents taxed themselves for parks, parkways, schools, and libraries. They elected leaders, such as Mayor Robert W. Speer, who may have taken for themselves but who also left a lasting legacy to those who live here. Residents supported landscape architects and planners who gave Denver a park and parkway system that took too much thought to be a miracle. Denver's "emerald necklace" had to be coaxed out of high plains desert, a refuge from city life. Citizens voted in a tax to support cultural and historic organizations. They primed the pump – more formally known as civic reinvestment – for projects that ranged from social amenities (libraries, an art museum expansion) to development schemes (an airport, a convention center expansion, various hotel deals).

As this book goes to press, Denver continues in the tradition of facing turning points that result from repeated booms and busts.

In the late 1980s, when the oil money dried up and blew away, so did many residents (and architects). Those who stayed began a period of soul-searching, looking to improve on the gleaming downtown oil money had bought. Then-Mayor Federico Peña asked people to imagine a great city – corny? Of course – and they tried.

But as good times came again to push out yet another bust, the rush to build became more manic. Every project under the sun had to be completed, and every bare bit of land filled in. While Mayor Wellington Webb's push to create it all during three terms was understandable, this fast-track building blitz caused a certain disconnect between the reality of many residents and the goals of many developers. The two groups can work together, if money is not the only goal.

This influx of development outside of downtown created another challenge, and it's not just economic. Ironically, as New Urbanists have worked to convince wide-open-spaces westerners about the virtues of increased density and mass transit, it has left a certain void in the arena of discrete design. What has moved in? A suburban aesthetic, a bland, cheap-material way of doing business that has produced projects that are neither urban nor urbane.

As Mayor John Hickenlooper instructed the city's planning department to bring Denver's zoning code into the 21st century, another disconnect seemed to appear: Neighborhoods had become more and more fearful of massive developments damaging the integrity of their immediate surroundings, and it was not clear if anyone at City Hall was listening. Preservationists saw pushback to their work, and to the city's landmark ordinance, and at times seemed to lose their voice in the increasing noise. Hickenlooper announced that "Denver is open for business" in his first inaugural speech, and, boy, was it ever.

Mayor Michael Hancock, elected in 2011 after an interim mayor took the reins when Hickenlooper became governor, finally named a planning director, who comes from a smart growth background. I hope his design instincts are as strong. How this will affect Denver – from downtown through neighborhoods – remains to be seen, even as a sweep of eye-catching infill has sprung up in older neighborhoods.

There have been moves forward as the metro area continues to regain a sure footing. Denver's economy has become much more diversified, not relying on one market sector that could be easily wiped out by economic losses. And though home prices in some areas became dizzying, the vast overbuilding and inflated prices found in states such as Nevada, Arizona, and Florida did not happen here. Yes, many people here have been hurt, but mortgage irregularities did not sink Denver. Architecture firms, contractors, and the building trades, however, were hurt by others' folly.

As for design, if anyone who loves architecture were to get three wishes, they should be: ban synthetic stucco and use honest materials, abandon phony historicism, and operate on the concept that thought is as important as money. The sigh, followed by the resigned "It's not as bad as it could have been," can stop when the will is there to make it so.

Guide to Denver Architecture

Second Edition

Downtown Denver

Like many American downtowns, Denver's has changed with regional prosperity – and, just as often, lack thereof, as is evident over the past decade of plentiful money and deep recession.

That paragraph opened the "Downtown Denver" chapter in the 2001 *Guide to Denver Architecture*. Twelve years later, it's difficult to think of a better way to begin the same section in the book's second edition.

Economic ups and downs still mark the city's architectural complexion, but so do other factors that have rendered downtown a more lively, walkable city. There were more losses, to be sure, including the forward-thinking Currigan Exhibition Hall and the evocative design of Skyline Park. Yet several factors have made the central city feel more mature: the introduction of connections formed by light rail and a Downtown Circulator, the continued presence of the unusual Downtown Denver Historic District, an increase in downtown residential projects (back to the future, so to speak), continued development along 14th Street, and improvements to the 16th Street Mall.

Still, the city's genesis bears repeating. Denver began in what is now lower downtown and Auraria, but the commercial center soon spread east, where different types of enterprises drifted into specific parts of town. Sixteenth Street housed retail stores and theaters galore. Seventeenth Street was where banks and financiers built the Wall Street of the West. Homes, apartments, and hotels made the term "downtown neighborhood" real.

Like other cities, Denver after World War II faced two challenges: migration to the suburbs, taking families and stores along, and the impact of a massive urban renewal program that led to the destruction of good buildings along with the blight (or "wrong" people) that was the intended target: Some 27 square blocks of the business area and lower downtown were cleared in the late 1960s and early 1970s as part of the Skyline Urban Renewal Project.

During the Skyline era, and later, many streets lost buildings, leaving a gap-toothed effect. Most of those holes have been filled in with varying success, many following a Skyline urban design scheme crafted in the 1960s by Baume, Polivnick, and Hatami, the last serving as primary designer. Yet major streets kept their initial purposes: The transformation of 16th Street into the 16th Street Mall didn't change its role as a mercantile spine; instead, the transit mall became an important connector between the Civic Center and lower downtown – and now, beyond, to the crucial Union Station redevelopment as a transit hub and into the ever-evolving Highlands neighborhoods. Seventeenth Street remains a banking and investment center, and home to the grande dames of Denver – the Equitable and Boston Buildings.

The oil boom of the 1970s and early 1980s brought tremendous growth, skyscrapers and urban complexes that gave the city a new, if sometimes disappointing, any-town face. Out-of-town architectural firms – especially Skidmore, Owings, and Merrill – became major players in the design and development of the city.

The bust of the mid-1980s prompted a sense of civic reinvestment, cooled by a tangled banking market that led to preservation defeats. The elegant Central Bank was lost to a botched financial deal, a wound that partially healed in the formation of the voluntary downtown historic district.

In the 1990s and first decade of the 21st century, there were losses, but also victories. Some buildings once threatened by neglect or demolition came back from the brink, massaged by perceptive architects and developers into residential or commercial use. Several small buildings have become boutique hotels, the almost forgotten Buerger Brothers and old Chamber of Commerce Buildings gained new life through thoughtful renovation, and the once-endangered Guaranty Bank Building, stripped of its riches by a greedy investor, now shelters apartments.

The historic Colorado National Bank, with stellar murals by Colorado artist Allen Tupper True, found a savvy developer to turn it into a hotel, keeping the singular interior decoration. The long-forlorn Fontius Building has a new face and new standing as the Sage Building, thanks to architects, artists, and a developer who saw the beauty beneath the grime. And the General Services Administration, through its green modernization program, has brought continued attention and upgrades to the eclectic mix of buildings in the city's Federal District, with the addition of an exceptional new federal courthouse.

The prosperity of the 1990s through the economic downturn of 2008 also brought another force to bear: pressure to destroy existing structures and build bigger. Denver lost the important hyperbolic paraboloid that had made I.M. Pei's Courthouse Square complex a geometric masterpiece. The replacement? A faceless hotel lobby. The beautiful marble that faced the tower of Colorado National Bank/U.S. Bank was stripped, to be replaced by granite, and a noteworthy outdoor sculpture by Harry Bertoia was removed. The Art Moderne Denver Post Building fell to hotel speculation, though the project that resulted is a sleek hotel filled with art – setting a design standard that other new hotels along 14th Street do not achieve.

We learned the answer to the question, "If a beautiful, eminently lovable Neoclassical structure such as Central Bank could be lost, what chance did Modernism have?" Exemplars such as Currigan Exhibition Hall and the urban canyon of Skyline Park gave way to demands by business interests, augmented by a lack of understanding of the style. A belief in context goes only so far in a city that is not sure how to honor the full spectrum of design.

As the "downturn" turned into the "Great Recession," more than one downtown project never made it out of the ground. Two new towers eventually emerged, though only one goes beyond mere workmanlike design. Other building owners decided to update their properties, making them more colorful and sustainable, while upgrading dated facades that hid fine lines.

Downtown now anchors close-in, vibrant neighborhoods that had gone flat – or barely existed – transforming the city at large. Despite more than 150 years on an economic roller coaster, downtown has survived.

LIST OF BUILDINGS

LoDo
20TH STREET
19TH STREET
18TH STREET
17TH STREET
16TH STREET MALL
15TH STREET
14TH STREET
MARKET STREET
LARIMER STREET
LAWRENCE STREET
ARAPAHOE STREET
CURTIS STREET
CHAMPA STREET
STOUT STREET
CALIFORNIA STREET
WELTON STREET
16TH STREET MALL
GLENARM PLACE
TREMONT PLACE
COURT PLACE
CLEVELAND PLACE
13TH STREET
SPEER BOULEVARD
20TH AVENUE
19TH AVENUE
18TH AVENUE
17TH AVENUE
16TH AVENUE
COLFAX AVENUE
COLFAX AVENUE
FOX STREET
ELATI STREET
DELAWARE STREET
CHEROKEE STREET
BANNOCK STREET
CIVIC CENTER
BROADWAY
LINCOLN STREET
N
Golden Triangle

1 **16th Street Transit Mall**
Between Broadway and Market Streets
I.M. Pei & Partners, 1982

The city's retail row lost cars but gained transit during conversion into a pedestrian/bus mall in the earlier 1980s. Henry Cobb of I.M. Pei's office designed the mall's 13 linear blocks in gray and pink stone laid to resemble the back of a rattlesnake when viewed from above.

Since then, the mall has seen its share of problems (cracked pavers from the buses, empty stores during economic downturns), but its drawing power and popularity have made the mall a huge draw for tourists and residents alike. An extension of the mall beyond Market Street has made it an adjunct to the FasTracks program's light rail system and the sweeping redevelopment of the Union Station area into a regional transit hub.

Zimmer Gunsul Frasca Architects – with the Olin Studio, ELS, and studioINSITE – completed the first 16th Street Mall Urban Design Plan in 2009, which is being carried out as funding becomes available. Ongoing incremental improvements to the mall include cleaning and protecting pavers, rehabbing street furniture to conform to the mall's original color palette, and adding new amenities.
AIA Colorado 25 Year Award, 2010

2 **Republic Plaza**
370 17th Street
Skidmore, Owings, and Merrill, 1984

Republic Plaza is the tallest building in Denver and in Colorado: 56 stories (714 feet) of granite and glass set back from 16th Street to create a generous plaza and pierce the sky with deceptive simplicity.

Deceptive? As with Skidmore, Owings, and Merrill's earlier building at 1225 17th Street, Republic's designer went even further in defining the traditionally conceived composition of a skyscraper: the base, a stark composition of oversized windows; and doors; a shaft that gains power from the regular progression of square windows, and a top that appears elongated because of the introduction of a more vertical window type.

For all its size, however, Republic Plaza retains an unusual transparency, serving as a supersized mirror by which to follow the ever-shifting Colorado clouds and skies. Perhaps that is the best way to approach this testament to the power of geometry. It escapes the lure of the fancy hat on top, allowing its rigorous design progression to triumph.
AIA Colorado 25 Year Award, 2009

3 **Courthouse Square / Radisson / Hilton Hotel and May D&F/ Adam's Mark Hotel / Sheraton Hotel**
1550 Court Place
I.M. Pei, 1958 through 1960. Hyperbolic paraboloid component at Zeckendorf Plaza destroyed in 1996 to create new hotel lobby; a later renovation performed for Sheraton.

On the site of the old Arapahoe County Courthouse, New York developer William Zeckendorf placed the granddaddy of mixed-use projects, Courthouse Square. He hired I.M. Pei to fit the parts together, and the architect found a solution in geometry. He designed the department store portion as a box, the hotel as a tall, rectangular slab, and set everything off with a plaza and a hyperbolic paraboloid with a thin-shell concrete roof that seemed to float over the pavement. (See "Rest in Peace" for further information on the paraboloid and plaza.)

If the demolition of the old courthouse was controversial, so was Pei's solution to his commission. It was ingenious, as well. The box was faced with aluminum panels, while the hotel sported a latticework facade that created a decorative sunscreen. The hotel's precast building material was made from stone excavated from the hotel site, a rough reddish-brown mosaic of sand and gravel that addressed the concept of a building's need to fit in its surroundings. The light-as-air paraboloid and plaza linked the two at a human scale.

In the early 1990s, developers began to eye the location as key to boosting business at the upper end of the 16th Street Mall. The Adam's Mark Hotel chain's entry into the market led to changes in the former department store's exterior facade, swapping out metal for glass. The city's refusal to shut a public right-of-way led then-hotel owner Fred Kummer to scrape the plaza and the paraboloid, replacing it with what various architects seeking the commission termed "an elegant box." In reality, the new lobby is a clunky could-be-anywhere holdover from the 1980s, a less-than-distinctive (and hardly elegant) granite and glass bunker fronted by sculptures of elongated dancers. Billed as the answer to the city's need for a convention center hotel, the new complex instead meant the destruction of a unique design and construction of a new structure that was dated by the time it opened.

Under the new flag of Sheraton Denver Downtown, more changes came in the form of individually detailed ground-floor retail, including a corner given over to a pub facade that recalls a Disneyfied Dublin, again chipping away at the overall Modernist form.
Original complex: AIA Honor Award, 1959

4 **Kittredge Building**
511 16th Street
A. Morris Stuckert, 1890; renovation by C.W. Fentress and Associates, 1992

The Kittredge Building has been called Denver's first modern skyscraper, a seven-story structure supported by steel beams and iron columns and the all-important inclusion of an elevator. But the heavily worked facade in native granite and rhyolite, and sturdy, finely crafted windows speak of Richardsonian Romanesque intent. The Kittredge is a solid part of downtown, too lively to be considered a gray ghost, too much of its era to flaunt technology.
Renovation: AIA Colorado Honor Award, 1992. National Register of Historic Places, a Denver Landmark, and part of the Downtown Denver Historic District.

5 1600 Glenarm
1600 Glenarm Place
1964, Sorey, Hill, and Sorey Architects, Oklahoma City; reconfiguration by Davis Partnership Architects, 2006

Built as the much-heralded second Security Life Building, this primarily concrete Formalist structure at its opening was the tallest building in Denver: 31 stories, including a three-level set back at the top. The insurance firm was its main tenant, and the famed Top of the Rockies restaurant overlooked downtown. In the 1980s, Security Life built a new home on the edge of Civic Center (now 1290 Broadway), and the downtown high-rise eventually went dark.

Recognizing a market in the central business district for high-end apartments, a development firm hired Davis Partnership to remake this well-ordered building into upscale residences, with street-level retail. The building's facade has been cleaned up and its central bay has been highlighted, adding to its street presence on the 16th Street Mall, though denting the integrity of original design elements.
Renovation: AIA Denver Chapter Citation Award, 2007

6 Paramount Theatre
1621 Glenarm Place
Temple Buell, and C.W. and George L. Rapp, 1930

Denver architect Temple Buell worked with the firm that specialized in theater architecture to design what is now the last picture palace left downtown. The Depression blues didn't stop him from producing an exuberant Art Deco delight, liberally frosted with terra-cotta and reaching to the sky with Buell-esque spires and plumes.

A restoration in 1985 cost the Paramount some features, and its lobby orientation was shifted. But the plaster and gilded detailing inside were saved, along with wall tapestries featuring commedia dell'arte figures.
National Register of Historic Places, Denver Landmark, and part of the Downtown Denver Historic District

7 The Denver Pavilions
16th Street between Tremont Place and Welton Street
ELS / Elbasoni & Logan Architects, 1998; reconfiguration and refreshing, Semple Brown Design, Communications Arts, 2009

For years, city planners worried about the two huge blocks along the 16th Street Mall relegated to the role of parking lot.

But when it came time to fill this gap at the southeast end, the choice was a two-block-long shopping mall that is neither suburban nor urban in its appearance or attitude. The architects tried, adding abundant windows and some stone and metal beams to break up the synthetic stucco. The Pavilions covers the blocks between Tremont and Welton, with boxes broken up to mimic the rhythm of the historic buildings across from it on the 16th Street Mall. In effect, this divided two

blocks into what appear to be four "buildings," tacked on a contemporary interpretation of a cornice, and looked to the historic stone buildings for some sense of scale.

A decade later, new owners brought in a new architecture and graphics team to update the Pavilions, improving circulation and color palette, moving and replacing clunky escalators, and painting a stylish grid pattern over a bland, beige, two-block-long back wall. The shimmery "Denver" sign, created by Texas-based Irideon Corp., remains, intended as public art for what was touted as "entertainment architecture" when first completed. But the heart of the Pavilions has become easier to navigate, making it more at home downtown.

8 The Steel / Sage / Fontius Building
610 16th Street
Merrill Hoyt, 1923; renovation by klipp, 2008

Built as the Steel Building to house a department store but long known as the Fontius Building, this Renaissance design was a vacant mess by the end of the 20th century. Perceived as a blight on the 16th Street Mall, its good lines and generous windows survived, and eventually the building was brought back to life by klipp terra-cotta expert and artist Barry Rose and developer Evan Makovsky. The work ranged from restoration of numerous building details (Rose estimates he used 14 tons of clay on the project) to installation of windows that please both those interested in preservation and sustainability. The building's new name is derived from its current major tenant. Significant work on the four-story, 59,000-square-foot building included replacing the street-level facade, with new exterior lighting, canopies, a roof terrace, and the addition of skylights for daylighting. The new facade is a modern interpretation of the original retail storefront. The result: The Sage has become a major presence downtown.
Denver Landmark and part of the Downtown Denver Historic District

9 Masonic Building
1614 Welton Street
Frank Edbrooke, 1889

Architect Frank Edbrooke placed gable-like parapets near the corners of this sandstone mix of commercial and ritual space. Following Richardsonian style, the stone facade is rough and the entry pronounced, flanked by heavily worked columns and upper panel. Massive arches at the granite base play against the arcade of arches on the fifth floor.

A fire in the mid-1980s led to a renovation by C.W. Fentress and Associates that added penthouse floors and saved the Masonic as popular retail and office space.
National Register of Historic Places, Denver Landmark, and part of the Downtown Denver Historic District

10 Colorado Building
1615 California Street
John W. Roberts, 1891; addition by Frank E. Edbrooke, 1909;
renovation by Jacques J.B. Benedict, 1935

Art Deco eventually came to Denver, to be interpreted in several buildings by designers who found terra-cotta the perfect material with which to create elaborate ornamentation inherent to that style. That was true of the Colorado Building, which began as the brick commercial-style Hayden, Dickinson, and Feldhauser Building. Renowned commercial architect Frank Edbrooke contributed additional stories, though it was Benedict who later gave the newly named Colorado Building its overlay of Deco detailing.
Part of the Downtown Denver Historic District

11 The Denver Dry
700 16th Street
Frank Edbrooke, 1889; renovation by John Carney and Associates,
with Urban Design Group and Communications Arts, 1993

For years, the mammoth former Denver Dry Goods Company sat shrouded in white paint, ungainly while it was a thriving department store, ghostly after the crowds left.

A renovation that included an infusion of public funds revealed the building's hidden beauty. A reported 30 coats of paint were stripped from the Denver Dry, and color was added at the roofline (though not necessarily the original hues). The sad brown awnings were removed, and the place glowed as only solid red Denver brick can.

Frank Edbrooke had designed a three-story building here for builder John J. Riethmann, fronting 16th Street and extending down California Street. A fourth floor was added in 1898 (the original cornice line is still evident); another addition in 1906 again extended the Denver Dry (originally the McNamara Dry Goods Company), this time all the way to California Street. More floors were added in the 1920s. In the 1930s the complex was painted white – for a reason apparently lost to history.

Edbrooke worked in the disparate modes of regularity (the California Street side can seem very long) and highly detailed Victorian Commercial style. Pilasters sport banded sandstone, while arched windows give a sense of rhythm to this large red brick structure. The existing cornice is elaborate and bracketed, and underscored by a festooned frieze. Arcaded, rounded windows – an Edbrooke signature – add an Italianate touch.

After the Denver Dry closed, the building faced the threat of demolition but was purchased by the Denver Urban Renewal Authority, which spurred renovation and the conversion of the Denver Dry to offices, retail, and residences. Though the

Denver City Council had opposed landmarking the structure for fear of burdening an owner with a white (or not) elephant, that process eventually succeeded. It helps assure the continued presence of a Frank Edbrooke design that grew in parts as it rose in stature.
National Register of Historic Places, Denver Landmark, and part of the Downtown Denver Historic District

12 The Neusteter Building
720 16th Street
Fisher and Fisher, 1924, with 1950s addition of parking garage at 1520 Stout Street

If the Denver Dry is robust red brick in a basically Victorian Commercial style, its neighbor on 16th Street shows the Classical elegance that would appeal to an upscale clientele. Known for residential as well as commercial architecture, the firm of Fisher and Fisher consistently brought intelligence to its work. Iron columns at the base provide a slimming effect to the gray brick and stone structure, which is marked by strong horizontal lines and a restrained cornice. Turn the corner, and the carefully shielded garage displays a more restrained contemporary appearance.

The store closed in 1985, leading to a renovation into apartments and then condominiums in 1991, an early example of conversion of a retail gem into downtown residences.
National Register of Historic Places, Denver Landmark, and part of the Downtown Denver Historic District

13 A.C. Foster Building / University Building
912 16th Street
Fisher and Fisher, 1911

The design firm that brought Classical elegance to both commercial and residential projects here produced a tripart building with clearly delineated base, shaft, and capital. White terra-cotta marks the building's center bays, with a green pinstripe decoration, while dark red brick provides the corner supports. A flaring cornice tops the structure, which was renovated to show off its brass-doored elevators and mosaic accents.

Built by broker A.C. Foster, the structure was renamed the University Building when one of Foster's one-time partners, James H. Causey, purchased it for the school. The Foster/University Building long has housed many jewelers.
National Register of Historic Places and part of the Downtown Denver Historic District

  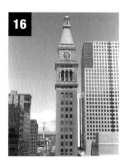

14 Odd Fellows Hall
1543–45 Champa Street
Emmett Anthony, 1889; 1983 renovation and reconfiguration by Curt Fentress

The International Order of Odd Fellows bestowed upon the city one of its most exuberant Victorian Eclectic facades, featuring well-worked stone, arched windows, a cupola, and pressed tin trim. An early 1980s renovation added a set-back fourth story and skylit atrium, while protecting a massive stained glass window that marks the fraternal order's presence.
Denver Landmark and part of the Downtown Denver Historic District. Western Mountain Region Merit Award for Adaptive Reuse, 1984; AIA Colorado Honor Award, 1985

15 Federal Reserve Branch Bank
1020 16th Street
William C. Muchow Associates, and Ken R. White Co., engineers, 1968

Low and sleek, the design for Modernist building makes it appear more a contemplative zen statement than a storehouse for money. William Muchow created a deeply recessed first floor, protected by a formal colonnade. An over-hang of pendant-like forms is cantilevered from above, serving as a sunscreen. The aggregate material is a soft, cream-colored counterpoint to the stone of neighboring historic buildings, yet hardly results in a background building. This bank merely claims its space and asks for respect. In the wave of security measures that swept the United States after 9/11, the building was surrounded by an iron fence that can't quite match the simplicity of what is being protected, though it tries.

16 The Daniels & Fisher Tower
1101 16th Street / 1601 Arapahoe Street
Frederick J. Sterner and George Williamson, 1911; renovation by Gensler and Associates, 1981

One of the most thought-provoking preservation stories in Denver is that of the D&F Tower. It has peril. It has hyperbole. It has a happy ending. And it illustrates how something considered old and worn out can take on new life.

When the tower was built, it was as a corner keynote for the Daniels & Fisher Department Store. William B. Daniels's son William Cooke Daniels bought out the interest of W.G. Fisher at the time of his death in 1897. When Daniels decided to expand the store, he became entranced with the idea of adding a tower. St. Mark's Campanile came to mind: The Venetian landmark had collapsed in 1902 and was being rebuilt. Why not import that concept?

The two structures do not really look alike, though St. Mark's was the inspiration. When the D&F Tower was dedicated in fall 1911, it stood 330 feet tall, 40 feet square at the ground. The Renaissance Revival design was constructed of brick set on a concrete base, then detailed on 19 floors with terra-cotta and stone.

Entablatures on the 13th and 16th floors serve to set up the tower for a belfry, which houses the machinery for a huge clock. Balustrades, painted stone guirlandes, and columns are part of the detailing. The spire begins at the 20th floor. A flagpole sits on top. Daniels had his beautiful tower.

When the Skyline Redevelopment Plan, administered by the Denver Urban Renewal Authority, moved to demolish store and tower, a fierce fight began. The tower was named a landmark in 1969. The store was razed in 1971, but DURA put the tower on the market, and developer French and Co. purchased it (for a reported $72,678) and rehabbed it for commercial use.

During the renovation, architects from Gensler wisely did not try to make the tower look as if it had just sprung up fully formed: Where the tower had touched the store, a different color brick was used for infill repair. In the late 1980s, the restoration firm Grammar of Ornament repaired and repainted the fanciful mural on the ground-floor ceiling, a sky of blue that matches the Wedgwood blue trim on the tower's exterior. At the time, a Grammar of Ornament artist described the murals as painted in an Etruscan/Pompeiian motif set within the Beaux Arts mode. (The original artists have not been documented.)

The D&F Tower, which has served as an anchor for Skyline Park, houses condominiumized offices that each occupy a single floor. It is an elegant landmark from all angles. And if it is no longer the third tallest tower in the country, as it reportedly was at the time of its construction, the building is a reminder that if you save something and wait a few years...
National Register of Historic Places, Denver Landmark, and part of the Downtown Denver Historic District

17 Park Central
1515 Arapahoe Street
W.C. Muchow and Partners, 1973; reorganization and refurbishment of lobby by HumphriesPoli Architects, 1996

One of the most complex projects in downtown involves unifying three office towers into one structure. In varying heights and with massing respectful toward Modernist practice, the architects looked to the future for one of the first structures in the Skyline Urban Renewal Project.

Black anodized aluminum and solar bronze glass give Park Central a somewhat foreboding appearance, though the addition of an arcade and plaza space tempered its impact on the street. The building's complicated interior could be irritating to navigate, though a reorganization of the lobby and installation of a floor in striking organic shapes helped end the confusion. Park Central served as the vertical foil to Skyline Park, when the park still dipped below street level to offer refuge from the buildings nearby.
Western Mountain Region Design Award, 1974; AIA Colorado 25 Year Award, 1998

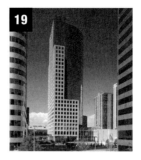

18 Writer Square
1512 Larimer Street
Barker Rinker Seacat and Partners, 1981

Flowing out of Larimer Square, Writer Square was built after land was cleared by the Denver Urban Renewal Authority's Skyline program. The complex is an early attempt in late 20th-century Denver to incorporate residential, office, and retail space in one location – in effect, return to the days when people lived above the store.

On the block bounded by 15th and 16th Streets, and Lawrence and Larimer Streets, the architects worked in varying building heights to create a project that pushed retail right onto the street, while creating a shopping street between the office and residential buildings. At the center is a simple clock tower.

Red brick on portions of the project, sparked by dentil trim, helped tie Writer Square to the historic buildings that remained in the district. Though the interior walkway offers abundant open space and leads easily back to Larimer Street, the cross axis placement can give a visitor the impression of walking into a blind alley. A refurbishment of Writer Square in 2009 provided updates in street furnishings, but without some of the more drastic changes originally announced by new owners. *Western Mountain Region Merit Award, 1981; AIA Colorado Merit Award, 1982; AIA Colorado 25 Year Award, 2006*

19 One Tabor Center
1200 17th Street (Shops: 1201 16th St.)
Master plan by Urban Design Group, with tower design by Kohn Pedersen Fox, construction drawings on tower by RNL Design and Urban Design Group, construction drawings on the shops and Westin Hotel by Urban Design Group, 1984

Conceived as the final portion of the Skyline Urban Renewal Project, Tabor Center brought Postmodernism to Denver in a complex – and very shiny – package. The project includes a sizable hotel, a bridge of shops (originally developed by the Rouse Co.), and an office tower, in which the simplicity of materials (of which there are many) is set aside for an emphasis on angles and a great curved wall. Reflective glass and precast mix with green and red granite, a glittering package on a prominent downtown block.

The architects' interpretation of an urban mall, with escalators and myriad entrances and segments, opened to great fanfare but didn't soar – the city's economy began a down cycle soon after. In the 1990s, some renovation work on the exterior began (including Neoclassical froufrou to signal the presence of a new chain restaurant at one corner). Talk also occasionally heats up about adding a second phase – the 750,000-square-foot Tabor Tower II; it was part of the original plan but was not built in the 1980s. A renovation, involving Anthony Belluschi Architects, has accommodated new retail, with the addition of a light sculpture by Ken Ambrosini on the shopping bridge.

20 17th St. Plaza
1225 17th Street
Skidmore, Owings, and Merrill, 1982

The first rule of skyscrapers: They're divided into three parts, and so is this highly abstracted version by Skidmore, Owings, and Merrill.

In a search to find a contemporary way to interpret the base, the shaft, and the top, the architects began with a stark but beautiful plaza and a recessed base. The shaft is a field of alternating glass and rosy granite strips, offering the merest hint of a separation – a few rectangular voids – to define a top. This top-tier 20th-century addition to Denver's skyline is set off at the base by the floating glitter of Kenneth Snelson's sculpture *Soft Landing*.'

21 Skyline Park
Arapahoe Street between 15th and 18th Streets
Lawrence Halprin, 1973; partial reconstruction by Thomas Balsley Associates,
2003; addition of Skyline Park Pavilion, Humphries Poli Architects, 2007

The seismic impact of the Skyline Urban Renewal Project hinged not only on what was removed and what grew out of the ground, but also what grew below grade. That was Skyline Park. The sophisticated urban canyon was sited at the foot of the D&F Tower, placed so as to link downtown blocks via Arapahoe Street to the Auraria Higher Education Center in one direction and Broadway in another. Until the creation of Commons Park in the Central Platte Valley, Skyline was the only green space downtown – far from the park-like ensemble of Civic Center.

Lawrence Halprin's plan was to provide an oasis away from the construction that enveloped downtown during that era. He drew on the materials and colors of the Rockies (and Red Rocks) to create terraced interior walls and block-built fountains, all protected by side berms and generous landscaping. (The plan was created in conjunction with the overall Skyline program developed by Marvin Hatami of Baum, Polivnik, and Hatami, and Floyd Tanaka of Tanaka and Associates.)

Through three blocks, Skyline presented a different world, narrowing at the ends to create areas for rest and reflection, yet near the tower providing more of a space for gatherings and activity. It was a city park that looks like a park in the city.

Though once a popular place admired for its unusual materials and configuration, Skyline became the subject of fierce debate over its role in life at the city's core.

A series of events worked against the Modernist landscape design as perceived among downtown business interests. When Skyline was constructed, it was alone, the kickoff for the Skyline Urban Renewal Project that remade almost 30 square blocks of downtown. The buildings around the park came later and were not as compatible as they could have been with the park's unusual sunken design. The 16th Street Mall, built in the early 1980s, drew people out of the park. When the old Central Bank was demolished in 1990, the resulting vacant lot left one edge open. Societal and economic changes brought park visitors that did not please downtown business leaders. The fountains rarely functioned, and the landscaping was not consistently attended. Many deemed it a failed space, and

a contentious process began to change Skyline – whether funding was available or not.

In the 1990s, downtown business owners and city leaders began a campaign to alter the park, studying plans that eventually resulted in sponsoring a 2001 competition to alter the three blocks along Arapahoe Street. Lawrence Halprin, then still practicing in San Francisco, was not contacted for advice until very late in the game. Thomas Balsley Associates of New York was selected from a short list of five firms and teams, including Ken Kay Associates, Hargreaves Associates, then-EDAW Inc., and DHM Design and CTLK.

Landscape architect Balsley's plan called for bringing the park up to street level, adding abundant grass, and removing fountains, while trying to weave some Halprin elements into the "new" park. Many features of the plan were not completed because there wasn't enough money to finish the new Skyline, by then a $9 million project with a $6.5 million budget. Missing in action: a shade structure and information/food kiosk in the southern block, although in 2007 a Skyline Park Pavilion, with restrooms and information booth, was constructed to a beautiful design that had virtually no relationship to the Park Central complex. In abundance, though, was lots of grass in a drought-prone city. Public art – bronze sculptures by artist Ann Weber – was installed in 2006.

At the opening of the "new" park, then-mayor John Hickenlooper said that funding would be found to finish what had become an example of neither fish nor fowl design. That didn't happen, and another key Modernist element in Denver's development was lost.

22 Colorado National Bank / Marriott Renaissance Hotel
17th and Champa Streets
Fisher and Fisher, 1915; addition, Burnham and Merrill Hoyt, 1926;
upper stories addition, Rogers Nagel, 1963; renovation and reconfiguration,
klipp, a division of gkkworks, 2013

Fisher and Fisher selected only the finest Yule marble and worked in the most perfect proportions for this superb example of Neoclassical architecture. It was a true temple of commerce, a refined and graceful structure that was all about quality, from its graceful Ionic columns to its carefully matched stone.

That extended to the soaring lobby featured a suite of 16 murals – *Indian Memories* – by preeminent Colorado artist Allen Tupper True. The bank later was joined by a Modernist tower designed by Minoru Yamasaki, in which the vertical elements were constructed of the same type of marble, unfortunately later replaced by granite. The Neoclassical gem went dark in 2007, and preservationists worried about the fate of the building and True's work, as plan after plan fell through.

A developer found a deal that could work to resuscitate the building by adding two floors, set back to the six-story structure, and basically cutting a hole in the center of the bank's top floors in order to create a light well. In the process, architects from klipp will transform the bank into a hotel. The great metal doors will again serve as an entrance, and the murals will be saved.
National Register of Historic Places, seeking to become a Denver Landmark,
and part of the Downtown Denver Historic District

23 **Boston Building / Boston Lofts**
828 17th Street
Andrews, Jacques, and Rantoul, 1890

Businessman Henry R. Wolcott commissioned this building in a time of technological change. Although the Boston Building was among the last of the all-masonry office buildings constructed downtown, his charge to the architects was to create a modern building.

Andrews, Jacques, and Rantoul, which also designed the more refined Equitable Building, responded by creating an adaptation of the Richardsonian Romanesque style, using huge blocks of Colorado red sandstone. For all its heavy stone, the Boston Building also includes Renaissance Revival flourishes. Its windows are arcaded, with a symmetrical arrangement of flat lintel and round arched windows grouped together vertically within those arcades. A ground floor below street grade supports eight stories above a cubed block base.

Carved arches abound, though some areas have weathered, and fanciful touches include stone colonnettes and mullions. Over the years, the building has gone through renovations, with the doors especially attracting attention. Built on the site of Wolfe Hall, an Episcopal school for girls torn down in 1889, the Boston Building was transformed into apartments in the 1990s.
National Register of Historic Places, Denver Landmark, and part of the Downtown Denver Landmark District

24 **Ideal Building / Denver National Bank / Colorado Business Bank Building**
821 17th Street
Montana Fallis and John J. Stein, 1907

Built by a holding company controlled by Claude Boettcher and F.A. Bonfils, the Ideal (as in Ideal Cement) is described as the first reinforced concrete multistory building constructed west of the Mississippi. A basic commercial style building, the Ideal features fine travertine facing and a heavily decorated cornice including arches and insets.

In the 1920s, Fisher and Fisher added a penthouse, along with generous decorative touches by notable artists with regional emphasis. These include reliefs of the history of money and banking by Arnold Ronnebeck, doors featuring images of Indian dances by Nena de Brennecke, exterior column heads of animals and geometric plaques by Clara S. Dieman, and a painted ceiling by John E. Thompson. To show off the value of concrete construction, the developers supposedly set a fire to test the basement's safety. Construction may rest on a basic material, but the building's textured stone veneer makes it appear more elegant. An early 21st-century renovation included restoration of the elaborate interior artwork, with updates to the facade, lobby, and main banking room.
National Register of Historic Places, Denver Landmark, and part of the Downtown Denver Historic District

25 Chamber of Commerce Building
1720–30 Champa Street
Willis Marean and Albert Norton, 1910; renovation by OZ Architects, 1998

Taken with the Buerger Brothers Beauty Supply Building and Denver Fire Clay Building next door, the old chamber building is one of the preservation success stories of the 1990s. All three were given not only new uses but also their old distinctive appearance during renovations that brought them back to life as apartments.

That their years of origin span four decades and three styles is part of the appeal of this ensemble. The Chamber Building, for instance, is a Neoclassical gem that had been covered with a metal facade in a process that damaged some original elements.

Renovation restored the granite and terra cotta-facade of the five-story structure, which is marked by garlands and Ionic columns. Also restored were some 400 lights that outlined the facade's features in its heyday, making the building glow again.
National Register of Historic Places and part of the Downtown Denver Historic District

26 Buerger Brothers Beauty Supply Building and Denver Fire Clay Building
1732–40 Champa Street, 1742 Champa Street
M.S. Fallis Co. (Buerger Brothers), 1929, and J.S. Brien (original design of Fire Clay), 1892; renovation by OZ Architects, 1998

The five-story Buerger Brothers building was an office and manufacturing center devoted to the promotion of beauty and fantasy. So what better facade than one devoted to exactly the same thing, expressed in terra-cotta and elaborate Art Deco decoration? In this, Buerger Brothers is rich, with chevrons, plumes, and floral elements formed in colorful terra-cotta along decorative spandrels and at the roofline. The renovation included repair work, especially at the stone base and on the original signage.

The Fire Clay Building next door is a more streamlined affair. Gutted by fire, the structure was rebuilt to connect to Buerger Brothers, though the facades remain separate.
National Register of Historic Places and part of the Downtown Denver Historic District

27 U.S. National Bank / Guaranty Bank Building / Bank Lofts
817 17th Street
Fisher and Fisher, 1921; reconfiguration, C.W. Fentress J.H Bradburn and Associates, 1997

Guaranty Bank may not have been as richly detailed as the neighboring Boston and Equitable Buildings, but Guaranty carried the air of a sober financial institution, with Classical Revival lines in solid limestone. It had housed a succession of banks, beginning with U.S. National and ending with Guaranty.

The Guaranty Building is not defined by complexity. What exists is restrained, including Ionic pilasters along the lower two floors, paired along 17th Street, single along Stout Street. The base is separated from the upper stories by a heavy entablature – topped off by a broad cornice marked by dentiling and other ornament.

For years, the Guaranty sat empty. It was considered too old-fashioned for office space, and stripped of much of its elegant interior fittings by a developer who planned to raze it; then it went broke. As a result, the Guaranty site almost became a parking lot on 17th Street. It was saved by landmark status and savvy reuse.

Lower floors now house retail and support residences above; lower interior "skylights" were removed and one installed at the roof to re-create the original atrium interior. Coffered ceilings were restored and painted marble (of what remained) uncovered.
National Register of Historic Places, Denver Landmark, and part of the Downtown Denver Historic District

28 Equitable Building
730 17th Street
Andrews, Jacques and Rantoul, 1892

How proud Denver must have been when this elegant Italian Renaissance Revival building was completed.

Designed so that it is like two "E's" laid back to back, the Equitable thus featured lightwells that provided natural light to most offices. It was built at the tail end of the pre–Silver Crash boom, as the western office for the Equitable Assurance Co. of New York. The Equitable helped attract other financial concerns to 17th Street, though by 1893 it also served as home for Colorado's executive offices during construction of the State Capitol.

United throughout at the street level by a darker, granite base, the Equitable rises nine stories – becoming more ornately decorated as it climbs – with granite on the first two floors and pressed brick above. The architects employed as much Classical embellishment as possible, including dentils, egg-and-dart molding, a bound acanthus, and a window in a Palladian arrangement. Terra-cotta is used for courses between floors and on the elaborate cornice.

Equitable obviously wanted nothing but the best, and that is apparent also in the interior, one of the most beautiful in town: The lobby is lined with buttery yellow marble, with deep-red marble floors, marble pillars, a glass-mosaic-lined groin vault ceiling, a grand bronze staircase, and Tiffany windows. It is now an office condominium.
National Register of Historic Places, Denver Landmark, and part of the Downtown Denver Historic District

29 First Interstate Towers / Colorado Plaza
621 17th Street and 633 17th Street
Raymond Harry Ervin, 1958; second tower Welton Becket and Associates,1973

Raymond Harry Ervin's original tower is a vertical Modernist sentinel in polished precast, terrazzo, aluminum, and glass, facing California Street as 621 17th Street. Across the plaza is a second tower, 633 17th Street, set at a right angle and completed 15 years later by the firm that evolved into Ellerbe Becket. There, rigid steel and precast support a glass curtain wall.

Both are uncompromising designs that epitomize conservative civic architecture, though updates designed to freshen the buildings have been ongoing in lobbies, entry elements, and names. M. Paul Freedburg's silver cylinders have been removed from a plaza that for years was a constant in downtown open spaces.

30 555 17th Street / Anaconda Tower
555 17th Street
Skidmore, Owings, and Merrill, 1978

If SOM's Republic Plaza manages transparency through the use of copious square windows and lightstone, the firm's earlier Anaconda Tower achieves a timeless state through an abundance of black glass and metal. Its severe lines and elegant simplicity make it as much sculptural object as building, and indicate another means – through shifts in structural elements – by which an architect can define the parts of a skyscraper. An interior mural and furnishings by Herbert Bayer were removed during a mid-1990s renovation, an attempt to modernize by eliminating Modern elements.

31 Brinker Collegiate Institute / The Navarre
1725–27 Tremont Place
Planned by Frank Edbrooke, 1880

If one historic Denver building has seen change, it is the old Navarre.

Built as the Brinker Collegiate Institute, the first coed college west of the Mississippi, this small but powerful brick confection later became the Richelieu Hotel and then the Navarre (gambling hall and brothel), a restaurant and a jazz club, and a home for art (William Foxley's Museum of Western Art, after a fine interior renovation by C.W. Fentress and Associates and John M. Prosser). The building now houses the American Museum of Western Art, which is devoted to the fine collection owned by businessman Philip Anschutz.

Over the decades, porches have been opened and enclosed (and added and removed) and a cupola and chimneys excised, but the basic Victorian building remains. Brick walls are divided by a wide stone belt course between the first and second floors. The hipped roof features pedimented gables with returns on three sides. At the roofline are double bracketed cornices, with segmental window openings with elaborate arched surrounds. In all, the Navarre is fancy and fanciful, and typical of the stylistic flourishes popular in the era.
National Register of Historic Places, Denver Landmark, and part of the Downtown Denver Historic District

32 Brown Palace Hotel
321 17th Street, at Tremont Place
Frank Edbrooke, 1892

In luxurious dressed and carved sandstone on a granite base, the Brown is a historic showpiece of pre–Silver Crash Denver. Edbrooke built on a triangle, claiming one of the city's awkward grid-changing corners with a beautifully proportioned building – Denver's own pre-Flatiron Flatiron. Richardsonian Romanesque principals and materials gained grace from Neoclassical attitudes. Henry C. Brown, who helped develop the Capitol Hill area, reportedly spent $2 million on the hotel, which took four years to construct.

Because of weathering to the stone, reliefs by sculptor James Whitehouse are almost gone, except for a few roundels and the cherub-and-garland decoration over the heavily corbelled entrance on 17th Street. The removal of Whitehouse's work ended some of the sense of whimsy on this powerful building set on an early steel skeleton.

Inside, a nine-story atrium lifts the visitor up from the central lobby, while a second-level walkway leads to the concrete guest-room tower addition next door (W.B. Tabler Associates). And despite attempts by historians to refute it, the tale persists of tunnels from the Brown to the nearby Navarre, a supposed guest amenity during the latter's term as a brothel.
National Register of Historic Places, Denver Landmark, and part of the Downtown Denver Historic District

33 Mile High Center / One United Bank Tower / Wells Fargo Center
1700 Broadway
I.M. Pei & Partners, Kahn & Jacobs, and G. Meredith Musick, 1955 / Johnson and Burgee, 1980–83

The 23-story Mile High Center was Pei's first project for Denver, as a designer for developer William Zeckendorf. The main building covered just a portion of the land, reserving space for an exhibition hall – called a "transportation center" and styled to look like an airport terminal – as well as such public amenities as a plaza and fountains. In a move to make the ground floor less cluttered, retail was moved underground.

Pei saved the tower's facade from a static feel and promoted the importance of new technology by weaving dark gray cast aluminum panels (covering the columns and spandrel beams) over and under buff porcelain panels that concealed mechanical elements. (According to a story on the building's opening in the magazine *Architectural Record*, Mile High brought air conditioning to Denver's office scene.) Interiors were designed by Denver architect James Sudler.

Along with introducing an element of urban planning into the site and using two unusual materials in a modern office building, Mile High challenged the city's height limit ordinance – and won. But Mile High was not allowed its spacious splendor for long.

Philip Johnson and John Burgee's pink granite, 50-story, cash-register-shape-topped One United Bank Tower (now named after the most recent successor,

Wells Fargo) went up on an adjacent block in the early 1980s. The two buildings coexisted nicely. But the later addition of atrium-style entries swallows a portion of the Pei building, which had attracted attention for its sense of all four sides floating free. The cash-register shape, echoed at street level entrances added in 1986, has contributed a memorable element to the city's skyline, but marred part of its streetscape and the integrity of a worthy earlier design. A luxurious interior – especially the elevators – speaks of the 1980s sense of wealth, while Ed Carpenter's ethereal dichroic glass and fabric *Altaflora* (2002) helps define the double-vaulted atrium.

34 Amoco Tower / 1670 Broadway
1670 Broadway
Kohn Pedersen Fox, 1980

For one of the early glitzy buildings of the 1980s boom, Kohn Pedersen Fox designed a 36-story aluminum and glass-clad office tower originally known as Columbia Plaza.

The structure provides a terminus to the 17th Street financial district, yet manages to relate to the neighboring Brown Palace Hotel. Rounded corners soften the effect of the strong horizontality produced by bands of metal and glass. Its sleek lines sparkle at the edge of the business district, bringing together one of Denver's many intersections that include a shift in street grid. Though splendid by day, the building really shines at night, or at least the lobby decoration installed by tenant UMB Bank does: a flutter of Dale Chihuly glass wall sculptures, titled *Colorado Wild Flowers*, climbs a back wall and lights up the street.

35 Curry-Chucovich House
1439 Court Place
Fred A. Hale, 1888

Now an office building, the old Curry-Chucovich House sits alone in a sea of parking lots. Built on a 25-foot lot, standard in 19th-century Denver, the house has a sandstone facade with a rhyolite foundation. The Victorian vernacular architecture includes details such as crossetted lintels on the first floor, keystones and voussoirs on the second-floor windows, and a wooden cornice with a recessed, paneled frieze.

The lavish use of stone was a natural. Owner James Curry ran quarries in Douglas County, reportedly providing stone for buildings ranging from Trinity Methodist Church to the Kittredge Building – and his own house. After Curry's death in 1892, the house came into possession of Vasco L. Chucovich, an investor, politico, and gambler.
National Register of Historic Places and Denver Landmark

36 Denver Press Club
1330 Glenarm Place
Merrill and Burnham Hoyt, 1925

The Press Club has seen some ups and downs in its lifetime, including the addition of a metal canopy that detracts from the brick and terra-cotta attention the Hoyts lavished on this little building. Quoining continues the sense of propriety in a place that has often been lacking in that virtue.

The interior has been reconfigured over the years, including a renovation/restoration in 2001 that included moving the bar from the back of the first floor to the front of the house and in the process uncovering a fireplace in what was an entry parlor. Of note: A 1945 mural by Herndon Davis in the downstairs poker room was restored in the late 1990s, keeping alive the journalistic lights depicted there. Davis left murals around the state, some reportedly done in payment for his consumption of libations.
Denver Landmark

37 Denver Athletic Club
1325 Glenarm Place
Lester Varian & Frederick Sterner, 1890, with several additions and reconstructions: Varian and Sterner in 1892; Lindner, Hodgson ,and Wright in 1951; Rodney S. Davis in 1973; James Sudler and Joal Cronenwett in 1984, and Pouw and Associates in 1996

The club is a rare downtown building to exhibit stylistic shifts so openly through more than a century of construction in Denver.

A gathering place for the health-minded was on the minds of the men who founded the DAC in 1884. By 1889, the group had mustered the resources to commission noted architects Varian and Sterner to create a Richardsonian Romanesque stone and brick building on Glenarm Place. The stone is worked in the manner of that popular style, and the entry arch is a welcoming signal of the original building. Tight eyebrow arches added rhythm and regularity to the design. Heavy iron ornamentation signaled the club as a society haunt.

Over the years, growth and change have prompted the club to expand, first with a wing to the east designed by the same architects. A replacement for the gymnasium, destroyed in a 1951 fire, added more contemporary lines, as did Rodney S. Davis's athletic wing, which extended the club to 13th Street.

The Sudler-Cronenwett addition, a new athletic wing, indicated the club's shifts in emphasis. Civic functions and events were scheduled at the club, which needed space to serve its members' needs. A 1996 fitness center and outdoor roof deck for parties capped off the corner of 14th Street at Glenarm; the design by Pouw and Associates included a stylized cornice that helped tie the addition to older portions of the club while not mimicking the past.
National Register of Historic Places and Denver Landmark

38 Colorado Convention Center
14th Street between Speer Boulevard and Welton Street
Fentress Bradburn Architects, 2004

During the oil bust era in which Denver hit bottom, the city began a program of civic reinvestment that paid off in a better economy. But whether it paid off in better buildings was another matter entirely.

That certainly was the case with the first Colorado Convention Center, completed in 1990 by the firm then known as Curt Fentress, J.H. Bradburn, and Associates. Focus groups and trade organizations had a lot of input into the design of the convention center, which included 292,000 square feet of exhibit space and about 100,000 square feet for meetings and functions. Among their judgments: No windows, thus producing a building that had very little interaction with the streets outside. Built from gray and pink precast concrete through an early design-build process, the convention center opened up only at its entrances, with the liberal use of glass and white tubular elements that appeared to create a gothic arch by way of Tinker Toys.
Western Mountain Region Merit Award, 1990; AIA Colorado Honor Award, 1990

Even as the first edition of the convention center opened, plans were brewing to double its size. A wall along Stout Street had been left totally blank with the intention of at some point expanding the center onto adjacent space. Despite pleas to somehow incorporate the forward-looking Currigan Hall into the expansion, the building was torn down – one of many lost in the quest for more meeting space and a convention center hotel.

The expanded convention center, which incorporated the first one, now covers nine city blocks, but as a structure marked by panoramic curtain walls and sweeping metal prows that help link Speer Boulevard to the central business district. The addition of a parking garage and 5,000-seat auditorium with its own lobby and entrance has formed connections, as has a light rail station integrated into the building. The latter required a bump-out curve in Stout Street, which shoots travelers from Speer to 14th Street. Those soaring glass walls also connect with the city's life outside.

Inside, the decor is neutral, with an abundance of white walls and spaces for numerous works funded by the city's Percent for Art Program. One massive exterior sculpture – Lawrence Argent's *I See What You Mean* – is fondly referred to as the Big Blue Bear, which is sited to look as if were peering inside the convention center. It has helped the convention center become an unexpected landmark.
AIA Colorado Citation Award, 2006

39 14th Street Streetscaping Project
Parsons Brinkerhoff and studioINSITE, 2011

The opening of a greatly expanded Colorado Convention Center – and a healthy economy in much of the first decade of the 21st century – led to a construction boom along 14th Street, once considered a dark spot in Denver's downtown business district. Funds from the 2007 Better Denver Bond Program – and $4 million in assessments from members of a new 14th Street General Improvement

District – raised a total of $14 million for improvements along a 12-block stretch of 14th Street, beginning at Market Street and heading toward Civic Center. This entailed expanding sidewalks and introducing decorative elements, adding a bicycle lane, better lighting and signage, planters, and additional trees. The city is now using the term "Ambassador Street" to refer to 14th, since it links so many attractions that cater to visitors as well as residents, and reflects more than $1.5 billion in public-private investment.

40 The Spire
891 14th Street
RNL Design, 2009

Despite being hit by financial drawbacks, developer Randy Nichols completed the Spire to a contemporary design that relies on glass and steel to create a smart-looking high-rise that earned LEED certification – NC. The 41-story structure, containing 33 floors of condominiums set atop 8 stories of parking and retail, continued the growth along 14th Street, taking design cues from the Colorado Convention Center and adding some street interest with a shimmering kinetic glass art wall fronting 14th. It may not actually sport a spire, but the Spire has added drama and density to downtown.

Two blocks away, at 1111 14th Street, the **Four Seasons Hotel and Residences** opened in 2010 as the new high-rise with a spire. Built to a design by Carney Burke Logan Architects of Jackson, Wyoming, with HKS Inc. of Dallas, the 45-story Four Seasons includes 16 floors of hotel rooms, with the rest devoted to upscale condominiums. The primary materials are concrete and glass, with dark bronze–colored mullions. Though a spire helps bump the building into the very-tall category, the design is more serviceable than inspired – despite elements intended to emphasize its vertical sensibility.

41 Mountain States Telephone Building
931 14th Street
William N. Bowman, 1929

Before communications went digital, the high-tech telephone company operated out of a building designed in the unusual American perpendicular style. Gothic elements, setbacks and soaring entry arches are expressed in terra-cotta, brick, and granite, producing an elaborate facade and imposing street presence. The interior surfaces of the entry arches are richly detailed, resembling brocaded fabric.

Historians note that the Mountain States Telephone Building is the first structure under the 1927 zoning code to be allowed extra height because of the setbacks included as it climbed. William N. Bowman stressed Gothic elements in this ultravertical design, while working an Art Deco impulse into the mix. Inside are notable murals by Colorado artist Allen Tupper True.
Part of the Downtown Denver Historic District

42 Hyatt Regency at the Convention Center Hotel
650 15th Street
klipp, with Brennan Beer Gorman Architects, 2005

Denver's long-sought "convention center hotel" debuted about a year after the expanded Colorado Convention Center, adding another project that stressed public art while including many privately funded paintings, sculptures, and photographs.

The city's hotel authority, created for this project, oversaw design and construction of a $285 million 538-foot-tall building that seems almost weightless against the sky, while presenting four sides at street level that exhibit a sense of rhythm and movement. The lower-level facades are bounded by 14th, 15th, California, and Welton Streets, and disappear at a distance, while not overwhelming passersby on the street nearby.

The architects' vision produced two streamlined towers that appear to pull against each other in a play of welcome tension. A beacon element adds drama, while Art Deco–flavored touches lend an urban sensibility, recalling to the former Denver Post building on that site until its demolition in 1998. The entry facade is a little uneasy meeting the street, and the wall along Welton Street is turned over to service entries and parking access.

But a dark granite base, some of it the background medium for the Percent for Art installation by Joseph Kosuth, helps tie together a project constructed of limestone, precast concrete, copious amounts of glass, and zinc panels, all in shifting patterns and popped-out planes. Some walls appear to float, windows range from ribbon-like strips of glass to unexpected slits, as at the corner of Welton and 14th Streets. The metal-framed glass wall facing California features a raised stone square that marks the presence of a boardroom inside. Matte metal protrusions off the 14th Street facade are a nod to the metal blades on the convention center. Several entryways, and all that glass, energize the entire composition.
AIA Colorado Citation Award, 2006

43 Gas and Electric Building / Insurance Exchange Building
910 15th Street
Frank Edbrooke and Co. (H.W.J. Edbrooke), 1910

The 15th Street Investment Co. commissioned Harry Edbrooke to design a building for the Denver Gas and Electric Light Co. What he produced amounted to an advertisement for electric lights, set against the strict formal structure of the style of commercial architecture propelled into prominence by Chicago architect Louis Sullivan.

Harry Edbrooke's 10-story pressed brick building is resplendent with white terra-cotta facing and green marble accents – and more than 13,000 electric lights. (Edbrooke was a nephew of Frank Edbrooke and worked in that office until founding his own firm.) Arched windows on the 10th floor, a shift from the rectangular shapes below, signal the beginning of a prominent cornice. In the 1960s, the building was sold, renamed the Insurance Exchange Building, and

received a renovation by Gass-Gay Architects. In the 1990s, another renovation took place, putting the lights back into action after going dark during the energy crisis of the 1970s.
National Register of Historic Places, Denver Landmark, and part of the Downtown Denver Historic District

44 Denver Performing Arts Complex
Speer Boulevard at Arapahoe Street
Master plan: John Dinkeloo and Kevin Roche; Boettcher Hall: Hardy, Holzman, Pfeiffer Associates (1978); Denver Center for the Performing Arts theaters: Kevin Roche, John Dinkeloo and Associates (1979); Galleria Theatre: Muchow & Associates (and parking garages, which opened 1977); Temple Hoyne Buell Theatre, replacing the old arena: Beyer Blinder Belle (lobby and facade), Van Dijk, Johnson & Partners (interior), Semple Brown Roberts (restoration work) (1991); Donald R. Seawell Grand Ballroom: Roche Dinkeloo Associates (1998); Sculpture Park: EDAW with various city agencies (1998); Ellie Caulkins Opera House (2005), Semple Brown Design, constructed inside what is now the Quigg Newton Denver Municipal Auditorium, Robert O. Willison (1908); proposed reconstruction of Boettcher Concert Hall by Diamond & Schmitt

What is now the city's mega-complex of theaters and performance spaces started in 1908 with the hearty Denver Municipal Auditorium. The big Neoclassical structure opened just in time to host that year's Democratic National Convention.

But over the decades, the auditorium suffered through various exterior and interior shufflings that diminished its presence. Its street orientation was shifted, and part of its pediment was removed during construction of glass-grid vaults over the street-like Galleria. By the 1990s, the auditorium theater was ripe for an exterior cleanup and refurbishment of the lights that had made it sparkle 80 years before. The occasion for the early 1990s cleanup was the addition to the complex of a new component, the Buell Theatre, as well as the construction of a third vault.

All this reworking revolved around the Denver Performing Arts Center, developed in the late 1970s by Helen Bonfils and Donald Seawell. These keepers of the cash box that resulted from the Bonfils family fortune (derived from ownership of the *Denver Post*) rebuilt four city blocks to make their dream come true.

The idea wasn't exactly to trump New York's Lincoln Center – the DPAC ranks itself as number 2 in the nation in terms of assembled seating – but the firm brought in to create a master plan was East Coast born and bred. So were the architects charged with designing Boettcher Hall, the in-the-round concert space in a square shell that plays off the rounded exterior form of the theater complex nearby.

The designers overall worked in a late Modern style that touched on brutalism, in gray-brown poured-in-place concrete and brick with hard edges and an uncompromising presentation. Viewed from Speer Boulevard, the Plex, as it has come to be called, appeared to turn its back on the city, buffered from Speer by a broad lawn of green that evolved into a park and open space for events.

Though the geometry of the space and the integrity of the materials made for a memorable complex, the cry went up in the late 1980s to add another hall, one that would serve to pull in additional profitable road shows. After a slow fund-raising program, the city kicked in bond money, and the Buell Theatre was born where an old arena had stood.

In squeezing the Buell into an existing space, the architects also added color to the complex, in a glass and steel facade that sported eggplant and rose and the fillip of Juliet balconies. Eventually, signage on the entire complex was jazzed up on both the facades facing in to the Galleria and the outer edge facing Speer. The addition of a ballroom with stunning views has further opened the complex with generous windows facing Speer.

Playful artwork by Fernando Botero was installed in the Galleria to augment an abstract sculpture by Victor Contreras. The park between the complex and Speer Boulevard became the site of occasional sculptural installations, though Jonathan Borofsky's *Dancers* – ungainly androgynous white figures – has taken up residence among the light posts and concrete forms out of scale even for a broad expanse of lawn.

The most important addition to the complex came in the form of the Ellie Caulkins Opera House, or Ellie, constructed in 2005 for $92 million in public and private funds inside the dark, tattered, and potentially dangerous Auditorium Theatre. Most original elements had been scraped years ago, but architects left portions of stone walls and steel beams exposed as a nod to history. Designed as a lyric opera house in form, the 2,268-seat venue for opera and ballet is marked by gleaming cherry wood panels on side walls, balcony fronts, and ceiling insets, as well as sand-colored terrazzo floors in the lobby. The entry was reoriented back to the Galleria, and marked inside by a Dale Chihuly glass sculpture. The Studio Loft rehearsal and event space in the Municipal Auditorium was completed in 2011, funded by 2007 bond money.

Soon Boettcher Concert Hall became the next candidate for renewal, as the leadership of the Colorado Symphony Orchestra complained about bad acoustics, the barrier to connecting to Speer Boulevard, and the drawbacks of the in-the-round configuration. In 2008, city officials selected Toronto-based Diamond & Schmitt, with OZ Architects, to remake Boettcher. Although bond money was in place, the symphony's required private contributions were hurt by a sinking economy, postponing initiation of the $90 million project focused on building a glass facade facing Speer.
Denver Center for the Performing Arts: AIA Denver 25 year Award, 2011

45 Tramway Building / Teatro Hotel
1100 14th Street
William E. Fisher and Arthur A. Fisher, 1911; renovation into a hotel,
David Owen Tryba Architects, 1999

Built on the site of former governor John Evans's house by his son, William Gray Evans, the Denver Tramway Co. headquarters was linked to attached trolley car barns down to 13th Street. The eight-story office building and two-story barns were linked by the same dark red brick facade and heady dose of white terra-cotta trim.

In the 1950s, the structure became part of the University of Colorado Denver, which moved back onto campus in the 1980s and sold the facilities to the Denver Center for the Performing Arts.

Eventually, developers saw an opening to renovate the office building portion into a boutique hotel with interiors that follow a performance theme prompted by its proximity to the Denver Center for Performing Arts. Meanwhile, the car barns at 1101 13th Street received a 2003 renovation by Eric Bartczak Architects and Pamela Bartczak Interior Design, as facilities for the DCPA.
National Register of Historic Places, Denver Landmark, and part of Downtown Denver Historic District

46 Residences at Lawrence Street Center
1350–80 Lawrence Street,
McOg Architects, 1982

Office and residential space came together – joined with a jolt of red neon – in a project that early on brought condos to the edge of downtown. The architects worked in an L-shaped space and inventive angles to minimize the bulk of the project. Generous use of glass is key to the project's success, in a prominent part of the city.

47 Denver City Cable Railway Building / Denver Tramway Company Building / Spaghetti Factory
1215 18th Street
Architect not known, 1889; 1974 renovation by James Sudler

Offices and a restaurant now fill a Romanesque Revival building that had been used for power generators for Denver's cable car system and later a home for trolleys and mass transit offices. Elaborate arches, starburst roundels, and magnificent corbelled brick at the entry mark what could have been a simple utilitarian building. Sudler moved his offices into the building after renovation, a pioneering venture into that part of Denver.
National Register of Historic Places and Denver Landmark

48 The A.H. Ghost Building
800 18th Street
William Lang, 1889

Moved to this location in 1985, the Ghost Building lived up to (part of) its name by vanishing for several years. It was torn down from its original site near 15th Street and Glenarm Place in the late 1970s. The building, which actually refers to pioneer developer A.H. Ghost, sat in storage for several years before developer Sandy Brown bought the 1,700 or so stones and found it a new home.

The North Dakota limestone blocks originally had been fashioned into a Romanesque structure by an architect better known for residential design. Lang worked wonders in stone, and that shows in the Ghost, which continues to house a restaurant.
Part of the Downtown Denver Landmark District

49 Church of the Holy Ghost / 1999 Broadway
1900 California Street / 19th Street at Broadway
Jacques J.B. Benedict, 1943, with addition by John Monroe;
C.W. Fentress and Associates, 1985

When the Church of the Holy Ghost sold its air rights for development, 1999 Broadway was the result. On land upon which a cloister and rectory had stood, the architects wrapped a 43-story triangular tower around the Renaissance-style church. In the process, one of the city's more unusual pairings was created.

1999 Broadway uses the church's cruciform plan as a focal point and the intersection as a triangular edge. Facing the church, the new building is concave; away from the church, a corner wall addresses the city's central business district and acts as a terminus for the Broadway axis. The glass of the office building plays off the church's green tile roof, while its limestone quoining recalls the church's terra-cotta-trimmed brick exterior. A stepped arcade – on 50-foot columns – created a plaza to allow some space around the old church, which was restored as part of the development project. A later office building owner added lighted green dash lines that define the building's edges at night.

Though the 1999 Broadway interior is suited for an office building, the Holy Ghost sanctuary is resplendent in lush colocreme marble, with elaborate iron chandeliers, a soaring arched and coffered ceiling, and elegant details throughout.
Western Mountain Region Honor Award, 1985; AIA Colorado Merit Award, 1990

50 One Lincoln Park
100 E. 20th Avenue
Buchanan Yonushewski Group, 2008

This 32-story residential tower is sited in a somewhat desolate part of town at an intersection that can be one big tangle, making it seem abandoned on its own private island. If you're viewing One Lincoln Park from that intersection, it becomes apparent that the architects placed this high-rise on a fairly pedestrian podium. Move away a few blocks, and suddenly the high-rise takes its place on the skyline. The most memorable feature: its curved roofline, topping upper floors that are set back and more detailed than the lower level.

FEDERAL DISTRICT

51 Byron White U.S. Courthouse (former Court of Appeals) / U.S. Post Office
1823 Stout Street
Tracy, Swarthout & Litchfield, 1916; renovation into courts by Michael Barber Architecture, 1994 (one courtroom had been renovated in 1983 by Hoover Berg Desmond); 2011 window design study by Bennett Wagner & Grody Architects

In 1901, Denver businessmen began to campaign for a real federal building, and eight years later, their quest paid off. The U.S. Treasury Department asked a dozen architectural firms to apply for a competition to design a new post office

and courthouse in Denver. The firm chosen, Tracy, Swartwout, and Litchfield, also designed St. John's Cathedral and included two alumni of McKim, Mead & White – Tracy and Swartwout.

Their proposal set the standard for Neoclassical Revival architecture in Denver. The imposing exterior facades featured a three-story portico of 16 Ionic columns along Stout Street, with modified Ionic columns on the other three elevations. An eagle motif was worked into the Ionic form, and the facades were capped by a generous entablature that wraps around the building. Details include dentils, acanthus leaves, and medallions, all used to set off exterior marble walls. The building, which occupies a full city block, appears elevated by being placed on a platform, reached by elevated stairs. The architects shifted gears for the interior light courts, there working in a Renaissance Revival style, with walls faced in limestone.

The original interior included a lobby and court functions, with a section devoted to the post office. Construction delays were common because of glitches in appropriating money for the project. Eventually, though, the courthouse/post office was completed. The building went through its share of change, including one brutal 1960s remodel in which the vaulted appeals courtroom was cut in two – horizontally – despite the architects' protests. Hallways and other beautiful spaces were reworked into offices, degrading the building's style and status.

A $28 million renovation ended with the building's dedication in 1994 as the Byron White U.S. Courthouse. Architects removed false walls and ceilings, restored fittings, uncovered skylights, cleaned the exterior, and made the once-proud building proud again. Some post office apparatus was kept as a reminder of that era. Four courtrooms and chambers were built over two floors, with color added through carpeting and furnishings; the appeals courtroom was restored. During the process, art with a western theme was installed throughout. These pieces joined one of the city's best known public art projects: Gladys Caldwell Fisher's two, six-and-one-half ton sheep at the 18th Street entrance were completed in 1936 through the Works Progress Administration, and murals on agriculture and mining by H.T. Schladermundt of New York had been installed in 1918. *National Register, Denver Landmark, and part of the Downtown Denver Historic District*

52 U.S. Post Office, Denver Downtown Station
951 20th Street
Hoover Berg Desmond, 1991

In a design about as far from traditional Federal fare as possible, the architects relied on cast block and glass grids to add presence to the block. There are, though, references to a more Neoclassical postal facility, in the form of an arcaded walkway along the center section of the building, with the addition of prominent square arches protruding from the 20th Street facade. The back of the structure, facing the parking lot, is almost devoid of detail, though the other aspects reveal a play of recessed spaces and geometric forms.

53 U.S. Courthouse and Byron G. Rogers Federal Building
1929–61 Stout Street
James Sudler Associates, design architect, and Fisher and Davis, 1965;
GSA First Impressions reconfiguration and energy improvements, Gensler,
2002, and Bennett Wagner & Grody, Architects, 2006; GSA green
modernization, HOK, design architect, and Bennett Wagner & Grody Architects,
architect of record, projected completion in 2013

This mid-1960s Modernist design for a court and federal office facility relied on a combination of complementary geometric shapes and elegant Formalist lines to express a forward-thinking view of government services, which were expanding in the Denver metro area.

For the 18-story federal office tower, the architects created a tall rectangle that is not quite a true rectangle, since its sides pull in from a middle point as if to touch. For the courthouse, the design was more straightforward: a low, simple rectangle, compatible with the scale of nearby traditional federal buildings. The courthouse is marked at the center of its facade by an abstract aluminum screen designed by Alan Gass.

The structures differ in height, but Sudler used similar materials for both, including various elements in marble and aggregate panels for walls, base, windows, and top. The components are linked by a plaza and walkways, which were redesigned in a sensitive manner to accommodate security needs as well as retain the covered walkway – a task undertaken in 2002 through 2006 to respect suggestions made by the preservation community. The result: a subtle glass pavilion to house security screening. The exterior artwork includes a massive bronze Great Seal of the United States by William Joseph and a bronze column by Edgar Britton on the plaza. These notable pieces mark a complex made timeless by its composition and materials.

The most recent work on the Rogers Federal Building involves the interiors only, introducing energy-saving practices, retrofitting windows, and installing new systems, such as chilled beams and a heat sink, with the goal of achieving LEED Gold certification.
Renovation: AIA Denver Honor Award, 2006

54 U.S. Custom House
721 19th Street
James A. Wetmore, 1931; addition in 1937 by G. Meredith Musick and
Temple H. Buell; green modernization design-build project, Bennett Wagner &
Grody Architects, architect of record

The original five-story Italian Renaissance Revival Custom House is partially faced with Colorado Yule marble on a granite foundation, with granite steps rising to arched doorways. Marble continues in surrounds and lobby trim, though the fifth floor is light-colored brick. Even though the contract called for limestone, Colorado legislators insisted on the Yule marble, adding to the cost, but with tremendous payback. Terra-cotta is used liberally on the spandrels and banding separating the first floor from upper stories, as well as on the cornice and reliefs.

Wetmore, a supervisory architect with the U.S. Treasury Department, designed each facade with a different sensibility, relying on symmetry on the 19th Street side, but asymmetrical forms on California Street. The Stout Street side was reduced in importance during the addition of a basement entrance.

A 1937 addition extended the building to 20th Street, while adding penthouse features and filling in an interior courtyard. A Works Progress Administration project, the addition again used Yule marble instead of cheaper non-Colorado stone. Repairs after a 1971 bombing included the addition of another section but removal of the old doors. The most recent work includes architectural upgrades and installation of mechanical and electrical systems that will improve energy efficiency, part of the General Services Administration's sweeping green modernization program.
National Register

55 Alfred A. Arraj U.S. Courthouse
901 19th Street
Hellmuth Obata + Kassabaum, with Anderson Mason Dale, 2002

The addition of this new U.S. courthouse confirmed Denver's Federal Court Campus as eclectic in the best sense of the word. The charge was to provide more court and office space for the fine 1965 Modernist U.S. Courthouse and Byron G. Rogers Federal Building. But the Arraj was to be sited next to that complex and facing the same direction. The ability to make a connection was limited, even if the project that became the Arraj for years was referred to as an annex. Still, the new courthouse turned to the Neoclassical Byron White U.S. Courthouse for cues.

The result was using a pavilion to form the entry to the Arraj, a 10-story building containing 14 courtrooms that impresses with its clean lines and stone and brick construction. Its sleek aluminum columns reference the Ionic columns of the Byron G. White U.S. Courthouse. A metal web of cables and supports back the glass walls of the pavilion – a security measure as much as a design element. Constructed of buff brick on a limestone base, the courthouse retains a sense of transparency through its windows and an airy cornice, and openness through the addition of a low retaining wall that serves as a platform.

It is an elusive yet imposing posture, made even more so with the installation of Sol LeWitt's abstracted *Irregular Form*, with slabs of gray slate on a black ground.
AIA Denver Citation Award, 2003; AIA Colorado Honor Award 2003

Lower Downtown & Larimer Square

Lower downtown – bounded roughly by Wynkoop and the alley between Larimer and Market Streets, and between Speer Boulevard and 20th Street – is where Denver's commercial core took hold. The first mint was here, along with the merchants, the government, and the brothels. By turns rowdy and resplendent, lower downtown, now known as LoDo, has seen its reputation rise and fall with the times. Over the years, lower downtown became home to the Denver Union Terminal, after the consolidation of several depots scattered around town. It was where manufacturers supplying the region built their warehouses along Wynkoop Street. These boom-time barons hired architects of note – from Frank Edbrooke to Montana Fallis – who brought quality materials and impeccable detailing to the job.

From Victorian Commercial to Eclectic, these stately brick structures began to show a subtle stylistic shift to the more spare design tendencies growing out of Chicago as the 19th century turned into the 20th. Among those who imported the new sensibility here were Aaron Gove and Thomas Walsh, who had worked in Chicago (Walsh at Edbrooke and Burnham) and then Denver. Gove and Walsh designed several timeless commercial structures in the district.

Some mercantile buildings became hotels, while other, more grand buildings devoted to that purpose began to spring up, many along 17th Street, in order to serve business travelers who poured through nearby Union Station.

But that was the resplendent period. As the Denver economy performed one of its regular flip-flops, and as commerce shifted more into the center city, lower downtown's fortunes sank. Bars and flophouses took up more than their share of space. Demolitions began.

Organized urban renewal and its twin – not-so-benign neglect – were major forces in the loss of dozens of buildings and the scattering of people who actually lived in the neighborhood. By the time lower downtown was designated a historic district in 1988, more than one-fourth of the land there had been turned into parking lots. Landmark approval was a hard-fought battle, though forces led by then-mayor Federico Peña prevailed against property owners who complained that restrictions on their property would cost them money (thus the irregular district boundaries). Just the opposite would prove true. In the tapped-out late 1980s, designation instead brought financial help and the beneficial forum of design review. Artists and architects found cheap space for offices, studios, and galleries, cleaning up and improving property.

That adaptive reuse could pay shouldn't have been news. A group of preservation-minded developers had rescued the 1400 block of Larimer Street in the mid-1960s. Larimer Square became Denver's first historic district and a tourist magnet. Lower downtown also is a National Register historic district.

It was the recognition of the area's history and architectural importance – not the mid-1990s debut of nearby Coors Field – that turned lower downtown around. Renovations certainly began before then, when lofts truly were lofts, along with some small but important in-fill projects. Some of the gritty character and industrial edge were lost when viaducts at 15th and 16th Streets were moved, though suddenly it was possible to see buildings long hidden by iron trusses. More recently, construction has continued, with design statements primarily coming from striking new office buildings that share space with retail and residential, and work with the historic context.

Since baseball became a neighbor, lower downtown has undergone tremendous social change. Old warehouses now are home to (trendy) bars, restaurants, and, more importantly, residential property that has grown pricier and pricier. Artists and galleries are almost gone.

Always a neighborhood, lower downtown has become a star, although one feeling the pressures of balancing its status as an entertainment district with its growing popularity as a place to live and work. Just as fierce has been the struggle to maintain integrity in buildings whose owners wish to expand.

As building uses have shifted from commercial to residential, some familiar lower downtown addresses have changed, while other properties now have two addresses to reflect dual purposes. The good times have been good to lower downtown, the bad times remarkably gentle. Denver's party central now faces the debut of a regional transit hub in its midst: a repurposed Union Station, designed for the 21st century equivalent of the railroad, as well as hotel and retail operations. Development pressures will again be felt in a neighborhood once given up for lost.

40

LIST OF BUILDINGS

Downtown Denver

01

1 **Denver Union Terminal / Union Station**
17th and Wynkoop Streets
William E. Taylor, original center section and wings, 1881; center rebuilt after a
fire in 1894 (design in some sources credited to Van Brundt and Howe), then
torn down in 1914; new, existing center section designed by Gove and Walsh.
Major update and redevelopment, transforming the station into a hotel and
retail attraction (Union Station Alliance, including Tryba Architects, J.G Johnson
Architects and Sage Hospitality), with master planning by Skidmore, Owings, and
Merrill, and wing buildings by Anderson Mason Dale and Semple Brown Design;
expected completion 2014

Calamity and progress have changed the face of Denver's train station, producing
a building in which the center section is of a different style than the wings. Its
construction marked the consolidation of several depots into one Union Station.
And, a century later, Union Station has not stopped changing.

Kansas City architect William E. Taylor designed the original stations and adjoining
wings in pink lava stone with limestone trim. His robust Romanesque mega-depot
featured rusticated stone. (Two smaller wings were added in the early 1890s.)
But fire demolished the main section in 1894. Though it was rebuilt and crowned
with a huge clock tower, the structure was deemed too small for boomtown
Denver, and in 1914 it was torn down.

In its place, Aaron Gove and Thomas Walsh created a Beaux Arts–influenced
building with a smooth granite skin and soaring arches to interpret the Classical
Revival style popular at the time. Rather than add a clock tower that could
have destroyed the building's sensitive lines, the architects set a clock into an
oculus-style dormer in the roof.

Though this newer center portion does not match its wings, the station offers the
pluses of fine lines and abundant windows that flood the interior with light. With
the growing popularity of lower downtown, restaurants began to move into the
station, mainly serving residents as rail traffic slowed substantially over the years.
Just as the arrival of the railroad put Denver on the map, so, too, the 21st century
is witnessing the evolution of Union Station into a regional transit hub that will
change the face of Colorado. This major step forward includes transformation of
much of the station proper into a hotel (Tryba Architects, J.G. Johnson Architects),
with public space and retail, a commuter rail train hall, a station for light rail and
for the 16th Street Mall shuttle, public spaces, and a regional bus facility.

The National Park Service gave the go ahead to developers to change some
aspects of the station to meet the requirements of a hotel and other 21st-
century uses. But sprucing up the Great Hall has been a preservation goal for
years. Construction of the wing buildings and plazas began in 2012, kick-starting
other development around that edge of lower downtown – based, as before,
on transportation and trade.
National Register of Historic Places, Denver Landmark

2 Denver City Railway Building / Hendrie & Bolthoff Manufacturing and Supply Co.

1635 17th Street, with loft entrance at 1720 Wynkoop Street
Baerresen Brothers, 1882; renovated in 1892

The home of the city's old transit system – with a car barn and stables – took on another life as the Hendrie & Bolthoff Manufacturing and Supply Co. As with other handsome structures in lower downtown, the old railway building has gone residential, as the Street Car Stables, with retail accompaniment at street level. In this case, it was a matter of dealing with more than an old warehouse: This sprawling brick industrial site brought with it a heavily timbered interior and the legacy of years as a stable.
National Register of Historic Places

As with the Denver City Railway Building, other structures in the district demonstrate that fine architectural detailing was not too good for the typical commercial buildings of the era. In the process, architects such as Aaron Gove and Thomas Walsh began to import significant design themes found in the evolving architecture of Chicago. Nearby Gove and Walsh buildings include:

2.1 – J. S. Brown Mercantile / Wynkoop Brewery, 1634 18th Street (commercial), 1792 Wynkoop Street (residential), 1899: Gove and Walsh drew mightily from their early arsenal of detailing to make a showplace of this longtime warehouse: sawtooth-style brickwork, corbelling, and fancy masonry pendants below the cornice. Romanesque arches on the fifth floor top off the building, which is accented with stone and enlivened by deeply recessed windows. Renovation into a brewpub and popular restaurant in 1988 was among the early moves to bring entertainment to a then-sleepy neighborhood, with the addition of lofts a decade later.
National Register of Historic Places

2.2 – Edward W. Wynkoop Building / Spice and Commission Warehouse, 1738 Wynkoop Street, 1901: This neighbor of the elaborately detailed J.S. Brown Mercantile is crafted in a darker brick, with simpler lines. But it is hardly plain. The architects arranged the four stories in two bays, and repeated the brick pendants below the cornice.

3 Struby-Estabrook Building

1660 17th Street
Frank Edbrooke, 1885

Frank Edbrooke's combination of red brick with strong stone accents and a variegated stone base created a Victorian Commercial building that appears to grow lighter as it rises. An early conversion into an office building, the Struby-Estabrook Building begins a rhythmic progression of color and material leading from Union Station along 17th Street into the downtown business district.

4 **Oxford Hotel Annex**
1612 17th Street
Montana Fallis and Robert Willison, 1912; renovation by Emerson Design and W.C. Muchow & Partners

Between the red brick of Frank Edbrooke's Struby-Estabrook Building and the red brick of Frank Edbrooke's Oxford Hotel sits a vision in glazed white terra-cotta designed by Montana Fallis and Robert Willison. With its curved front bay and heavy, ornate decoration, the annex was renovated at the same time the Oxford Hotel was brought back to life in the early 1980s. The annex's richly textured facade stands out for its exotic motifs and a Beaux Arts sensibility of grace and elegance.
National Register of Historic Places

5 **Oxford Hotel**
1600 17th Street
Frank E. Edbrooke, 1891

Again working in a palette of red, Frank Edbrooke relied on Classic design elements for the Oxford, lightening the Richardsonian Romanesque tendencies of brick and carved sandstone perched atop a system of coffered first-floor metal supports. Corner decorations are part of the strong detailing. Long notable is a beloved remnant of a 1930s remodeling: the Cruise Room, architect Charles Jaka's Deco delight in black, pink, and neon. The Oxford's renovation in the early 1980s into an upscale historic hotel helped support the neighborhood's elevation into a Denver Landmark District. The entry canopy was restored several years ago to its original configuration.
National Register of Historic Places

6 **Peters Paper Co. Warehouse**
1625–31 Wazee Street
Aaron Gove and Thomas Walsh, 1899

Even at the turn of the 19th century, Gove and Walsh had their eye on simplifying design, a trend growing out of the Chicago School in which they had cut their teeth. Though in a somewhat off-kilter format, with a bay at one side protruding from the facade, this one-time warehouse introduced a certain formal element to lower downtown design. The fifth floor of the blond brick building features arched windows, though the lower levels show a more straightforward window treatment. A pilaster effect gives the building a sense of restraint.
National Register of Historic Places

7 **Millennium Building**
1550 17th Street
Parkhill-Ivins Architects, 2000

Back into the rhythm of 17th Street, a more contemporary property was designed with an eye to structures around it. The Denver firm of Parkhill-Ivins Architects placed the entrance on the corner to address both 17th and Wazee Streets, and introduced an unexpected color – a grayish taupe – into the cadence of red and white. Prominent elements include elaborate brickwork and detailing rarely found in contemporary construction, referencing buildings of a century ago.

Steel columns at regular focal points recall the cast-iron first-floor supports found throughout lower downtown, while triangular elements at the roofline offer a nod to the house-shaped finials of the Barth Hotel next door.

8 **Barth Hotel**
1514 17th Street
Frederick C. Eberley, 1882

Built as the Union Warehouse, this structure within a decade was converted into a hotel, one of many constructed to serve rail travelers of the era. Victorian to the bone, the Barth features a mix of window shapes, heavy decorative elements – an impressive cornice with brackets and finials – and a substantial feel lent by the mix of red brick and limestone. In the 1980s, the Barth became a residential center for the elderly and low income and has maintained its elegance through the district's popularity as an entertainment district.
National Register of Historic Places

9 **The Cactus Club**
1621 Blake Street
Peter Dominick, 1990

Back when lower downtown was considered merely an assemblage of classy buildings in need of loving care, architect Peter Dominick took on the task of creating something new with an eye to the old. The result is a small building that picks up cues from its much larger neighbors in the use of materials (brick and terra-cotta) and stylistic elements (pierced brick frieze, the rhythm of bays). Dominick did not try to mimic his surroundings, using glazed, colored brick – including an eye-popping green – to add interest to the predominantly gray structure. This edition of the Cactus Club, which over the years has had many homes in the city, is an early example of new construction adding life to the district.

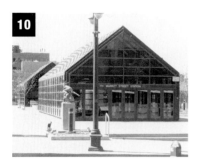 

10 Market Street Station / RTD Offices
16th and Market Streets / 1600 Blake Street, Johnson Hopson & Partners and Kohn Pedersen Fox (station); Dominick Associates (RTD headquarters renovation), 1982

To provide closure to the 16th Street Mall and a counterweight to the Civic Center Station, the architects worked in almost neutral materials and shed-like forms for this major RTD transit point. Putting the guts of the operation underground, and adding simple glass and steel buildings above allowed the inclusion of an ample plaza for the neighborhood. Nearby at 1600 Blake Street, two old hotels in a traditional Victorian Commercial style were refurbished and reconfigured into offices for RTD. Though the buildings back up to the Market Street Station plaza, they still feel connected because of an outside walkway.

With the sweeping redevelopment of Union Station, and RTD's planned move to that complex, the combination of transit station and office building faces future redevelopment as well.
AIA Colorado Honor Award (Johnson Hopson), 1983; AIA Western Mountain Region Excellence Award (Dominick), 1982

11 Columbia Hotel / Market Center
1350 17th Street and 1624 Market Street both used as addresses. Frank Goodnow, 1878; converted to a hotel in 1892; SLP Architects, 1981 renovation

One of the more complicated reworkings of a block in lower downtown, Market Center appears to wrap around several Victorian Commercial structures along Market Street. On the 17th Street side, historic arches and below-street-level retail access set off the rest of the brick building and give it breathing room from the street. (Built as a commercial structure, that portion of the complex had been converted to hotel use in 1892.) As the project turns the corner onto Market, other buildings gain prominence before the second part of Market Center emerges.

Among the buildings "sheltered" by the Market Center complex are two buildings whose architects are not known:

11.1 – Liebhardt-Lindner Building, *1624 Market Street*, 1881: This Victorian Commercial boasts an elaborate cornice decoration of corbelled brick pendants, flanked by massive Classical brackets. Built by Gustavus Liebhardt for his fruit company, the building has since been renovated as part of a row of historic structures with new, integrated facade treatments.

11.2 – Hitchings Block, *1620 Market Street*, 1893: United at street level by a glass grid, this structure was built for the Reverend Horace Baldwin Hitchings, who came to Denver in the 1860s to be minister of St. John's in the Wilderness. The Hitchings Block is a more solid structure, with notable iron trusses. Other commercial buildings in the project include the McCrary Building.

12 16 Market Square
1400 16th Street (commercial), 1560 Blake Street (residential)
Hartman-Cox Architects, with David Owen Tryba Architects, 2000

Though eight stories tall, this two-building complex emerges as a low-key addition to the stretch of the 16th Street Mall between Blake and Market Streets. Spanning an alley and wrapping around both corners, the structures reflect obvious references to other buildings in the district. However, 16 Market Square is more deferential in its homage than, say, the Millennium Building to the historic buildings on 17th Street. With the majority of 16 Market Square constructed in buff-blond brick and precast concrete, but red brick on the side-street segments, the first thought for inspiration for 16 Market Square is the Sugar Building a block away.

In the commercial section, window openings and treatments – especially at street level – are more contemporary, while the side portions are marked by soaring arches that reference elements in the district's former warehouses. The architects have chosen to break up the commercial facades with panels of mini-pilasters, which help link the two predominant portions of the complex and add some movement to the design. Not quite retro, not quite witty enough to be daring, 16 Market Square has settled in as a solid background building.

13 Sugar Building
1530 16th Street
Aaron Gove and Thomas Walsh, 1906, with the addition of an annex in 1912;
1999 renovation by Josh Comfort Architecture

There's a reason new buildings pay respect to the Sugar Building. Architects Gove and Walsh created a dignified yet stylish structure with elements that pulled from the design vocabulary of Louis Sullivan, the Chicago-based architect who was setting a new standard for defining a building's most basic aspects with elegance. Ample, yet restrained decorative impulses carry over to the adjoining annex.

As the Great Western Sugar Co. grew, so did the building that served this early Denver conglomerate. The buff-blond-brick office structure on 16th Street was joined by the red brick warehouse next door on Wazee Street, which was expanded later.

Gove and Walsh divided the main building into three parts, using a decorative course at the top of the fourth floor to add emphasis to the floors above. This also gave the architects the opportunity to add geometric terra-cotta pendants on the piers separating windows at that level; they saved the more exuberant designs of stylized fronds for the cornice and the small openings that pierce the band of brick below. A thoughtful renovation several years ago by new owners retained the Sugar Building's original birdcage elevator, while ushering it into a new century.
National Register of Historic Places

14 Sugar Cube Building
1555 Blake Street
Kuwabara Payne McKenna Blumberg Architects (KPMB), 2008

Architecture lovers were thrilled when this star Toronto firm was selected to design a building in Denver, especially one next to the distinguished, high-profile Sugar Building on the 16th Street Mall. The process included working with the Lower Downtown Design Review Board to achieve clarity, but that has paid off in a handsome contemporary design. KPMB created a building-within-a-building format to combine spaces for retail, office, and residential use on varying levels.

The 10-story, grayish brick mini-tower is wrapped by two lower structures in blond brick that play off the cornice line of the adjacent Sugar Building. Among standout elements is the use of contrasting colors to delineate different sections of the building, demonstrating a complexity that remains respectful of its neighbors. In addition the structure meets the street in true urban form, but on upper levels, it appears deeply set back, allowing assertive balconies to punctuate the facades.

15 1755 Blake
1755 Blake Street
RNL Design, 2009

The five-story office building offers corner facades that combine stone, brick, concrete and glass in a way that promotes a sense of rhythm, scale, and character, especially along Blake Street. The result is a busy mix of inset balconies, columns, and glass panels that pit a strong horizontal feel against a vertical emphasis at the entry. As is the custom in development these days, the first floor is reserved for retail, with the upper four levels devoted to office space.

The building relates to lower downtown through the material of choice – brick – with liberally applied contemporary elements of stone, concrete, and glass. The last material informs a canopy that swoops up and over the entry. A corner is anchored by a concrete column rather than the entry, as found in many historic buildings. Overall, 1755 Blake speaks of today, while appearing at home in its historic context.
AIA Denver Merit Award, 2009; AIA Colorado Citation Award, 2010

16 Mercantile Square / Morey Mercantile Building / Tattered Cover
1528 16th Street
Aaron Gove and Thomas Walsh, 1896, with 1994 renovation by David Owen Tryba Architects

For one of the early buildings in their large lower downtown portfolio, Gove and Walsh used buff-blond brick in a more elaborately decorated structure with Neoclassical sensibilities. The first floor displays horizontal brick banding, while upper levels are marked by recessed vertical windows. The cornice is pronounced, as was true with many commercial buildings of the era. The changes in the district and the flexibility of its buildings can be noted in a door that appears to open onto thin air: The former entrance for years was lined up to lead to the now-gone 16th Street Viaduct.
AIA Colorado Honor Award, 1998

17 **Spratlen-Anderson Wholesale Grocery / Edbrooke Lofts**
1450 Wynkoop Street
Frank E. Edbrooke, 1906

Architect Frank Edbrooke again used the pattern of paired arched windows separated by roundels, a motif he also employed in the much grander Brown Palace Hotel. Yet Spratlen-Anderson, in 1990 renovated into the Edbrooke Lofts, was hardly a run-of-the-mill building. Edbrooke decorated with cartouches and swags, adding a Classical touch to one of the warehouses that lined Wynkoop Street.
National Register of Historic Places

18 **EPA Region 8 Headquarters**
1595 Wynkoop Street
Zimmer Gunsul Frasca Architects, with Opus Architects & Engineers Inc. and Shears Adkins Architects, 2006

The new EPA Region 8 Headquarters Building, designed by Portland, Oregon-based Zimmer Gunsul Frasca, is the result of discussions between the client and the lower downtown neighborhood, as much as the client and the architect. The way in which the building addresses the corner of Wynkoop and 16th Streets, its setback, its materials, and its massing were subject to review – fitting for a building in a location that serves as a transition between lower downtown and the booming Central Platte Valley.

The building serves as a teaching tool for environmentally conscious practices (it achieved LEED Gold certification), but it also has succeeded in fitting into its context. Organized in the form of two "Ls," the nine-story building fronts on Wynkoop Street but has a strong facade on 16th Street and a presence on Little Raven Street. In the process, the building has balanced its goal of achieving both civic presence and security needs.

The mix of brick segments and glass walls, with windows set off by fin-like elements, continues around the building – except for the face it turns toward 15th Street, which has been obscured to some extent by another infill building. (The site of both projects previously held Denver's stocky blond brick Postal Annex.) The EPA building's 15th Street facade is glass and a rougher material, concrete, but has not been unattended in terms of detail. A wedge-like shape shoots off the facade on Wynkoop in the direction of Union Station, in an attempt to add a sense of motion.

As for sustainable strategies, two features are standouts: green roofs planted with sedum, part of a pilot program to gauge its effectiveness in slowing and cleansing storm water runoff, and a series of sails that top the soaring atrium, swaths of canvas that direct natural light to the nine floors below, or shade the area below, depending on time of day.

19 Wynkoop Street Railroad Bridge / Manny's Bridge
Wynkoop Street at Cherry Creek
Pennsylvania Steel Co., 1908

The district's viaducts may be gone, and once-busy loading docks converted to spaces for outdoor dining, but the solid trusses of this bridge are a welcome souvenir of the earlier dominance of commerce and cargo. This bridge has been nicknamed Manny's Bridge to honor Manny Saltzman, a LoDo pioneer who was instrumental in getting the bridge rehabilitated. The Wynkoop Street Railroad Bridge is one of several to survive, with the rest located in the Central Platte Valley area.

20 Brecht Candy Company / Acme Upholstery / Acme Lofts
1615 14th Street
Architect not known, 1909

Using dark red brick, tightly composed windows, and a simple cornice, the unknown designer of this building created one of the more restrained structures in the district. Its history, in a way, is told on the remaining signs: years as a space for manufacturing sweets, followed by a short stint as an upholstery factory. The Acme was a natural for conversion to lofts in the mid-1990s.

21 Windsor Stables and Storefront and Blake Street Bath and Racquet Club Building
1420–1430 18th Street / 1732–1770 Blake Street
John W. Roberts, 1881

An L-shaped building that turns from 18th Street onto Blake, the complex was among the first conversions to residential and retail in the district. The pioneering late-1970s project resulted in entry to common areas off of 18th, with retail behind and above. Ten regular segments front on Blake Street, with large glass windows and cast-iron support columns that add a sense of motion while preserving a historic structure. Decorative elements are simple, mainly stylized brick panels above the center of each bay.

22 The Red House / Mayer House
1702 Wazee Street
Olson Sundburg Architects, 1998

When arts patrons–philanthropists Frederick and Jan Mayer decided to leave suburban quiet for life in lower downtown, they wanted space for their artwork, a house adaptable for entertaining, and an exterior that would coexist but not try to replicate the historic brick buildings around them. They chose a Seattle-based firm that had designed the first new structure to be built in decades in that city's famed Pike Place Market, a reborn urban neighborhood somewhat comparable to lower downtown.

Olson Sundburg created what has come to be called the Red House because of its imposing, flat facade of red sandstone, broken by a huge bronze gated entry with a contrasting annex-like structure to one side. Precast offers a counterpoint to the stone, while a circular metal element and generous use of glass on the upper level create a different kind of roofline in a neighborhood full of broad cornices. Like the older buildings, the Red House fronts right on the street, though its restrained decorative elements introduce a sense of modernity into a historic place.

23 Hendrie & Bolthoff Warehouse Building / Bradford Publishing
1743 Wazee Street
Frank Edbrooke, 1907

Simply designed in a relatively spare 20th-century commercial style, this former warehouse includes four stories marked mainly by brick pendant cornice decorations and pier-like columns featuring chevron-shaped stone forms. Two entries and the hint of a courtyard are part of the building's street-level facade.
National Register of Historic Places

24 Burke-Donaldson-Taylor Building / 18th Street Atrium
1621 18th Street
Fisher and Fisher, 1919

A mega-building featuring generous gridded windows, this office space is notable along Wynkoop Street for a series of imposing arches set off by smaller circular windows and regularly spaced tile insets. Its presence on 18th Street is more controlled, with a symmetrical facade and simple cornice. In restoring this building into offices, the Urban Design Group made the atrium the focus, aiding circulation and interior lighting.

25 Littleton Creamery / Beatrice Foods Cold Storage Warehouse / Ice House
1801 Wynkoop Street
Aaron Gove and Thomas Walsh, 1903, with an addition in 1912 (Mountjoy and Frewen are credited with a 1916 addition), renovation by Josh Comfort, 1997

The Ice House is one of lower downtown's most remarkable buildings. The Littleton Creamery built what eventually included 1 million square feet of storage space and wrapped it in some of the most fanciful brickwork in a district known for fanciful brickwork: polychromed patterning that looked as if the bricklayers were weaving cloth as much as constructing walls. The diamonds and stripes and latticework all were set on a sandstone base.

Sold to Beatrice Foods in 1912, the huge structure eventually became a to-the-trade design center that failed in the bad economy of the early 1990s. Left behind were tiled dairy processing rooms and fine interior brick walls balanced by a grand marble entryway. The next step, naturally, was to turn the Ice House into lofts and apartments, a renovation by Josh Comfort Architecture in 1997. That process included the innovative use of vinyl window screening to help protect the

building's historic signage. Holes punched through for windows were covered with a material usually used on buses, a move that stirred discussion at the time of the conversion. Those inside can see out with little interference, while changes to the basic structure are less noticeable from the outside. But still noticeable. *National Register of Historic Places*

26 Union Pacific Freight Depot
1735 19th Street
Architect not known, circa 1923

Though somewhat overwhelmed today by the addition of a restaurant and lofts, the basic bones of Uncle Pete's freight depot show how serious the railroad took its design. The Neoclassical brick gem includes towering columns at the entry, with a scroll decoration on the upper course and terra-cotta accents. With demolition of the 20th Street Viaduct, portions of the building also were razed, though the dramatic entry was retained.

27 Eurobath + Tile / Euro Lofts
1923 Market Street
David Owen Tryba Architects, 1994

Though constructed several years after the Cactus Club, plans for this mixed-use retail and residential structure provoked just as much interest. Growing out of a squat metal building and a vacant lot next door, the project was to be built in materials that did not include masonry – a first since lower downtown was designated a landmark district, and regular design review began. The architect's design and materials palette included a false cornice, block and rusticated block, mixed with slate in various colors, topped by a crenelated portion of roofline at one side. An entry constructed in steel recalls the district's industrial roots.

28 1800 Larimer
1800 Larimer Street
RNL Design, 2010

As the first high-rise office building to debut in downtown in more than two decades, 1800 Larimer represents a mix of high-tech attributes and intense design impact. (It was designed by Michael Brendle, who folded his firm into RNL in 2005.) Home to a major utility, 1800 Larimer achieved LEED Platinum certification and introduced numerous sustainable measures in its construction and interior finish.

For mere spectators, however, the building is notable for its facade, where large blue glass panels form a random sense of dimension set against its neomodernist facade. An eye-catching roofline gives the 22-story office tower a presence on the skyline, while a carefully established street-level setback has formed a plaza along both 18th and Larimer Streets. The building is a compelling reflective object, a sculptural building sited in an area of lower downtown that begins the urban transition into a developing area north of downtown.

29 Larimer Square
1400 block of Larimer Street

From gin joints to festivals in one generation: The commercial structures of Larimer Square were spared demolition when a group of preservation-minded developers banded together to save the old buildings on a street named after the city's founder, General William Larimer. The structures were part of the 27 square blocks of downtown being targeted for massive clearance as part of the Skyline Urban Renewal Project administered by the Denver Urban Renewal Authority.

Part of the city's first commercial strip, this one-block-long suite of buildings was renovated by Larimer Square Associates, with architect Langdon Morris. In the process, the developers and designers created courtyards and arcades and added a street presence that continues today.

This block of Larimer Street includes almost 20 structures built between 1870 and 1890; they have been renovated into uses as diverse as restaurants, ad agencies, and clothing stores. Homes and buildings constructed before 1870 – General Larimer's own dated from 1858 – were demolished to make way for brick structures.

The buildings exhibit architectural styles representative of the 1870s and 1880s, with Italianate, high Victorian, and traditional commercial made notable by superb detailing. Cast-iron facades, elaborate cornices, and masterful stonework mark the buildings of Larimer Square, which now serves as home to city celebrations and public events.

Larimer Square became Denver's first historic district in 1971, and soon after was placed on the National Register of Historic Places. AIA Colorado Merit Award, 1990; Western Mountain Region Citation for Revitalization Work, 1990

Three buildings that stand out include:

29.1 – Clayton / Granite Building, *1460 Larimer Street*, 1882: As with many of Denver's historic buildings, this one has served many purposes. (It sits on the site of General Larimer's cabin.) It began as a store, a fancy four-story mercantile built by George W. and William N. Clayton where their smaller store had stood. It's not difficult to see why it was renamed the Granite Building in the 1890s: Colorado stone in all manner of pinks and grays makes up the structure's exuberant facade. A bay front adds depth, and portions of the original elaborate filigree railing survive atop the imposing cornice.

29.2 – Kettle Building / Kettle Arcade, *1426 Larimer Street*, 1873: George Kettle, a butcher, built his shop to be both economical and showy: He used walls from adjacent buildings to support his own facade, which became an elaborate face for a tiny building. Cut "stone" supports a large, molded cornice that adds height and bravado to Kettle's legacy. The nearby arcade was reconfigured in the late 1980s by architects Semple Brown Roberts.

29.3 – Gallup-Stanbury Building, *1445–51 Larimer Street*, 1873: Merchants Andrew Stanbury and Avery Gallup teamed up to build this pleasantly symmetrical three-story brick building, in which a central, arched tier of windows and main entry separates two equal parts of the facade. Though the building housed retail, it was hardly a simple structure, with triangular finials at the roofline, stone

accents, and a floral motif in decoration on the cast-iron pilasters on the first floor. According to the National Register nomination, the roofline at one point included four minarets lost to history.

30 Wells Fargo Building
1338 15th Street
Architect not known, circa 1875

The Wells Fargo Building is among the original structures from the city's era of brick construction in lower downtown. Marked by generous arches capped by keystones, the structure is small but displays powerful design elements, including nicely spaced windows and a course of stone near the top of each opening that gives the illusion of pilasters or columns. Built on the site of the original 1866 Wells Fargo Co. building, this structure lost its top story to deterioration after World War II. Portions of former window openings still are visible.

North of Downtown / River North (RiNo) District / Ballpark Historic District

While some of the close-in neighborhoods that ring downtown Denver attract attention for their meticulously restored homes and hard-won historic districts, areas better known as industrial districts have fought for survival and recognition. In the case of the River North District and the Ballpark Historic District, a recent influx of creative industries and residential conversions have pumped new blood into buildings whose original owners are known only by historic signage.

For a century, these neighborhoods were blighted by smelters and other heavy industry, including the plants that attracted immigrant workers to Globeville, Swansea, and Elyria north of downtown. Then, the settlements were chopped up by railroad tracks and a major highway, which left truncated streets and a stark concrete skyscape. Although the debate continues about how to address the presence of Interstate 70 in these important ethnic communities – remove it? reroute it? – other areas closer in to downtown have begun to show a vitality unimagined a decade ago.

Back then, the River North District, or RiNo, and the Ballpark Historic District still were areas defined by numerous rail lines, warehouses, open lots, low rents, abundant opportunities to build new or remake a historic structure – and complete civic disinterest. Today, both stand as growing neighborhoods divided by the major thoroughfare of Broadway, but connected by aesthetic pursuits.

The sprawling area known as RiNo is now home to dozens of galleries, studios, design firms, and residences in a groundbreaking contemporary development, as well as dozens of historic buildings that span decades of architectural styles, and streets cut through by rail lines.

Two factors kick-started this metamorphosis into RiNo: construction of the growing Taxi complex that began in 2001 with a renovated cab dispatch center turned into quirky offices followed by high-style residential and retail; and the influx of artists, architects, graphic design firms, and other entrepreneurial enterprises looking for cheaper space after lower downtown became a high-rent entertainment district. The arts community had been priced out after making improvement to the old skid row of Denver, but that is not likely to happen in RiNo, with its boundless space for creative growth. Artistic impulse is building this still-industrial neighborhood, opening up a whole new view of the South Platte River that helped give birth to Denver, while tackling a host of buildings ripe for rehab or rebirth.

The Ballpark Neighborhood, too, has begun to emerge as a magnet for artistic endeavors, drawn by historic buildings and plentiful infill space (i.e., parking lots). Anchored by Coors Field to the south, Ballpark is an evolving community packed with a mix of urban nightlife and creative businesses. Once a sort of no-man's-land of open space and deteriorating buildings, Ballpark's once-gloomy prospects have brightened, fueled by grit, perseverance, and a renewed interest in the importance of the urban experience. Development has been bolstered by the neighborhood's designation as a historic district by the Denver Landmark Preservation Commission. This growth demonstrates that Coors Field no longer is the northern border to lower downtown, but an entrée to areas with a diversity of fine architecture reflecting numerous styles.

LIST OF BUILDINGS

1	St. Joseph Polish Roman Catholic Church	10	Taxi 1 and Taxi 2 / Freight
2	Valdez Perry Branch Library	11	Silver Square
3	Harrington Elementary School	12	Pattern Shop Studio
4	RiNo District Gateway	13	Blake Street Flats
5	Dry Ice Factory / Ice Cube	14	Riverside Cemetery
6	Benjamin Moore Paint Factory / 2500 Walnut Lofts	15	Coors Field
		16	Zi Lofts
7	Chroma Townhomes / Plus Gallery	17	Silver State Laundry / Silver State Lofts
8	RedLine	18	Paris Hotel / Hamburger Block
9	Weilworks	19	Engine House No. 5 / SLATERPAULL Architects

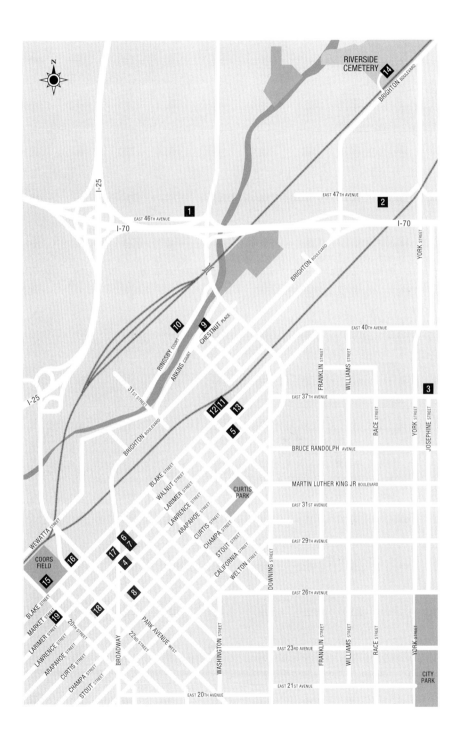

NORTH OF DOWNTOWN

1 St. Joseph Polish Roman Catholic Church
517 E. 46th Avenue
Architect known only as Mr. Parrot, 1902

Just as industry attracted immigrant labor to the neighborhoods to the north, so these workers and their families developed institutions to remind them of home. That included churches in various denominations that were key to cultural identity. Among these is St. Joseph Polish Catholic Church, a solid red brick building whose main feature is an elaborately corbelled entrance and a standout rubble rock shrine to the front. (Nearby is the 1898 Russian Orthodox Church, Transfiguration of Christ, at 4711 Logan Street) Church records note only that a Mr. Parrot designed St. Joseph, and that the Frank Kirchoff Co. of Denver acted as contractor. The adjacent parish house also includes a highly detailed entryway.
National Register of Historic Places

2 Valdez Perry Branch Library
4690 Vine Street
ArchitectureDenver, 1996

When neighborhood demand for library services outstripped bookmobile service, the city's library system decided to go the experimental route. ArchitectureDenver took into account the small-scale buildings throughout surrounding Swansea, Globeville, and Elyria to design a compact building with stunning accents. A forecourt at the entry is marked by a sleek canopy, while angles are predominate in the design. To counter simple exterior materials such as block and metal, the architects relied on clerestory windows and punched openings to add interest and light to the interior. There, slate and wood add a touch of elegance and color.
AIA Denver, Honor Award, 1996

3 Harrington Elementary School
2491 E. 37th Avenue
Anderson Mason Dale Architects, 1994

To replace the old Harrington School a few blocks away, Anderson Mason Dale turned away from the almost-standard vision of a contemporary school as a horizontal design. Able to use nearby Shafer Park as an extension of the play area, the architects built up – not out – on the small school site. Still, Harrington is a long, two-story rectangle interrupted by three rotundas; each circular space is topped by a skylight and broken by a mezzanine-type balcony that lets light into both stories. What the designers called a "decorated box" sports a buff brick exterior marked by red brick stripes. That, along with windows of various sizes, adds a sense of movement to the design.

RIVER NORTH NEIGHBORHOOD, or RiNo:

4 RiNo District Gateway
Broadway at Lawrence, Larimer, and Blake Streets
Artist Joe Riché, 2009

Denver-based artist Joe Riché capitalized on a commission from the city's Percent for Art Program to find a conceptual link between RiNo's past as a railroad hub and its present as a district known for making and showing art and other creative pursuits. To that end, he used discarded freight containers painted in different colors and stacked in different configurations to form a gateway to the district. The piece at Blake and Broadway stands out for its exuberance, with bold colors that note the strong personality and future of RiNo.

5 Dry Ice Factory / Ice Cube
3300 Walnut Street
1929; founder Matthew Palmer, renovation 2007

Once home to the Liquid Carbonic Corp. plant – boon to early soda fountains as a supplier of dry ice and carbon dioxide – the Dry Ice Factory shelters more than 30 studios and the spacious, beautifully proportioned Ice Cube gallery for the resident artists/members of this thriving co-op. Rule Gallery moved next door to Ice Cube in a small annex space, helping to make this an important destination in the RiNo neighborhood. Numerous historic soda-centric ads hang in the hallway linking Ice Cube and the studios, giving flavor to another industrial building that has been transformed into a new vision. The renovation achieved the project LEED-NC certification.

6 Benjamin Moore Paint Factory / 2500 Walnut Lofts
2500 Walnut Street
Sections built starting in 1921; renovation by OZ Architecture, 2005

This proud brick building is part of a complex of structures where thousands – if not millions – of gallons of paints were manufactured over the years. That colorful history originally was reflected in the historic structure's window surrounds being painted in a rainbow of shades. That decorative element is gone, but the distinguished building with terra-cotta accents now has a new life, while keeping the imposing neon sign that has signaled its presence for decades. Careful conversion into residential units has accompanied the influx of people into a part of Denver once basically devoted to industrial and manufacturing purposes but is now opening up to other uses.
Denver Historic Landmark

7 Chroma Townhomes / Plus Gallery
25th and Larimer Streets / 2501 Larimer Street
Craine Frahm Architects / Steve Chucovich (then at Gensler) /
both projects, 2009

This two-part complex signals development that plays Neomodernist infill off of the historic commercial architecture of a prominent former paint factory – a clear delineation between new and old.

A three-story townhome development, Chroma stretches along Larimer, designed in the popular contemporary style that stresses verticality and urban views. Windows and glass balcony shields sport squares of colored glass, a reference to the rainbow of hues once produced in the nearby Benjamin Moore Paint Factory.

Meanwhile, fronting on 25th, Plus Gallery grows out of the factory's former flue building, a tall, red brick element that resembles a flight of stairs and houses the entry of the gallery and storage area. Atop the most horizontal portion of that building, architect Steve Chucovich created additional gallery space in a cube-shaped structure covered in stainless steel. Inside, this small, but beautifully proportioned, exhibition area is indeed the definition of White Cube, adroitly connected to the section below. The gallery proprietors have redeveloped an adjacent small factory building as their residence.

8 RedLine
2350 Arapahoe Street
Semple Brown Design renovation, 2008

Artist and philanthropist Laura Merage had a vision years ago that an exhibition space, an artist-in-residence program, and community outreach could coexist happily in an urban setting. The result, several millions of dollars later, is the beautiful renovated warehouse now known as RedLine.

Semple Brown Design created a plan in which the interior exhibition space is ringed with studios, a library/conference room, and an entryway that also leads to a smaller community gallery on the other side. Interior walls do not fully reach the ceiling, linking the studios to the exhibition space; natural light is dependent on several small skylights and a flexible lighting grid. Movable hanging walls allow for creativity in installation in this expansive space, where a large plaza lifts the space from the street, even as it welcomes visitors.
AIA Colorado Citation Award, 2008

9 Weilworks
3611 Chestnut Place
David Lynn Wise, 2004

Artist and arts advocate Tracy Weil – who with painter Jill Hadley Hooper got the promotional ball rolling for the sprawling and important River North Arts District – turned to architect David Lynn Wise to create a low-cost, high-impact home that

also includes work space and an exhibition gallery. (This began as an unremarkable existing building; Wise did the same transformation for Plinth Gallery on Brighton Boulevard, which specializes in ceramic art.)

An unusual viewing tower helps unify the parts of Weilwork's low-tech structure, while making it part of the skyline on this site near the South Platte River. Wise chose durable materials that carry through the industrial feel of the area, while referencing Weil's family farm. The siding is steel, the stair tower is cement board screwed into place, and the interior features an open floor plan on the lower, public level. Still, the tower's interior walls have been called into service to display art, whether by Weil or other area artists. An adjacent greenhouse helps define a project that is both welcoming and firmly grounded in the industrial history of the district.

Across the street from Weilworks, the Ironton Gallery and Studios – managed by Hadley Hooper – presents shows and houses studios as well as space for the noted Juno Ironworks.

10 Taxi 1 and Taxi 2 / Freight
3455–57 Ringsby Court
Taxi 1: Alan Eban Brown and Semple Brown Design, 2001; Taxi 2: Will Bruder, David Baker, Harry Teague, and Alan Eban Brown, 2006; Drive: Stephen Dynia Architects, 2012

Developer and art lover Mickey Zeppelin and his band of respected architects have worked magic on a complex of rambling cab buildings and an industrial site on the edge of nowhere. Over more than a decade, they have created offices for creative enterprises, residences, and retail amenities with a mix of high-tech, western, and bohemian flair.

Taxi 1 transformed the old Yellow Cab terminal building into offices, later joined by a from-scratch residential project that brings together an innovative spirit and convenience to downtown Denver in the form of a series of bar-like buildings that scrape the land. The next step was Freight, a truck terminal building converted into offices. Wenk Associates designed the landscape for the project, fitting for a firm that created the city's most unusual new (or old) park in the Taxi neighborhood. Northside Park, at Franklin Street south of 58th Street, is a green space carved out of an old sewage treatment plant, with remnants that remain to tell that story. What is now known as Taxi includes numerous projects, including Fuel, Diesel, and BioDiesel.

The Taxi development epitomizes the best of bravura risktaking, serving as an anchor for the growth of the River North neighborhood while establishing its own personality of gumption and the avant-garde.
AIA Colorado Merit Award, 2009; AIA Denver Honor Award, 2008 (Taxi 2)

11 Silver Square
3377 Blake Street
1909; Alan Eban Brown, 1985–88 conversion into live/work spaces and eventually condominiums

This early adaptive reuse of a large-scale manufacturing facility kept the industrial spirit alive, including preservation of remnants of large-scale equipment used in the making of everything from machinery to refine sugar to machinery to fabricate oil field equipment.

The project's bold appearance relies on the preservation of a large, shed-like metal structure that enlivens buildings in the more conventional commercial brick style prevalent in Denver's industrial areas. Among the more notable portions of Silver Square is the Pattern Shop Studio, which was repurposed into a home, studio, office, and gallery for a single family.
AIA Denver Design Award, 1988

12 Pattern Shop Studio
3349 Blake Street
Circa 1908; David Owen Tryba Architects, conversion 1991

Wordplay and reality figure into the story of this innovative reuse of a brick manufacturing building in one of Denver's oldest industrial neighborhoods. The owners of Pattern Shop Studio and their architect turned to Christopher Alexander's revered 1977 book *A Pattern Language* to create an open but well-organized home out of a building that had manufactured wooden patterns for machine parts for the Silver Engineering Works. Views, living spaces, and the mixing of old and new were carefully considered to produce a timeless live-work space out of simple materials.

The Pattern Shop Studio is in the heart of Denver's groundbreaking Silver Square development, a renovation that provides an outdoor garden/courtyard and generous space for entertaining, as well as the making of art. Reworking the interior meant removing a warren of small offices to produce a series of public spaces on the first level built around a soaring atrium, with kitchen, sleeping, and living areas upstairs. Numerous historic elements were retained (art storage is in the old company vault), as was the original structural configuration. The building has no columns; the second floor is hung from roof trusses, though additional beams were added to provide more support. Simplicity of design has resulted in an elegant, welcoming space for art openings and events – and life.

13 Blake Street Flats
3432 Blake Street
Humphries Poli Architects, 2002

Many of the materials and references to the prevalent industrial character of the area make this affordable housing infill project comfortable in its context. But the use of primary colors for exterior cladding differentiates the Blake Street Flats from

its historic neighbors. Clean lines, attention to detail, and a distinct corner cornice element elevate this three-story, 24-unit building constructed on a modest budget.
2006 AIA / National HUD Secretary's Housing Community Design Awards, 2006

14 Riverside Cemetery
5201 Brighton Boulevard
1876

As Denver's oldest operating cemetery, Riverside has faced its share of challenges. These range from now being part of a diverse and evolving industrial district that reaches from Denver to Adams County, to the need to resolve the ability of Riverside to have access to water from the South Platte River, which it lost in 2001. Trees have died and toppled, damaging grave markers; the grass is essentially gone.

But caring supporters who recognize an irreplaceable cultural and historic asset have been working to preserve and improve Riverside's condition and garner aid for this early example of a park-like cemetery in the region.

In Riverside's 77 acres, visitors will find the often elaborate and fanciful graves of some of the state's most significant early settlers and civic stalwarts (and characters), from Augusta Tabor to governors such as John Evans and John Routt. More than 1,000 veterans reportedly share the soil of Riverside with 60,000-plus other souls. A special attraction is the stone "cabin" that is a remembrance of Lester Drake, as well as intricate and touching markers of all types that speak to the aesthetic vision of their era.
National Register of Historic Places Historic District

BALLPARK NEIGHBORHOOD

15 Coors Field
2000 Blake Street
HOK Sports Facilities Group (Brad Schrock), with RNL Design, 1995

As the preference began to fade for saucer-shaped ballparks surrounded by seas of parking, the reversion to historicism that shot through Postmodern design landed on home plate. Thus was born the drive to create a Coors Field that looked as if it had been sitting at 20th and Blake Streets since the days when players wore uniforms made out of natural fiber.

Hot off their success with Camden Yards in Baltimore, HOK next turned to the Denver commission. Though Joe Spear and Ray Chandler were heavily involved in the process of working with the neighborhood, as were designers at RNL, the design of Coors Field eventually fell to young architect Brad Schrock. What Schrock – and others – did was make the park look as if it had indeed been pinned down in a tight space, though it meant demolishing a few old structures (and plenty of parking sites nearby).

In well-laid brick set in a design reminiscent of part of the historic Ice House, Coors combines that rosy material with rich dark green steel, creating an entry plaza at Wazee Street, space for a big clock where Blake meets 20th, and an open concourse area that allows fans to be out of their seats, yet remain aware of the action on the field. The field is sunk deep, so that the surrounding walls can be tall enough to contain the game but stay at a par with surrounding structures. Seats are close to the field (though more were added than originally proposed).

As a nod to the area, designers asked Denver artist Barry Rose to create terra-cotta columbines set into the piers in the outer wall. An art program administered by the Metropolitan Baseball District Board commissioned work by Lonnie Hanzon, Erick Johnson, and Matt O'Neill and Jeff Starr. Hanzon's playful sculpture *Evolution of the Ball* has become a favorite, and an intellectual delight at that.

The architects were able – mostly – to avoid the trap of nostalgia in the brick and steel complex. Among the most successful of Denver's 1990s buildings, Coors Field has worn well in terms of its exterior impact and its relationship to the district's historic buildings. That it spawned what seems to be a million sports bars has, over time, changed the dynamic of the area. But in the process, Coors Field has opened an entryway into what is now the Baseball Historic District and to River North beyond.

16 Zi Lofts
2229 Blake Street
OZ Architecture, 2008

A new entry in the Ballpark neighborhood, Zi is visible from three sides in a design that plays off an industrial feel in different ways. That does not, however, include stucco, a material that has crept into too many downtown projects of late. Instead, the architects chose materials that reflect the neighborhood's predominant warehouse/Coors Field brick aesthetic.

In this instance, the brick is used as a foil to a concrete frame and columns. The result is a subtle six-story wrapper for lofts and two-story townhomes, a parking garage, and first-floor retail and office space. The building's wavy metal top is intended to reference the nearby ballpark's series of metal arches along the roofline, plus add an identifying element as infill construction continues in the area. Metal is used as an accent material in several portions of the facade, including window frames and the grating over the parking area. Inside, the goal is to create a sense of calm, with large windows, a level in which there is an interior pool/rock garden, and glass panels on which artist Lynn Heitler has applied nature-related subjects.

17 Silver State Laundry / Silver State Lofts
2441 Broadway
1911 (later additions by Mountjoy and Frewen); renovation by
Buchanan Yonushewski Group, 2006

Built through the 1930s in phases of steel, wood and concrete, the old Silver State Laundry is a gateway building into the Ballpark Historic District that began to coalesce after the construction of Coors Field. Empty for years, the Silver State Laundry retained its clean lines, with an emphasis on brick and expansive windows. During renovation into lofts, the architects added a third-floor penthouse, with the attendant requirement to strengthen the original building so it could support the additional load.

18 Paris Hotel / Hamburger Block
2199 Arapahoe Street
Richard Phillips, 1891

George Hamburger, maker of harnesses and saddles, hired Richard Phillips to design a three-story business block on four lots. The result was a well-crafted example of 19th-century commercial architecture, with an ornate metal cornice, modestly arched windows, a center parapet, and detailed brickwork – all set on a rusticated stone foundation. The three-bay cast-iron storefront took up the first floor of the Arapahoe Street facade, with living space above on floors given definition by brick pilasters.

Over time, a restaurant was installed on the first floor, a hotel above, and in 1935, the building became the Paris Hotel, operated by proprietor Paris Hargis and his wife until the mid-1950s. Extensive renovation in the late 1980s, with design work by William Adams Design, resulted in a reborn Paris Hotel, with living space above and room for retail /restaurant on the first floor.
National Register of Historic Places

19 Engine House No. 5 / SLATERPAULL Architects
1331 19th Street
1922; renovation by SLATERPAULL Architects, 2007

The historic Engine House No. 5, a bi-level building with an imposing cornice and brackets on its taller section, served the city for decades before it was sold to an architecture firm known for its work in historic preservation. The renovation and adaptive reuse was completed with an eye toward sustainability, leading to its status as the first LEED Platinum certified historic building in the state. Strategies to boost energy efficiency and create a high-performance building – from chilled beam technology to a photovoltaic system – were a large part of the renovation inside and out.
Denver Landmark, National Register of Historic Places

Civic Center & Golden Triangle

The core of Denver's civic and cultural life comes in three parts: the Civic Center, Civic Center Park, and the historic district that encompasses most of the area.

Civic Center proper, anchored and balanced by the State Capitol and the Denver City and County Building, includes various state, county, city, and federal government buildings on an east-west axis that is reaching toward Speer Boulevard. Civic Center's north-south axis forms a link between downtown Denver and a cultural complex to the south that includes the Denver Central Library, the expanded Denver Art Museum, the Clyfford Still Museum, and, a bit farther, a new History Colorado Center.

Thus Civic Center, in effect, is growing, extending the scope of an area dedicated to the life of the community. In the first decade of the 21st century, Civic Center witnessed an enormous amount of development, most of it through public or public-private investment, along with the addition of a corporate presence on the park's edge facing the central business district.

The Civic Center Historic District, as listed on the National Register of Historic Places, ranges from Grant to Delaware Streets, bounded on the south by West 13th Avenue and on the north by, variously, West Colfax Avenue, Cheyenne Place, and Court Place. The city also has designated a portion of Civic Center as a Denver Landmark District, using slightly different – and exclusionary – boundary lines.

Civic Center grew out of several plans considered after the Denver Art Commission suggested in 1904 to Mayor Robert Speer that "a civic center" or "city center" was a good idea for Denver. Speer concurred. The powerful mayor was enamored with the City Beautiful movement sweeping the United States (inspired by the 1893 Columbian Exposition in Chicago), and a devotee of the urban design work in Europe in the latter part of the 19th century.

Planners, artists, and architects such as Charles M. Robinson, Frederick MacMonnies, Frederick Law Olmsted Jr., and Denver's influential landscape architect S.R. DeBoer all made proposals for a civic center, but either Speer or voters turned them down. Eventually, Chicago architect Edward H. Bennett, a successor to Daniel Burnham, put together the design that basically survives today.

Bit by bit, Civic Center began to evolve as a response to the Capitol. The first move was to clear a residential neighborhood on the site, which the city had purchased in 1912. In the early 1920s, Colfax Avenue was rerouted out of the park, and since then various planners have worked to improve landscaping and pedestrian access.

And, over the years, the prevailing design ethos has shifted from Neoclassicism to Neomodernism and related styles. The late 20th century brought the addition of color in a new central library. A decade later, the art museum's Hamilton Building introduced a gleaming titanium skin, and the Still Museum a rough but gentle concrete exterior.

Ironically, Civic Center – in 2012 named a National Historic Landmark – also is a place where the evolution of design is clearly viewed in Denver. What's old remains new.

Just south of Civic Center, the area dubbed the Golden Triangle is bounded by Colfax Avenue, Lincoln Street, and Speer Boulevard. The former home of low-rise industrial and commercial structures has attracted renovation and new construction. In the first instance, architects and designers found fertile ground for offices in quirky old buildings. In the second, developers heartened by strong public investment and the lure of a growing cultural presence began to mine a neighborhood close to downtown yet with buildings in a more human and humane scale.

Downtown Denver

LIST OF BUILDINGS

1   Civic Center Park
2   The City and County Building
3   The Denver Mint
4   Denver Police Crime Laboratory
5   Denver Justice Center Complex
6   The Van Cise-Simonet Detention Center
7   The Lindsey-Flanigan Courthouse
8   Wellington E. Webb Municipal Office
    Building and City and County Annex No. 1
9   Denver Newspaper Agency
10 Voorhies Memorial
11 The Pioneer Monument
12 The McNichols Civic Center Building
13 Greek Theater and Colonnade of
    Civic Benefactors
14 Byers-Evans House
15 The Denver Art Museum
15.1 Denver Art Museum Hamilton Building
15.2 Denver Art Museum Residences
16 Denver Central Library
17 Clyfford Still Museum
18 Ralph L. Carr Colorado Judicial Center
19 History Colorado Center
20 One Civic Center
21 Civic Center Station
22 Colorado State Office Building
23 The State Capitol
24 The State Capitol Annex
25 The Colorado State Museum Building

26 First Baptist Church
27 Evans School
28 Cullen-Thompson Motor Company /
    Gart Bros. Sports Castle / Sports Authority
    Sportscastle
29 Anthem Blue Cross / Blue Shield
30 Grand Cherokee Lofts
31 Rocky Mountain Bank Note / Galvanize
32 Century Lofts
33 1200 Delaware
34 Cesar E. Chavez Federal Building

1 Civic Center Park
Bounded by West Colfax and West 14th Avenues, Broadway and Bannock Street
Various architects

The long process of developing a civic center for Denver included a plan by Frederick Law Olmsted Jr. Beginning in 1913, plantings and walkways were undertaken for a few years, although the city in 1916 hired Edward H. Bennett to develop a new plan. By 1919, the Beaux Arts format of the park was established, with axes and lawns in place. Yet urban design proposals and master plans have continued to be devised for the park, including a plan authored by noted Denver landscape architect S.R. DeBoer.

Each mayor – and other architects – has labored to leave his mark on Civic Center. These ideas have ranged from respectful (continuing and laudable calls to bring new life to the now-McNichols Building) to harebrained (Daniel Libeskind's proposed addition of numerous angular "elements") to puzzling (the then-Colorado History Museum's short-lived plan to put part of its new home underground before selecting a new site altogether).

New design guidelines and a bond-financed boost resulted in a renovation of the Broadway Terrace area, including new brick pavers, more benches, a restored balustrade, restoration of the Voorhies Memorial and Greek Theater, more lighting, and the removal of a right-turn lane onto Broadway, which had made pedestrian movement hazardous. Still, much work continues, including efforts to clean up a place that helps define Denver's civic identity. In 2012, the U.S. Department of Interior designated Civic Center Denver's first National Historic Landmark.
National Register of Historic Places, Denver Landmark District, and Denver's first National Historic Landmark

2 The City and County Building
1437 Bannock Street
Allied Architects Association; Robert K. Fuller, 1932 (more than 30 local architects formed the Allied Architects Association to win the contract for this building. Robert K. Fuller served as president. When a court ordered the association to disband, Fuller was named lead architect.)

A site for Denver's city government was chosen by voters in 1923 as a location that could offer a response to the Colorado State Capitol. After that, little went smoothly, with challenges to the association of architects offering a design as well as to the choice of building materials. (One Denver architect of note, Jacques J.B. Benedict, even offered a competing design for a more vertical, less Classical structure.)

But Classicism won: The City and County Building's design works off a convex curved facade of engaged Doric columns with a focus on a large central Corinthian portico and clock tower (the tower was designed by George Koyl of McKim, Mead, and White). The exterior is brick with dressed Cotopaxi granite facing. Inside are a dozen varieties of marble and travertine walls. The four-story building is 435 feet long. The tower is topped by a six-foot-plus bronze eagle. The original massive bronze doors were removed in the 1960s, and early in the project artwork planned for niches around the building fell by the wayside. In the 1960s, George Thorson

and Dudley Tyler Smith oversaw a renovation of the courts in the building, and in the early 1990s, Michael Barber Architecture produced a master plan for repairs and renovations funded by bond money.

Bond programs have funded needed maintenance to the City and County Building, including cleaning and waterproofing the stone, and repairing the stairs and windows. In 2010, most court functions housed in the City and County Building moved to the Lindsey-Flanigan Courthouse in the Denver Justice Center Complex.

3 The Denver Mint
320 W. Colfax Avenue
James Knox Taylor, 1906, with a series of later additions

Established by an act of Congress in 1862, the Denver Mint operated until 1904 at 16th and Market Streets. The Colfax Avenue building, which opened in 1906, is designed in a Renaissance Revival style (inspiration is said to have come, variously, from the 15th-century Florentine palazzi Riccardi and Strozzi). The Mint's creamy-pink stone facade, topped with a tile roof, is a symmetrical structure with arches and medallions.

A 1980s addition by RNL Design added glass vaults toward the rear, making the structure look like an Italian train station jutting out of the palazzo. A visitor's entrance on Cherokee Street, added in 1991, is bound by glass to a small 1935 addition. The gatehouse style entryway, by JH/P Architecture Interior Design Planning, is constructed of precast, but incising matches up to belt courses on the original building. A skylight floods the waiting area with light, and the new building's iron doors work with touches of iron on the original Mint.

Of note: Interior murals by Vincent Aderente symbolize mining, manufacturing, and commerce, and the lobby chandeliers are reportedly by Tiffany.
National Register of Historic Places

4 Denver Police Crime Laboratory
1371 Cherokee Street
The SmithGroup, with Durrant, 2012

Financed by the Better Denver Bond Program, this 60,000-square-foot building adds a complex glass and metal facade and clean lines to the Civic Center design vocabulary. A combination of shooting range, laboratories, and office facilities, the crime lab building reads as two structures from an oblique view; a glass-walled centerpiece links a building sporting those upper floor undulations, with another that is more about articulated extensions providing rhythm and texture. The greatly expanded crime lab facility also succeeds in diminishing the lonely desert of a plaza that was the approach to the Denver Police Administration Building and bringing a civic presence to the block catty-corner from the Denver Justice Center Complex. Artist Cliff Garten's shimmering suspended sculptures – *Bullet* and *Suspect* – complement the lab's open and airy interior.

5 **Denver Justice Center Complex**
Bounded by W. 14th and W. Colfax Avenues
between Delaware and Fox Streets

This massive project began in 2005 with the best of intentions: provide more secure conditions for the city's judicial system than possible at the City and County Building, relieve overcrowding at the city's existing detention facilities, create an extension of Civic Center that would serve as a city landmark and important terminus to Tremont Place, and heed then-mayor John Hickenlooper's call to bring on board an internationally acclaimed architect to attract attention to Denver.

Things did not go quite as intended.

Indeed, the new Lindsey-Flanigan Courthouse is a striking contemporary building, with sophisticated security circulation and a folded glass facade that provides a rewarding view at the end of Tremont. The Van Cise-Simonet Detention Center, on the other hand, is a Neotraditional building that is not compatible with its peer on a plaza that is well landscaped but whose vastness cannot link the two buildings – even with a major public art installation by a renowned artist.

As for that internationally acclaimed architect? Steven Holl, winner of the American Institute of Architects 2012 Gold Medal, was bounced from the job – along with his stellar, light-oriented design – because the city and its project managers could not figure out how to work with an architectural force such as Steven Holl. He took his exceptional design with him. In advance of the construction of the Denver Justice Center, a new post office/parking garage was built at 450 W. Colfax Avenue. Designed by then-AR7 Hoover Desmond Architects, the building suffered from a trimmed budget, losing its cornice and other detailing. The result is a bland structure that does not meet the level of design expected in Civic Center or its surroundings. It did, however, achieve LEED Silver certification.

6 **The Van Cise-Simonet Detention Center**
490 W. Colfax Avenue
Hartman Cox Architects, in association with Ricci Greene Associates and
OZ Architecture, 2010

This 460,000-square-foot Indiana limestone building includes 1,500 beds, two courtrooms, 25 housing units, and recreation yards. Managing to be at once stolid and overbearing, it sports Neoclassical elements and decorative touches more traditionally found in the typical American courthouse. But while an overarching framework plan helped keep both buildings in the same scale as other Civic Center buildings such as City and County and the Mint, the panel that selected the designers was intent on splitting the stylistic pie, choosing a traditional design for the jail and contemporary for the courthouse.
In the end, the buildings do not relate. The detention center has achieved LEED Gold certification.

7 The Lindsey-Flanigan Courthouse
520 W. Colfax Avenue
klipp, with Ricci Greene Associates and Harold Massop Associates
Architects, 2010

Once Steven Holl had departed, the project struggled to recover but found its footing through the design produced by klipp, the architecture and planning firm that had been the local firm on the project. It is quite a save: The focal point of the resulting five-story, 317,000-square-foot building is a technically demanding folded glass facade that not only opens up the building to outside, but lets the world see in.

The glass also complements the pale Alabama limestone, stretching in bands on the east face of the courthouse to offer views of the city. The west face presents a more discreet view toward Speer Boulevard, with windows marked by protruding sun shields and walls that feature slits of glass. The north side, especially, is a study in contrasts, with a mix of horizontal and vertical glass elements that adds rhythm facing the busy Colfax corridor. The interior is set off by a pearl-white terrazzo floor, which boosts the light allowed in by the sweep of glass. Entries to courtrooms sport wood surrounds, leading to sedate interiors finished in a neutral palette.

Though its two green roofs may be au courant features, the courthouse's diamond-shaped jury assembly room is more memorable, with its fritted glass panels and comfortable, bright interior. For anyone used to sitting in the stark assembly room of the City and County Building waiting to be summoned for jury selection, this new space is quite a change, marked by the dreamy and colorful public art piece *Cloudbreak*, by Catherine Widgery.

The Dale Tooley Plaza, intended to tie together the detention center and the courthouse, features attractive natural landscaping by studioINSITE that is more free-form than manicured. And perhaps this windswept vista someday will feel welcoming. However, the placement of Dennis Oppenheim's subtly illuminated *Light Chamber*, intended as a beacon where Colfax and Tremont meet, might have been better served if placed closer to the center of the plaza, making it more convenient to explore to find the solace the late artist intended.

8 Wellington E. Webb Municipal Office Building and City and County Annex No. 1
201 W. Colfax Avenue
Dudley Smith, Casper Hegner, and Thomas Moore, with G. Meredith Musick (Hegner and Moore principal designers, technical support by Musick), 1949; David Tryba Architects and RNL Architects, 2002

During a limited competition, the city in early 2000 chose a design by David Tryba Architects with RNL Design for an office tower that would consolidate numerous agencies on a prime Civic Center location. In the process, the building became more than a much-debated exception to the rule about naming a city structure after a living person.

The Webb Building, with its appearance of an elliptical building interlocked with a rectangular wing, also became linked to and in effect subsumed the highly regarded, if threatened, International Style City and County Annex 1. Intended as a

classroom for the University of Denver's downtown campus, but eventually used for city offices, the Annex demonstrated a purity of form that won it a singular place on the National Register of Historic Places.

This architectural ripple effect came about through the inclusion of a glass-covered atrium that provided space for frequently used city services, staff and public gatherings, and copious public art. Though the Webb building's materials and forms helped link Civic Center with downtown and complemented the Annex's lime-stone, the older building's strongest facade has been obscured. Further, to serve retail included on the Annex's street level interior, a door was cut in the wall facing Civic Center, a door never used because of security concerns.

Still, the Webb Building, a 12-story, 648,000-square-foot rich champagne–colored mix of metallic panels, granite, and limestone, was the first step to begin creating a full edge for Civic Center, a handsome Neomodern structure that maintains a strong identity while demonstrating respect for the historic district. The Webb Building has achieved LEED EB Gold Certification.

9 Denver Newspaper Agency
101 W. Colfax Avenue
Newman Cavender & Doane, 2006

The last open space on Civic Center – at the time – was filled by an 11-story, 310,000-square-foot building designed to house the *Rocky Mountain News*, the *Denver Post*, the Denver Newspaper Agency, and the Media News Group, owner of the *Post*.

Three years later, the *News* closed, but this key building still lights up Civic Center with a bright-white facade and a segmented form that helps link the Broadway and Colfax corridors and mark one of the most important intersections in the city. The structure's large windows, illuminated crawl of headlines, and first-floor retail helped fuel a relationship with its neighbors.

The building's expansive lobby also provides an informal walkway from the intersection into downtown, while the overall design offers a complement to the Webb Building by employing interlocking elliptical and rectangular forms. The DNA Building did more than add a corporate presence to a district usually associated with government and cultural entities. It also introduced the color white into the design discussion while emphasizing the architecture of its time.

10 Voorhies Memorial
W. Colfax Avenue at Cheyenne Place
W.E. and A.A. Fisher, 1922

Giving balance to the Greek Theater and Colonnade, the Fishers' memorial in Turkey Creek sandstone is another Classical structure, in Greek Revival with Ionic columns sheltering murals by noted artist Allen Tupper True and embracing a pool and fountain. This structure serves as a memorial to John H.P. Voorhies, an early Denver business leader who had lived nearby. A fountain designed by Robert Garrison includes sculptures of two sea lions; from each side, a double colonnade curves in toward Civic Center. When the memorial was built, Colfax Avenue was

closed and moved to the north, adding another curved edge to the district. Recent increased interest in Civic Center – and some helpful bond money – brought much-needed improvements and repairs to the memorial by the firm Andrews + Anderson, including repainting the turquoise pool basin a simple gray, ending the sense of walking into a 1950s Florida resort.

11 The Pioneer Monument
Colfax Avenue at Broadway
Dedicated in 1910

Sculptor Frederick MacMonnies originally planned to use the figure of an American Indian in his work in bronze, but popular sentiment was against that. Instead it's Kit Carson on horseback, with figures at the granite base of a miner, a hunter, and a pioneer woman. The fountain and its superior sculptures mark one of the city's most important intersections.

On the grounds of and around Civic Center are several other distinguished pieces of public art. They include: *Closing Era*, John Preston Powers's rendition of a buffalo and Indian was displayed at the 1893 Columbian Exposition; the soldier's monument at the State Capitol, 1909, by Captain John D. Howland, artist and Civil War veteran; in the park across Lincoln Street from the Capitol is the 1990 sandstone obelisk Veteran's Monument designed by Robert Root and Richard Farley; *The Broncho Buster*, a bronze by Alexander Phimister Proctor of a rider on a bucking horse (also by Proctor: *On the War Trail*, the Emily Griffith drinking fountain, and the Sadie Likens drinking fountain), and the library tile book mural by Barry Rose, a piece removed and reconstructed for the new library. Proctor's *Broncho Buster* and *On the War Trail* were cleaned and restored in 2011.

12 The McNichols Civic Center Building
Former Carnegie Library, later known as City and County Annex 3
144 W. Colfax Avenue
Albert Randolph Ross of New York, 1910 renovation for adaptive reuse,
Humphries Poli Architects, 2012

Built as the city's library headquarters several years before there was an actual Civic Center, this Greek Revival structure features Corinthian columns in a strict Classical style. After the library funded by Andrew Carnegie moved to new quarters in 1956, its interior was "renovated" (Gordon D. White) to accommodate a series of city offices.

As interest grew in improving Civic Center, plans for the building now named for former Mayor William H. McNichols Jr. began to percolate – especially when it was tagged as the site of the city's 2010 Biennial of the Americas.

Renovation plans began to take shape later that year, including the replacement of windows installed during the conversion to an office building, bringing systems up to code to use the building for public events. The "new" McNichols Civic Center Building shows plenty of history, with exposed brick wall sections and iron beams. Yvonne Domengo's blue steel *Coral Sphere* seems to flutter on the front lawn.

13 Greek Theater and Colonnade of Civic Benefactors
W. 14th Avenue at Acoma Street
Marean & Norton, 1919

The architect designed an amphitheater that could seat 1,200, another Neoclassical Revival gem on axis with the Voorhies Memorial at the northern edge of Civic Center. The interior walls are Tennessee marble. A curved colonnade, on either side of a rectangular plaza, was decorated by murals by Allen Tupper True (a gift of Mrs. Charles Hansen Toll in memory of her husband). As with the Voorhies Memorial, the theater and its murals were repaired and restored in 2010 (Andrews + Anderson).

14 Byers-Evans House
1310 Bannock Street
Architect not known, 1883

This plum-colored brick home was built for William N. Byers, publisher of the *Rocky Mountain News*; later, the trim structure housed descendants of John Evans, the first Colorado territorial governor. An addition in 1898 and remodeling in 1910 changed the orientation of the rooms and entrance.

In a Victorian Eclectic style with Italianate touches, the Byers-Evans home features leaded glass, segmental and Tudor arches above the second-story bay window, a tin mansarded porch roof, and a cast-iron widow's walk.

The structure is now a house museum operated by History Colorado. Long-Haeft Architects guided the renovation in 1990 using the 1912–24 era as a guide to colors and circulation. A changing exhibit gallery opened in a back room several years ago, with a focus on the state's artists.

15 The Denver Art Museum
100 W. 14th Ave. Parkway
Gio Ponti of Milan and James Sudler of Denver, 1971
Studio Daniel Libeskind and Davis Partnership, 2006

With its strong vertical lines, its crenelated roofline and its scattered slit windows, the Gio Ponti Museum Building has been called everything from a fortress to a computer punch card. But this building of reinforced concrete and shimmering gray faceted glass tiles holds its position well, lending contemporary sophistication to Civic Center. Ponti is generally credited with designing the exterior, James Sudler with the interior public spaces, and then-museum director Otto Bach with the concept of twinned 10,000-square-foot gallery spaces on the floors devoted to exhibitions.

Over the years, there were several renovations and gallery shifts and a reorientation of the entry to the plaza built during construction of the new Denver Central Library. The original Ponti door – a sleek metal oval – was relegated to the status of an "emergency exit" and pristine design object.

A growing collection, the demand for galleries that could handle major traveling shows, and the need for a proper auditorium required an overall museum expansion: In 1999, the museum asked Denver voters for $62.5 million to construct a new

wing, with the caveat that trustees would raise another $50 million for the endowment and project support. A limited competition was sponsored by the city, with 18 architects responding to a request for proposals; from a field of five, three were chosen to offer ideas to the city. Of the three – Irata Isozaki, Daniel Libeskind, and Thom Mayne – Libeskind was selected to design the new 146,000-square-foot wing, working with Davis Partnership.

The result was a titanium-clad explosion of shards (15.1), a signature Libeskind statement, with a massive prow that stretches across West 13th Avenue toward the Ponti castle (the two are connected by a bridge two floors below). The metal panels and their coloration relate to the Ponti building's rectangular glass tiles, and the scale is proper. The $110 million Frederic J. Hamilton Building, named after the longtime DAM board president who donated $20 million toward the project, became an instant landmark, loved and reviled in equal measure.

But pattern and color end all similarities between old and new. The Hamilton Building's interior walls are canted and its layout heavy on angles. its galleries include occasional tight, difficult spaces, and its grand staircase presents an exhilarating way to become enveloped by the soaring ceilings. Since the Hamilton opened in 2006, museum administrators and curators have learned to work with this extravagant object, moving the gift shop into what had been a forlorn lobby, and refining installation techniques to take advantage of the angles and slopes.

The result, buoyed by a new museum administration, is an arts institution that has become an exhibition powerhouse in the region. Large sculptures including Beverly Pepper's *Denver Monoliths* and Claes Oldenburg and Coosje van Bruggen's *Big Sweep*, dot the Lanny and Sharon Martin Plaza. This welcoming space connects the Hamilton to a parking garage sheathed on two sides by the Museum Residences (15.2), designed by Libeskind and Davis Partnership using the same angular forms. An economic bust postponed plans for a hotel to wrap the Broadway side of the garage, leaving a bare concrete wall that blocks the view of what lies to the west.

16 Denver Central Library
10 W. 14th Ave. Parkway
Michael Graves Architect of Princeton, New Jersey., and Klipp Colussy Jenks Dubois Architects of Denver, 1995; Burnham Hoyt of Denver, 1956

A linchpin of Denver's Civic Center, Burnham Hoyt's modified International Style building relied on a graceful rotunda and crisp, well-defined fenestration to overcome a somewhat bulky back facing West 13th Avenue. And that rotunda – architects for the new Central Library referred to it as a "hemicycle" – is basically what was saved during the process of creating a building for the next century.

With bond money in hand, the city sponsored a competition that attracted dozens of firms. Three were chosen to create models and participate in a series of workshops: Robert A.M. Stern, Michael Graves, and George Hoover of the now-defunct Hoover Berg Desmond.

What competition winner Graves produced was a sort of Italian hill town – disparate geometric parts in colors that appeared even more striking than they were when

surrounded by the overwhelming gray Classicism of Civic Center. It is very much a Graves building, where Postmodernism and whimsy meet. In the process, these forms incorporated the rotunda salvaged from Hoyt's limestone building. Graves mixed stone and cast block, and introduced ornamentation in copper, a precursor to use of metal in projects on Civic Center.

During construction of a new library, a plaza was built to link the library with the Denver Art Museum above ground, just as a concourse and meeting rooms connect the two below grade. And more sculpture found a home in Civic Center. In 1996, private contributions funded the purchase of Mark di Suvero's *Lao Tzu*, a visually kinetic work sited so it is visible along Civic Center's north-south axis. Later, Donald Lipski's *The Yearling* was installed near the children's library, purchased with private contributions as well as some public money.

17 The Clyfford Still Museum
1250 Bannock Street
Allied Works Architecture, 2011

The debate over the relationship of container and contents in museum design finds harmony in a building devoted to the work of the reclusive artist whose powerful paintings were key to the evolution of the Abstract Expressionism movement in the 1940s. Still has a tenuous connection to Denver, but his widow in 2004 chose the city as recipient of some 94 percent of his work, with the requirement (one of many) that the city build a museum devoted solely to Still's work. The museum's new board selected Allied Works and Brad Cloepfil in an invited national competition; the final field also included Diller Scofidio + Renfro, and Ohlhausen DuBois Architects.

The result, after five years of fund-raising for the $29 million project, is a quiet, ribbed, cast-in-place concrete building with strategically placed wooden elements and windows that, respectively, bring rhythm to the exterior and a focused infusion of light to the interior. Nestled in the shadow of the Denver Art Museum's exuberant Hamilton Building, the Still is an elegant 28,000-square-foot counterpoint whose second, cantilevered level is dedicated to 10,000 square feet of gallery space.

The nine galleries are positioned to allow intelligent views into adjacent spaces, while the ceilings of perforated concrete allows in light courtesy of motorized skylight shades. Still's work – sometimes heavily painted, later more thinly covered allowing areas of raw canvas – pops in reaction to the carefully aimed light. The lower level is dedicated to an admissions desk, small shop, library and archives, collection storage, conservation laboratory, and subtle interactive educational displays. Throughout the interior, the walls' mix of concrete with rough "fins," aligned with wooden slats, demonstrates a high level of detailing, also visible in a grand, floating staircase and muted terrazzo floors.

Perhaps more than any other museum in Denver – scene of an early 21st-century boom in cultural facilities – the Still stands as an exemplar, where the container does not just understand the contents, it offers a true home. Notable is the bright blue Joel Shapiro sculptupre, *For Jennifer* installed on the lawn between the Still and the Hamilton Building. It is in the DAM collection, with funds raised to honor the late Denver planning director Jennifer Moulton. Moulton helped make the DAM project a reality.

18 Ralph L. Carr Colorado Judicial Center
2 E. 14th Avenue
Fentress Architects, 2013

Civic Center found itself with another gap on its edge with the decision to demolish the low-rise, idiosyncratic 1970s-era Judicial Heritage Center and then-Colorado History Museum in order to erect a new, consolidated state judicial center. The history museum moved south, ceding the land to a center that hews toward a Neoclassical vocabulary set off by overly dramatic lighting. (It is expected to achieve LEED Gold certification.)

Unfortunately, the result is a composition of two components that exhibit difficult proportions and exceptional bulk while working to hitch their star to the traditional buildings in the Civic Center ensemble. In addition, demolition of the old judicial building resulted in the destruction of Angelo Di Benedetto's sweeping evolution-of-law mural *Justice Through the Ages*; it was purportedly painted on panels that contain asbestos, and the state sentenced it to death.

This 600,000-square-foot combo of courthouse (for Colorado's supreme and appellate courts) and office tower (numerous state judicial agencies) is more than just large: It looms over the library while asserting its connection with the Colorado State Capitol immediately to the northeast.

The four-story granite courthouse is rooted in Neoclassicism, in stone chosen to match that of the Capitol, resting on a darker granite base. This component sports a shallow dome and glass-walled atrium, designed to flood the interior with natural light, establish a visual link with the Capitol, and represent the concept of transparency in the judicial system. An asymmetrical colonnade sweeps partway from Lincoln Street to Broadway, interrupted by a bulky portico denoting the entryway. Through this curved form the Carr aims to connect to architectural elements in Civic Center to the west. The wedge-shaped element along Lincoln sports a green roof and houses a facility devoted to education on the judicial system.

The 12-story tower, meanwhile, is made of similarly colored precast on a matching dark granite base – a rectangle marked by awkward proportions. This section is less highly detailed, and has its own truncated entry at Broadway and West 13th Avenue signaled by a puzzling partial colonnade, apparently designed to line up with the arcade on the Denver Central Library's south facade.

The state's judicial system benefited by keeping its home cheek-by-jowl with the Capitol, sending the now-History Colorado operation to a new site a couple of blocks south. In the process, however the relationship of Civic Center's buildings has been thrown off balance, the human scale shattered, the progression of architectural innovation on Civic Center stopped in its tracks.

19 History Colorado Center
1200 Broadway
Tryba Architects, 2012

When it became apparent that the Colorado Historical Society needed to move its offices and museum, the hunt was on for a new location. After some false starts, officials identified a site that provided a blank slate upon which to construct a new building, add parking, and get its exhibitions out of the basement.

The new $110.8 million, 200-square-foot History Colorado Center may not be right on Civic Center, but this Neomodern stone and glass structure carries on the spirit of architectural innovation inspired by that district.

Slightly mottled limestone blocks lend solidity and texture to a building that has a strong street presence and sense of buoyancy: an open and welcoming entrance, the inclusion of numerous materials, an elevated roof supported by metal pillars, and entry stairs that denote a sense of arrival without being monumental. Glass elements on all three sides (the fourth abuts the parking structure) add rhythm to a structure that houses a museum, its education and public programs, public spaces, and the Historical Society's Office of Archaeology and Historic Preservation, the State Historical Fund, and the Stephen H. Hart Research Library.

The skylighted four-story Great Hall features a terrazzo floor depicting a map of Colorado, and large media screens across the north wall above the first floor introduce a programmatic focus on interactive experiences throughout the museum. The spell is broken by the intrusion, from one corner, of a faux train depot painted a deep rose. Galleries are devoted to the display of bland, entertainment-heavy vignettes; spaces for traveling exhibitions have yet to open. History Colorado Center is designed to achieve LEED Gold certification.

20 One Civic Center
1560 Broadway
HOK Architects, 1983

21 Civic Center Station
Broadway at 16th Avenue
Johnson-Hopson and Partners, Architects and Planners, 1984

What appears to be three rosy brown buildings is really one, with a lopped-off prow that helps mitigate the office tower's bulk as it addresses the Capitol. With a silhouette defined by a series of angles, One Civic Center adds a commercial edge to the district's northern border.

The complex's plaza and landscaping form a roof for an RTD station, which also serves as a terminus to the transit mall that runs along the 16th Street Mall, linking the Capitol Hill neighborhood and Denver's business district.

22 Colorado State Office Building
1525 E. Colfax Avenue
William Norman Bowman, 1919, restored in 1985

This Neoclassical building of Yule marble and Cotopaxi granite (with some Tennessee marble in the interior) was built in a U-shape, with symmetrical fenestration and pilasters and cornices sympathetic to those of the Capitol itself. It is among notable state office buildings on the Capitol campus, once known as Brown's Bluff.

23 The State Capitol
East 14th Avenue at Lincoln Street
E.E. Myers of Detroit and Frank E. Edbrooke of Denver, cornerstone laid 1890, completed 1904; dome completed in 1908; Quinn Evans Architects, with Humphries Poli Architects, dome repairs, expected completion 2014

This Federal Revival gray granite structure features four symmetrical facades and porticos and a Greek-cross floor plan. E.E. Myers, who left the job early, ceded responsibilities to Frank Edbrooke. Myers had designed other state capitols, including that of his home state of Michigan.

Exterior granite for the Colorado Capitol came from quarries near Gunnison, although the central tower is a slightly different shade. The gold-covered dome stands 272 feet above ground; inside it is divided into 16 segments. The building's interior is of polished Colorado marble, with Colorado onyx on the interior columns and wainscots. Murals in the rotunda are by Allen Tupper True, with inscriptions by Denver poet Thomas Hornsby Ferril.

Like many large civic projects, Colorado's Capitol was a long time coming: Ground was broken in 1886, 18 years after developer Henry C. Brown had donated the land. The original gold applied in 1908 was donated by the Colorado Mining Association.

Fast-forward a century, and the Capitol has undergone safety improvements and some modernization. Most recently, critical repairs to the dome's weakened cast-iron infrastructure were identified after a large chunk of metal fell off the building. The solution to paying for this $17 million job has been controversial, though lawmakers finally settled on a mix of private contributions and support from the State Historical Fund, which has had a deep impact on its grant-making activities. About 72 ounces of gold to regild the dome have been donated by AngloGold Ashanti and the Cripple Creek and Victor Mining Co.

24 The State Capitol Annex
1375 Sherman Street
PMGW (architects who banded together to work on the state's office buildings included C. Francis Pillsbury, G. Meredith Musick, Arthur Fisher, and Gordon White), 1939

Pale limestone walls, rounded corners on the tower section, a dark gray granite entry surround, and geometric carvings that dance across the top of the first floor result in an Art Deco building that complements its Neoclassical neighbors.

 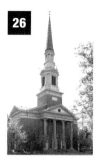 

25 The Colorado State Museum Building
200 E. 14th Avenue
Frank E. Edbrooke, 1915

Colorado building materials – Yule marble and Cotopaxi granite – form the exterior of this Neoclassical Revival building, which was designed to serve as the state's museum. The entrance portico features four fluted Ionic columns. It later served as headquarters of the Colorado Historical Society, until 1977, then stood vacant until a renovation by Pahl-Pahl-Pahl Architects in 1987. The building now houses the General Assembly's Legislative Services staff. Of note: stately hearing rooms in deep jewel tones, and stained glass windows in the stairwell added as part of the state's Art in Public Places Program.

26 First Baptist Church
200 E. 14th Avenue
G. Meredith Musick, 1938

G. Meridith Musick worked in a familiar material – rosy granite and brick – but an unusual style for this area: Georgian Revival mixed with Colonial. The heft of the building, especially its polished stone columns, contrasts with a delicate spire.

27 Evans School
1115 Acoma Street
David Dryden, 1904

David Dryden was the second accomplished architect to turn a great deal of his attention to designing schools for the city of Denver. Named after Colorado territorial Governor John Evans, this red brick building sports a generous hipped roof, Ionic columns, and elaborate detailing in line with Colonial Revival architecture. Closed in 1973, the building was sold to private individuals in 1974 and has been empty since. The city eventually ordered the owner to clean up this designated landmark building and convert it into a place suitable for offices.
Denver Landmark

28 Cullen-Thompson Motor Company / Gart Bros. Sports Castle / Sports Authority Sportscastle
1000 Broadway
Jacques J.B. Benedict, 1920

Many buildings in the neighborhood began as homes for businesses devoted to automobile sales or repair. But none was more elegant than the Cullen-Thompson Motor Company, designed in the early 1920s by noted Denver architect Jacques J.B. Benedict. A lover of Eclectic Classical design, Benedict chose French Gothic – with exotic touches – for this old Chrysler dealership. A terra-cotta facade is topped by minaret-style finials, and the stained glass windows sport the old Chrysler logo. The building has housed sporting good stores for several decades.

29 Anthem Blue Cross / Blue Shield
700 Broadway
The Ken R. White Co., with W.C. Muchow and Associates as design consultants
(George Hoover, design architect), 1973

With parking below and a penthouse floor at the top, what is now the Anthem Blue Cross/Blue Shield building was the height of functional modernity at the time of its construction. Energy-saving devices were included, and special safety features – such as a waterproofed garden level – were incorporated to build solidity into this glass-clad structure.

The massive concrete base – given the look of a train engine by its circular openings - supports an office tower built with a north-south spine and indentations that make it appear to be six towers. Walkways are poured-in-place concrete. Reflective glass covering the towers forms a large mirror for the surrounding area.

30 Grand Cherokee Lofts
1050 Cherokee Street
Humphries Poli Architects, 1998

The architects relied on cast-in-place concrete, aluminum windows, and infill masonry for a residential and retail development that celebrates Modernism at the end of the century. A courtyard designed for residents of the 39 units also serves as a sculpture garden, thanks to the presence of a light-filled gallery on Cherokee Street that specializes in contemporary art.

31 Rocky Mountain Bank Note / Galvanize
1062 Delaware Street
Frederick E. Mountjoy and Frank W. Frewen, 1929
Renovation/reconstruction by David Owen Tryba Architects, 1998

The challenge? To turn an old printing plant into a middle and high school that use the neighborhood as its textbook. It helped that the building was a distinguished one, with a factory interior cloaked in Classical grace and topped by a copper dome more fitting for a bank. For the school conversion, architects created a building within a building, so that classrooms and work spaces form an outer ring around a commons space. A remarkable set of sawtooth skylights provides ample light, while the lobby inside plays off the dome above. Wooden support trusses were left open for view. In 2012, a local investor and tech entrepreneur purchased the building to house Galvanize, a hub for digital start-ups and high-tech businesses.

32 Century Lofts
290 W. 12th Avenue
Humphries Poli Architects, 1998

This 30-unit condominium building is organized around a raised second-level courtyard built over the parking garage. The materials are a mix of concrete and light-gauge metal framing and synthetic stucco – practicality incarnate until the eye reaches the roofline, where designers mounted vintage hubcaps as an unusual cornice decoration.

33 1200 Delaware
Delaware Street at W. 12th Avenue
Bothwell Davis George Architects, 2008

The Golden Triangle has been a hub of infill projects, but usually in the form of condo and apartment buildings. This townhome development introduces early 21st-century Neomodern style into the neighborhood, with strong vertical planes defining the brick, block, and glass townhome sections. A deep band of metal mesh stretches along the upper level across the entire set of row houses, adding a complementary horizontal element that links components. As with many early 21st-century Neomodern infill developments throughout Denver, each unit is defined by a cap-style overhang that helps stretch the perception of height.

34 Cesar E. Chavez Federal Building
1244 Speer Boulevard
Murata Outland Architects, 1984
Tryba Architects, major building modernization, 2012

The federal government's General Services Administration, one of the nation's biggest landlords, announced several years ago that it was launching a major green modernization program for its holdings. The goal was more than a matter of aesthetics or repair: The GSA wanted to set an example for other developers in terms of energy conservation and sustainability.

Among the Denver properties undergoing such a modernization is the Chavez Federal Building, a handsome, early 1980s building that is gaining a new envelope in the form of a new energy-efficient glass and aluminum curtain wall. Also, the lobby is being expanded, the front courtyard/plaza and stretch of Fox Street reconfigured, and a parking garage constructed with a substantial rooftop solar sculpture anchored by an attention-grabbing curved space frame. The project is on track to achieve LEED Silver certification.

Auraria & the 9th Street Historic District

The old Auraria townsite – founded in 1858 across the rivers from Denver's birthplace on Larimer Street – has evolved into a district with several personalities, a far cry from its days as an immigrant community and industrial stronghold.

There is the quaint block of historic homes, saved in the mid-1970s by hard work and fund-raising by Historic Denver, Inc. and other organizations. There is a sweeping landscape of academic structures used by the three institutions of the Auraria Higher Education Center, or AHEC. There are several religious structures, two of which have found new uses. There is a fanciful former brewery, which for the past three decades has been both urban shopping mall and student center. And in the late 1980s, a historic home was trucked in – notable less for its design than for the fame of its former resident.

Absorbed by Denver in 1860, the modern Auraria was born of strife. In the Denver Urban Renewal Authority's 1960s rush to clean up by clearing out, the old residential neighborhood basically was demolished, breaking up a community and costing many buildings that had housed a largely Chicano and Hispanic population.

The reason: to create a campus for three schools, Metropolitan State University of Denver, the University of Colorado Denver, and the Community College of Denver. Each is a tenant of AHEC, with the stated goal to share facilities, although that has changed somewhat as each institution has begun to develop its own campus "neighborhood" of school-specific facilities. Although Auraria is still to some degree a commuter campus, the rise of students of a traditional college age has led to the development of several student housing projects, including one on campus.

Campus planning and construction have been centralized on a grid designed to maintain open spaces and walkways, with room for outdoor gatherings and art. The buildings that now stand on the "new" Auraria span more than 140 years, with the involvement of many architects, planners, contractors, and preservationists. Among the notable planners have been Chicago-based architect Jacques Brownson (of C.F. Murphy), who in the 1970s became director of planning and development for AHEC. As campus architect, he has been credited with establishing an architectural vocabulary for Auraria and bringing in Helmut Jahn to design the campus's award-winning library. Brownson was followed by Bob Kronewitter, and more recently, campus planner Jill Jennings Golich.

The boom in attendance has brought expansion across the campus, resulting in buildings that front Speer Boulevard and Auraria Parkway, and reach west toward residential areas and the city's football stadium. Campus and city officials see the move toward the central business district and lower downtown as a key element in bridging the gap between town and gown – though busy Speer Boulevard is a formidable impediment to easy access.

Downtown Denver

LIST OF BUILDINGS

1   Tivoli Brewery Company / Auraria Student Center
2   St. Cajetan's Center
3   The Auraria Library
4   9th Street Historic District
4.1   The Stephen Knight House
4.2   Groussman Grocery / Mercantile Cafe
4.3   The Charles R. Davis House
4.4   The Smedley-Cole House
4.5   The Golda Meir House
5   Emmanuel Gallery
6   Kenneth King Center for the Academic and
      Performing Arts
7   North Classroom Building
8   Auraria Science Building Addition and Renovation
9   Metro Student Success Building
10   Hotel and Hospitality Learning Center
11   Campus Village 1

1 **Tivoli Brewery Company / Auraria Student Center**
1320–48 10th Street
Various architects and renovations; major 2004 renovation included stripping paint and improvements, SlaterPaull Architects. 1860s

The Tivoli in a way was a precursor to the development in the Central Platte Valley, shifting from an industrial property to a more service-oriented purpose. This longtime brewery was reborn as a mall, an enterprise that failed. In the late 1990s, it lost its cluster of movie theaters. Built in phases over the years – and over numerous levels – what is now the Tivoli began in the mid-1860s with the historic Sigi's Hall.

Although the complex overall is designed in a Victorian Commercial style with arched windows in varying proportions marching around the facades, the Tivoli is dominated by a seven-story tower (1890) with a mansard roof and Second Empire elements. Architects for parts of the Tivoli include F.C. Eberly (the ornate 1881 two-story corner building) and Harold Baerresen (the 1882 Turnhalle section). In 1890, another building was added, with Italianate elements and even more decoration.

The Tivoli's taps went dry in 1969, and the buildings were purchased by the Denver Urban Renewal Authority and turned over to Auraria. A renovation by HOK in the early 1980s turned the complex into a shopping mall, but when stores began closing, Auraria bought the lease back a decade later and sought another renovation (Urban Design Group) to convert the property into a student and community center.

The most dramatic change at the Tivoli entailed structural and logistical improvements, plus the removal of numerous coats of white paint that had covered the complex for many years. The SlaterPaull project, funded by a student-approved fee boost, revealed instances of mismatched brick the original builder believed would never be exposed (the use of stain helped unify the appearance). The final results overshadowed that issue: What for years had appeared to be a jumble of forms clumped together on the edge of campus, suddenly emerged as individual structures that show fine, sometimes surprising detailing and a continuum of design influences.
Denver Landmark, National Register of Historic Places

2 **St. Cajetan's Center**
1190 9th Street
Robert Willison, circa 1920s (dates given variously as 1926 and 1929)

Robert Willison mixed details of Venetian Renaissance design with a bit of Spanish Colonial Revival to create a stucco mission topped by twin towers and a large rounded center parapet. Although imposing, St. Cajetan's is surprisingly simple in its decoration. It was renovated in the early 1990s by Auraria campus architects, and now hosts events.
Denver Landmark

Two other religious structures also grace the campus:
St. Elizabeth's Catholic Church, *1062 11th Street*, credited to Father Adrian,
O.F.M., 1898, and the adjacent **St. Francis Interfaith Center**, Marvin Hatami,
1978: Here, old and new meet along Speer Boulevard. Built of stone in a
Romanesque Revival style, St. Elizabeth's exhibits an asymmetrical face because
of its side tower and steeple. Eighty years later, Denver architect Hatami wrapped
a new building around part of the church, a conference and student center that
refers to the older structure's Classicism while adding a curved walkway,
Modernist crown, and contemporary materials.
St. Francis Interfaith Center: Western Mountain Region AIA, Honor Award, 1981

3 The Auraria Library
1100 Lawrence Street
Helmut Jahn, C.F. Murphy, 1976

The clean lines of this design stand out on a campus that mixes stately historical
structures with contemporary brick. Helmut Jahn used a glazed white surface
to clad a cube-like building that demonstrates a dignified interpretation of human
scale. Louvered window slats serve as sunscreens on a low-rise facility that
continues to anchor this part of a growing campus. Though at times threatened
with change, Jahn's Modernist design, with its light-filled interior, speaks to the
sense of optimism that fueled the development of the Auraria campus.
AIA Denver 25 Year Award, 2009

4 The 9th Street Historic District
9th Street between Curtis and Champa Streets

This district may be just one block long, but many of the small buildings rescued from
oblivion show the exuberance that early settlers coveted as they carved "civilization"
out of the high plains desert. Added to the mix farther up on 9th Street (originally
called Cheyenne Street) is a home moved to this site to save it from demolition.

Architects were not involved in the design of these buildings, but they are
notable for an attention to the detail and craftsmanship found in Victorian design
with Italianate and Empire variations. Residences for merchants and tradesmen
now shelter office and commercial space and stand as both reminder of the
short-lived town of Auraria, which became part of Denver in 1860, and a once-
vital neighborhood lost to civic "progress." These properties are among the oldest
in the city to survive demolition and disaster; seven date from before 1880.
Denver Landmark Historic District, National Register of Historic Places Historic District

The buildings include:
4.1 – The Stephen Knight House, *1015 9th Street*, 1885: Built by Charles Davis
for his daughter and her husband, Stephen Knight, the home is designed in the
Second Empire style, with a stepped-back mansard and imposing porch
columns. (Renovation by Hornbein & White and Long-Hoeft Architects.)

4.2 – Groussman Grocery / Mercantile Cafe, *9th and Curtis Streets*, 1906:
Albert B. Groussman first lived on the site in a frame house replaced in 1906
by this example of traditional early 20th-century commercial architecture. It
continues as a retail establishment.

4.3 – The Charles R. Davis House, *1068 9th Street*, circa 1872: Mill owner Davis
decorated his petite Italianate villa with the fruits of his labors: delicate wood
detailing on the porch entryway and balcony, including fancy brackets and a
quatrefoil design. (Renovation by Hornbein & White.)

4.4 – The Smedley-Cole House, *1020 9th Street*, circa 1872: Dentist William
Smedley built this fine Victorian with brackets to rival his neighbors'. (Renovation
by Hornbein & White.)

4.5 – The Golda Meir House, *1146 9th Street Park*, 1911: This humble duplex
was moved here in 1988 from its original location at 1606–1608 Julian Street.
The late Israeli leader was known as Goldie Mabowehz and a student at North
High School when she resided in this one-story brick home. The structure now
houses a conference and study center. (Renovation by Long-Hoeft Architects.)

5   Emmanuel Gallery
1205 10th Street Mall
Architect unknown; renovation by Gale Abels, 1876

This compact but well-proportioned stone building was built as an Episcopal
church, then in 1902 was purchased by Shearith Israel congregation and
converted to a synagogue. Almost a century later, it was renovated to gallery
space. Emmanuel gains a sense of height from slim buttresses and slender
arched Gothic windows.
Denver Landmark, National Register of Historic Places

6   Kenneth King Center for the Academic and Performing Arts
Between Lawrence Way and Larimer Street, at 8th and 9th Streets
AR7, with Semple Brown Design, 2001

The architects who also designed the nearby North Classroom Building conceived
of the King Center as a conduit through the Auraria campus, with a "Main Street"
corridor that links entries on the Lawrence Way and Larimer Street facades. In
the same vein, the building's design melds space for academic and performance
activities, serving the University of Colorado Denver, Metropolitan State University
of Denver, and the Community College of Denver.

While the earlier North Classroom Building introduced glass block to the campus's
vocabulary, the King Center has added a spotted brick and numerous concrete
accents and elements that help define the structure. The Larimer Street entry
is more subtle, though it leads to performance spaces. On Lawrence, the
approach is more open, with a facade that includes several stories of glass and
a concrete colonnade.

7 **North Classroom Building**
1200 Larimer Street
Hoover Berg Desmond, 1987

The architects relied on dark brick to create a modern academic sensibility, then added a generous amount of glass block to bring natural light into this distinguished building. The building has helped give the campus an edge on Speer Boulevard. The entrance visible from Speer is marked by a large lighted wagon-wheel "watch face" that kicked the traditional collegiate clock tower into the 20th century.
AIA Colorado Merit Award, 1989

8 **Auraria Science Building Addition and Renovation**
1151 Arapahoe Street
Original building, Charles S. Sink and Associates, 1976;
addition and renovation by Anderson Mason Dale Architects, 2009

This ambitious addition was intended as much to reach out to downtown from the campus as it was to provide more space for an overcrowded Science Building. The glazed "wedge" fronting on Speer Boulevard is an attention-getter for those driving the busy thoroughfare, which proved troublesome when a shutdown in state funding left the project a big hole in the ground for several months (the state of Colorado eventually provided funds).

The architects renovated the existing building and created a new structure that relates visually through the use of brick that is both compatible and distinctive. Extensive glass has been used in the four-story addition, allowing easy viewing into the equipment and classrooms that fill more than 180,000 square feet of new space. The angled design – it resembles a "7" if viewed from above – helped create a courtyard between the old and new structures, while making a sensitive connection. Donald Lipski's colorful *Psyche* (*The Butterfly*) is suspended at the entry of the new building that houses a cafe; the publicly funded sculpture's "wings" are composed of thousands of test tubes filled with amber-gold-orange material.

The building, apparently the last project designed to be shared by all three schools, has achieved LEED Gold certification.

9 **Metro Student Success Building**
890 Auraria Parkway
RNL Design, 2012

Along with extending the campus and helping to define an edge along Auraria
Parkway, the Student Success Building begins a trend of projects designed
for use by only one school's students, faculty, and staff. For Metropolitan State
University of Denver, that means a single-school "neighborhood" fronting the
parkway. Classrooms and administrative offices will share space with programs
(registrar, financial aid, etc.) designed to put new Metro students on the path to
success and aid retention of existing students. A bright red sign signals the way.
The four-story, 143,000-square-foot building is constructed in the shape of
an "L," with a skin that presents areas of blond brick, metal panels, and broad
horizontal expanses of glass. The building was designed to achieve LEED
Gold certification.

10 **Hotel and Hospitality Learning Center**
Speer Boulevard at Auraria Parkway
RNL Design, 2012

Metro State's Hospitality, Tourism, and Event Department makes its home in this
dramatic horizontal swath of dark gray-blue brick and glass that streams from
Speer Boulevard around the corner to Auraria Parkway.

A striking stretch of glass curtain wall serves as a bridge to connect classrooms
and academic facilities with a 150-room hotel and conference center – the
practical side of the learning experience. Glass elements help add rhythm to the
facade, which brings a commercial touch to a corner that stretches visually into
lower downtown. In effect, the wrapper effect linking Speer Boulevard and the
Auraria Parkway stresses the campus' continuing effort to connect with the rest
of the city. The project is designed to achieve LEED Silver certification.

11 **Campus Village 1**
318 Walnut Street
AR7, 2006

As attendance and facilities continued to expand at the three schools that
share the Auraria Higher Education Center, officials realized it was time to bring
something new to the mix: student housing, designed to foster a sense of
community, keep students in school, and make the Auraria experience feel more
like that of a traditional college campus. Work began on developing several
dorm-style settings, including one built from scratch (the others are located at
renovated former hotels off campus).

Campus Village 1, which pushes the boundaries of the campus toward residential neighborhoods and Sports Authority Field at Mile High, is the result of a partnership between a private developer and the CU Real Estate Foundation. Located on the former Atlas Metals Co. property, this "village" can house more than 680 students in a mix of buildings clad in brick and colorful corrugated metal.

From one angle, this combination of dorm and retail space appears to be a standard red brick housing block. But turn the corner, or peek inside a courtyard area, and the primary colors begin to pop, adding a sense of hominess to on-campus living.

Central Platte Valley / Prospect

Where the South Platte River and Cherry Creek come together is where the city first began. It is where Native Americans and early explorers met and traded. It is where the railroads later found the space needed to create a convergence of track.

And now, with the junkyards cleared and most rail lines ripped out, it is where a new mini-city of upscale high-rises (residential and office) and townhomes has grown, where the city and passionate citizens have built new parks that offer access to the rush of water, and open space for a tight environment. Along with residential and recreational opportunities, the Central Platte Valley also has become a locus of entertainment facilities, including an amusement park, a skate park, a contemporary art museum, and a football stadium whose curvy crown is an addition to the city's skyline.

Massive sections of Denver saw redevelopment in the late 1990s. The conversion of Lowry Air Force Base and Stapleton International Airport into residential neighborhoods is probably the most easily visible transformation. And the inner-ring neighborhoods (Highlands) and former industrial areas (RiNo) have come alive through infill projects and creative new development. But the Central Platte Valley has grown almost out of nothing.

Once the black hole of gone-to-seed space, the Valley now has an impact on the vitality of downtown as well as the evolution of transportation facilities that will affect the region. Acres of nothing have shifted from dregs to diamonds in just a few decades, while smart new connections – bridges, underpasses, pedestrian walkways – have made the interstate, the rivers, and the remaining rail system much less of an impediment between downtown and the neighborhoods to the northwest. As the Valley has grown, new development has moved to the north, including the residential area called Prospect. Throughout the Valley, new streets have been built and others have been extended, creating a grid that anchors a dense neighborhood.

One of the best vantage points to view the sweep of development in the Valley is to head to Highlands, and stand at the foot the pedestrian bridge spanning Interstate 25. There, the transformation becomes clear, illustrating how a tangle of rail lines has become a community for work and play.

OLD LIST OF BUILDINGS

1.1 15th Street Underpass
1.2 Speer Boulevard Bridge
1.3 Millennium Bridge
1.4 Platte Valley Pedestrian Bridge
1.5 18th Street Pedestrian Bridge
2 Moffat Depot
3.1 Confluence Park
3.2 Commons Park
3.3 Northside Park
4 MCA / Denver
5 ArtHouse Townhomes
6 Riverfront Park
7 Brownstones at Riverfront Park
8 Glasshouse
9 1900 Sixteenth
10 DaVita Headquarters
11 Denver Traffic Operations and
   Training Facility
12 Waterside Lofts
13 Denver Tramway Company Powerhouse /
   REI Flagship Store
14 Colorado Ocean Journey / Downtown
   Denver Aquarium
15 Pepsi Center
16 Children's Museum of Denver
17 Mile High Stadium / Invesco Field at
   Mile High / Sports Authority Field
   at Mile High
18 Flour Mill Lofts / Pride of the Rockies
   Flour Mill / Hungarian Flour Mill
19 Jack Kerouac Lofts
20 Ajax Lofts

THE CONNECTIONS

One of the key elements to development of the Central Platte Valley has been forging connections within the Valley while linking downtown Denver to the neighborhoods of nearby northwest Denver. Thus, numerous bridges and viaducts have been constructed to span waterways and railroad tracks that still chop up the area, including one structure that has become a modern landmark.

In the early 1990s, two of Denver's old viaducts came down. Demolition of the elevated 15th Street and 16th Street structures erased part of the city's gritty urban edge, but at the same time it revealed buildings that had been hidden for years and offered designers a chance to install sleek new connectors. (Eventually, other viaducts and overpasses to the north at 20th and 23rd Streets and at Broadway came on line, servicing traffic to Coors Field and lower downtown.)

These old and new connectors include:

1.1 – 15th Street Underpass, BRW Inc., 1992: Among the first steps after the old viaducts came down was the construction of the new 15th Street Underpass, which took traffic below grade rather than over a rickety elevated metal roadway. In this instance, BRW of Denver created somewhat of a plaza feel, widening 15th Street as it dipped and designing a graceful span above. Public art installed on the walls at either side may be difficult to see as drivers speed through, but the tile-and-brick murals by Ken and Judith Williams and Maria Alquilar incorporate items found during excavation on the site, a mingling of old and new.

1.2 – Speer Boulevard Bridge, URS-Greiner and BRW, 2001: This project takes drivers above the South Platte River along a broad roadway. Though the bridge speeds travel, it also includes somewhat unwieldy-looking structures, with spans in a combination of conventional steel girder construction and cable-stayed box-arch formation.

The old 16th Street Viaduct came down at about the same time. Its removal has literally opened up a new frontier, with the evolving extension of the 16th Street Mall, shuttle service and light rail near Union Station, and the introduction of three expressive pedestrian bridges that allow a trek from the Central Platte Valley, through Commons Park, over the Platte River, and eventually across Interstate 25 to reach the Highlands neighborhoods.

1.3 – Millennium Bridge, 16th and Little Raven streets, ArchitectureDenver, with Design Workshop, 2002: The continued extension of the 16th Street Mall toward the various Highlands neighborhoods required pedestrian links. This futuristic pedestrian bridge with a towering mast design by ArchitectureDenver, with Design Workshop, is a major part of the 16th Street extension and replaces the old 16th Street Viaduct over the remaining operational rail tracks, the Consolidated Main Line, or CML. The Millennium Bridge's 200-foot-tall white mast stands out as a signal for a new part of the city, though the construction of office buildings has somewhat obscured the view. The mast is canted back to hold stable the cables that suspend the walkway, becoming slimmer at the top and the bottom where the stress subsides. This nod to asymmetry and tension fronts a plaza that marks the earliest residential construction in the Valley, with an eye as much to the techtonic (engineering by Ove Arup of New York) as the aesthetic. The $9 million,

130-foot-long bridge was funded by the city of Denver, the Central Platte Valley Metropolitan District, and area developers – thus its new life as a logo.

Two more bridges later fell into line as part of the 16th Street extension: **1.4 – Platte Valley Pedestrian Bridge (Platte River at 16th Street, 2004), and Highlands Pedestrian Bridge (Carter & Burgess, 2006):** The former crosses the river at Commons Park with a much more straightforward span. The latter, at 325 feet long and costing more than $5 million, stretches over Interstate 25 as the final link in the chain. John McEnroe's public art sculptural installation, *National Velvet*, spurred much discussion in the area, with its glowing red resin forms sitting on a pedestal at the foot of the bridge on the Central Platte Valley side.

1.5 – 18th Street Pedestrian Bridge, 2010: Also known as the Union Gateway Bridge, this elevated pedestrian walkway connects the Riverfront Park and Union Station Districts in the Central Platte Valley. It crosses the CML freight tracks and tracks for the relocated light rail station near 17th Street.

Historic bridges that remain in the Valley include the somewhat disembodied but charming **19th Street Bridge** over the South Platte. This structure dates from 1889 and was built by the Missouri Valley Bridge and Iron Works. The **Wynkoop Street Railroad Bridge**, at Cherry Creek, was constructed by the Pennsylvania Steel Company (it's described in the chapter on lower downtown).

2 Moffat Depot
2101 15th Street
Edwin H. Moorman, 1906

Also called Moffat Station, this small Neoclassical structure was the Denver terminus for David Moffat's short (and short-lived) Denver, Northwestern, and Pacific Railroad. Time has not been particularly good to the depot, which was damaged by a fire in 1995. Still, it stands watch over the street as a bit of history, waiting for a ticket to the future. That almost came in 2006, when a new owner announced plans to design a senior care complex. With similar plans revised, the depot is poised to be part of the new construction that has surrounded it.
National Register of Historic Places, Denver Landmark

THE PLATTE RIVER PARK SYSTEM

People new to Denver learn many things. Among the first: People here love their parks. Not as if residents in other parts of the country don't love their parks, of course. But other parts of the country are not high plains desert, where early settlers encountered little vegetation and even less moisture to make it green.

In the early part of the 20th century, Denver's big three parks – Civic Center, Washington Park, and City Park – began to evolve. In the mid-1970s, the unlikely team of a former Republican state senator (Joe Shoemaker) and a Democratic mayor (William McNichols) took the bold step of trying to reintroduce residents to their river heritage. The Platte River Development Committee and Shoemaker's Greenway Foundation had parlayed a couple of million dollars in revenue-sharing

funds and private money into a place where residents could reach the confluence, augmented by bike paths and trails.

A decade later, the city released a Central Platte Valley plan that swept to the south and the north of Confluence Park, and in the 1989 Denver Comprehensive Plan, the Platte was deemed the "focus of Denver's natural open space system." Plans continued, and sometimes were shelved, as when a proposal died that would have placed the Colorado Convention Center in the Valley. But planning never really stopped. Design work on Rockmount Park (now City of Cuernavaca Park) began in 1992, and on Commons Park a few years later. Developers donated land, and the lottery-backed Greater Outdoors Colorado provided support. Former mayor Federico Peña and former mayor Wellington E. Webb both moved the planning forward.

The result is a string of urban oases carved out of what for years was considered lost land, with linked trails for bikes and people and activities that celebrate the waterways that helped Denver prosper. In 2012, a plan was announced to expand a greenway trail system that connects urban wildlife refuges and parks even further.

Among the highlights are:

3.1 – Confluence Park, bounded by Speer Boulevard and 15th Street, and by Little Raven and Water Streets; design by EDAW, 1976; updated by McLaughlin Water Engineers, 1990s; plaza by Architerra, 2001: Confluence Park takes its name from the fact that the South Platte River and Cherry Creek meet at this point – the site of Denver's first settlement. Though not the most dynamic of waterways, the two are Denver's close-in access to a host of recreational activities. Funded by the Greenway Foundation, public interests and the city, Confluence Park offers urban folk a spot for reflection as well as events. It is the anchor in the chain of the ever-evolving Platte Park System that reaches from Northside Park near the northern city limits to Grant-Frontier Park near the boundary to the south. In between are reconstructed bridges, public art, bike trails, and walkways that have opened the water to public enjoyment while attracting development to the Central Platte Valley. Improvements continue, with the development of design guidelines and plans that include reconstruction of amenities in Confluence Park's Shoemaker Plaza.

3.2 – Commons Park, bounded by Little Raven and Platte Streets and by 15th and 19th Streets; Civitas, 2000: Part of the Platte Park System developed over decades by the city, this 20-acre mix of wild and urban landscape opened to fanfare as an amenity to downtown workers as well as to residents of pricey new housing in lower downtown and the Central Platte Valley. Civitas accentuated access to the South Platte River with historic plantings, an amphitheater, and land sculpted to create both walkways and generous green space. A privately funded, ramplike installation by Barbara Grygutis – the serpentine rhyolite *Common Ground* – serves as an additional lure to view nature in context with new development.

3.3 – Northside Park, off Interstate 25 and south on Franklin Street from the 58th Avenue exit to the armory parking lot; Wenk and Associates, 2000: Northside Park was created from 70 acres of land and a sewage treatment plant – turning green into green in the greenest of ways. The plant is gone and paths are in place, following a plan by landscape architects Wenk and Associates. Many

materials were reused for fill, while several concrete structures – forms, really – have been preserved. Elegant (and finished for safety's sake), these details represent a link to the past as well as a proper frame for a park in an industrial neighborhood. It is, in the end, the ultimate in recycling, turning an eyesore into a place where people can breathe.

4 MCA / Denver
1485 Delgany Street
David Adjaye, Adjaye Associates, London, with Davis Partnership, Denver, 2007

From the outside, this cube-like structure may read as a smoky gray-black glass container for the Museum of Contemporary Art / Denver, or MCA but the interior tells a different story: Those glass walls are lined with white MonoPan, which allows the hallways and galleries to glow within during the day and emit diffused light at night. Clear windows are strategically placed to frame city views, and the roof garden area sports walkways and a cafe that are the soul of urbanity.

David Adjaye was chosen from a field that included the firms Snohetta, Gluckman Mayner Architects, TEC Arquitectos, Predock_Frane, and Rick Joy Architects – all of whom made presentations on their work to packed houses. MCA Denver, born in rental space and the longtime tenant of a former fish market, went the route of high style but low budget, costing about $16 million, on land donated by developer and board president Mark Falcone.

Adjaye's first U.S. project is a symbol of his serene, simple Neomodernism -- a fact that prompted compare-and-contrast discussions regarding Daniel Libeskind's 2006 Denver Art Museum Hamilton Building, an expressive study in explosive shapes. MCA's galleries and a lower-level program space are flexible, beautiful, and perfectly proportioned -- a quiet backdrop for cutting-edge art. The 27,000-square-foot building is marked by elegant details, from the lighting under the staircase railing, to a cantilevered Idea Box area upstairs that is scaled for young art lovers. MCA achieved LEED Gold certification.

5 ArtHouse Townhomes
1460 Delgany Street
Studio Completiva and David Adjaye, 2007

The Museum of Contemporary Art / Denver, or MCA, sits on a remarkably tight site, a corner of the Valley that also involves three residential projects, including one associated with the museum itself, two design firms, and two developers. All three projects almost caress the museum, separated by a fire lane and plaza MCA can use for events. However, all these elements are connected by an eye toward modernity.

The ArtHouse Townhomes were designed mainly by Denver-based Studio Completiva as high-end residences that would be simpatico with David Adjaye's mysterious glass MCA.

In two and three stories, the townhomes front on various thoroughfares, including 15th Street. Glass curtain walls and floating windows and planes provide rhythm

to the project, which utilizes black-and-white accents composed of materials such as Alphaton and Swiss Pearl.

In conjunction with the design of MCA, David Adjaye created an adjacent townhome for developer Mark Falcone, who donated the land for MCA and has served as board president. The home has special design elements, including the use of Cor-Ten steel.

The nearby mid-rise **Monarch Mills project, 1475 Delgany Street, 2007**, which includes affordable housing units to address that requirement in the Valley, was designed by Studio Completiva for a different developer. The project displays less finesse in its design and materials, with bright white stucco, accented by strips of raw concrete and a rain screen of a terra-cotta-colored, clay-based product called Alphaton.

The **Delgany Lofts**, a U-shaped complex designed by 4240 Architecture Inc., 1401 Delgany Street, 2005, stands right on Cherry Creek, helping create an edge for one of Denver's key natural markers. The Delgany project shelters a courtyard that adds a touch of green to the block. A street in front of the lofts separates it from its neighbors.

RIVERFRONT PARK

6.1 Riverfront Tower, Riverfront Plaza at Little Raven Street; Park Place Lofts, 1610 Little Raven Street; Promenade Lofts, 2100 16th Street, all 4240 Architecture Inc., 2002: This trio of high-rise towers early on set the tone for the design vocabulary in the Central Platte Valley. All rely on brick, glass, and stone used in ways to stress the Modernist design and the forward-thinking nature of this reclaimed neighborhood. The towers's location has a smart marker: the Millennium Bridge, which has become a symbol of the Valley's design ethos.
Riverfront Tower: AIA Colorado Merit Award, 2002

7 Brownstones at Riverfront Park
Little Raven and 18th Streets
Humphries Poli Architects, 2005

This 16-unit development farther up Little Raven displays a human scale and intriguing geometric compositions expressed in polychrome buff brick, metal, and glass forms and planes. Though more buff brick than brownstone, the project displays expert proportions, stressing individuality for each home while providing strong connections that unify the row of homes.

8 Glasshouse
1700 Bassett Street
Preston Partnership of Atlanta, 2007

The residential towers of Glasshouse in a way anchor the Valley's skyline because what is visible from the city and highway is glass curtain wall that expresses a stunning sense of transparency. Set on brick bases, these 23-story towers lose

some of their impact at ground level, where the design really comes down to earth. Still, Glasshouse is an intriguing addition to the Neomodernist design approach, especially for those who relish sweeping views.

9   1900 Sixteenth
1900 16th Street
Tryba Architects, 2009

1900 Sixteenth is sited at the heart of the Valley's entrée to the regional transit hub evolving around Union Station, near the multimodal light rail station, and on the extension of 16th Street that reaches into the neighborhoods northwest of Denver. Tryba Architects' project has introduced an office tower into this largely residential area, an 18-story project that has achieved LEED Gold certification. Abundant glass and clean lines mark Phase One of the project, which includes an adjacent parking structure, plaza, and space for street-level retail. Though the project has obscured views of the Millennium Bridge, its design is distinguished by an understated Neomodernist aesthetic.

10   DaVita Headquarters
2000 16th Street
MOA Architecture, 2012

The corporate home of this health care company stands out as the flashier younger brother of nearby 1900 Sixteenth. DaVita's glass is a little brighter shade of blue; it sports a wedge-like element on one facade, and its roof seems to float, tilted at a beguiling slant. While continuing the Neomodern aesthetic of the district, MOA Architecture has differentiated its building just enough through the use of bold elements, while working to complement the more restrained form of 1900 Sixteenth. The DaVita Building is pursuing LEED Gold certification, and contributes to the increased density of the area as another substantial transit-oriented development project.

11   Denver Traffic Operations and Training Facility
3375 Fox Street
Humphries Poli Architects, 2010

This Denver Police Department building may be located in a gritty area that is just starting to develop, but that doesn't mean it lacks style. Housing some basic law-enforcement needs, this off-the-beaten-path project features two components: a traffic operations area carved out of an old warehouse, and a separate, new firing range and training facility. Humphries Poli Architects introduced unexpected colors into the design, including a special piece of public art, Robert Zoell's untitled wall mural that reads as an American flag. The project is LEED Gold certified.

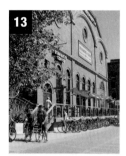

12 Waterside Lofts
1401 Wewatta Street
OZ Architecture, with Shears + Adkins Architects, 2002

Another early project in the Central Platte Valley, the Waterside Lofts helps form an edge on Speer Boulevard and is adjacent to both the banks of Cherry Creek and the bustle of lower downtown. With 13 stories and prominent balconies, this project claims its site. Exposed concrete structural elements, generous use of metal, and different types of brick give this building a sense of blending new and old, allowing it to serve as a connection between the historic structures of lower downtown and the more Neomodern aesthetic found in the Valley.
AIA Denver Special Recognition Award, 2003

13 Denver Tramway Company Powerhouse / REI Flagship Store
1416 Platte Street
Stearns Rogers Company, 1901; restoration by Mithun Partners, 2000

This purely industrial structure meant to create electricity for the Denver Tramway Company demonstrates how aesthetic standards have changed over the years. The powerhouse is decorated at the roofline with arches, lunette and half-lunette windows, and fan windows supported by elaborate wooden tracings. Romanesque windows and doors are notable features on the first story, with roundels and linked arches decorating the second.

Eventually, the building became home to Forney Transportation Museum, a labor of love and a home for a 400-piece collection of trains, automobiles, bicycles, buggies, and wagons. But the museum received little public support to maintain the building and in the late 1990s began moving the collection's many vehicles – including the mammoth "Big Boy" locomotive – to a new home in an industrial area to the north.

The outdoor equipment outfitters REI did find public help, however, and after restoration work to windows and rehabbing of the central building and attached battery house, the firm opened a store that offers access to water as well as a chance to savor the concept of "powerhouse chic." Works by local artists including Bernice Strawn, Erick Johnson, and Emmett Culligan fill the store.
Denver Landmark

14 Colorado Ocean Journey / Downtown Denver Aquarium
700 Water Street
Odyssea, a joint venture between AndersonMasonDale Architects and RNL Design, 1999

Talk of building an aquarium in high-and-dry Denver reaches back into dim memory, and at one point there were dueling projects on the drawing board. The winner was a husband-and-wife team that received tremendous local support and turned to local architects for a design rather than a national firm with a history of aquarium expertise. It was a wise decision, because the joint venture of Odyssea (AndersonMasonDale Architects and RNL Design) produced a fine building that helped set a standard for design in the Central Platte Valley.

With its mix of brick, steel, and glass, what is now the Downtown Denver Aquarium (and a seafood restaurant) reaches out to historic neighbors while bringing a forward-thinking look to a difficult site. Curving walls, vast expanses of windows, a wraparound observation deck, heavy trusses that serve as a reference to marine architecture and vehicles, and a park have contributed to the building's success.

The same cannot be said of Ocean Journey, which went belly up, doused in debt (and a bond default) and facing wavering attendance. A prominent restaurant chain reeled in the building in 2005, modifying the aquarium concept and making expensive modifications to the aquarium and the interior public spaces. Still, the former Colorado Ocean Journey remains one of the most successful buildings constructed in Denver in the 1990s.
AIA Denver Citation Award, 1999

15 Pepsi Center
1000 Chopper Place, off Auraria Parkway
HOK Sports Facilities Group, 1999

Even though the old McNichols Arena had undergone work in the late 1980s, the economics of sports was making the 1975 domed spaceship a dinosaur.

The replacement is an arena whose designer tried to connect to historic red brick structures in the area, while adding a floating roof and a fair amount of glass. The red-and-beige stucco cylinder needed that transparency to not only open it up to the neighborhood but also to add natural light to a building designed for concerts as much as for basketball and hockey.

A group of area architects worked as consultants on the project, insisting on treating all sides of the structure with features that kept it from being just one big red wall. From a distance – the best view is from Auraria campus – the colors of the center appear to stream in a horizontal format, broken by vertical elements and a great glass wedge that keep the building from being static. A mini-park, with a fake rock construction, contributes some greenery before entering the sea of parking set behind the center.

16 Children's Museum of Denver
2121 Children's Museum Drive, off Interstate 25
Barker Rinker Seacat, 1984

The museum was a pioneer in this district, a vast desert when this bright new building was constructed. The architects went for color and whimsy for their modern design. They added a box and a pyramid in aqua and purple as the decorative top for a simple brick structure that needed to attract attention from the highway. This party-hat look easily led to signature status for the museum, which has since expanded in a more quiet way.

17 Mile High Stadium / Invesco Field at Mile High / Sports Authority Field at Mile High

2755 W. 17th Avenue
James Tolle (Mile High), 1948; movable stands
added in 1977; HNTB Sports Architecture with Fentress Bradburn
Architects Ltd. and Bertram A. Burton and Associates (Invesco Field), 2001

Built in 1948 as the Denver Bears baseball stadium, the old Mile High was enlarged in the late 1950s to accommodate the new Denver Broncos football club. In 1977, additional seats were added, taking the stadium up to 76,000. The new stands slid via a hydraulic system on a pad of water, placed as necessary for various events. When Coors Field was constructed in the 1990s as a home for just baseball, the push began to build a stadium intended solely for football.

Constructed to the south of the old stadium, what is now called Sports Authority Field at Mile High aimed for distinction in design and siting. The old Mile High was demolished after the new stadium opened, allowing several months' worth of comparison between then and now.

Three firms competed for the new 76,000-plus-seat stadium, which later took the Sports Authority Field name. (The Metropolitan Football Stadium District selected the HNTB / Fentress Bradburn / Bruton team over HOK Sports, whose designers had created Coors Field and the Pepsi Center. A few days before the final selection, a district board committee had eliminated a third contender, NBBJ and Ellerbe Becket.)

The winning partnership's design evolved into a bowl in a horseshoe-shaped surround that registers on the skyline. A curvy metal framework lifts the stadium up and turns the edge into something almost like a roller coaster railway. A metal skin, mixed with brick and glass, offers a different look for a new stadium, which is surrounded by a ring of parkland and plazas. The horseshoe shape and noise-producing metal risers offer an homage to the old Mile High, while vastly more amenities, easier circulation, and a sense of openness are a hallmark of the new design. The Metropolitan Stadium District administered a public art program that has included work by Catherine Widgery, Melissa Smedley, Ante Marinovic and Mathieu Gregoire, and Ralph Helmick and Stuart Schecter, plus a giant bronze sculpture of horses by Sergio Benvenuti. Historic Bucky cantered over to the new stadium and seems at home there today.
AIA Denver Citation Award, 2003

PROSPECT

As development boomed in the lower section of the Central Platte Valley, new projects began to take hold in the upper area, which is referred to as Prospect. There, a historic loft transformation – from flour mill to bombed-out building to upscale residences – already was in place. As with the buildings elsewhere in the Valley, the new buildings in Prospect trend toward contemporary, with clean lines, but these projects reveal more of an industrial edge, befitting their surroundings.

18 Flour Mill Lofts / Pride of the Rockies Flour Mill / Hungarian Flour Mill
2000 Little Raven Street
Architect not known, 1906; rehabilitation and loft
conversion by Cuthbertson and DeSousa, 1998; second phase of development,
new construction designed by Shears + Leese Architects and John Williams
Architecture, 2000

The Longmont Farmers and Milling Company built this stark industrial structure as one of several milling plants in the Valley. (An old section, designed by Frank Edbrooke, was destroyed by fire in 1920.) The concrete and brick mill remained in operation until the 1940s, when it reverted to warehouse use. In the 1970s, it became nothing more than a desolate but intriguing sculptural object. A home for transients and a graffiti magnet, the mill picked up nicknames such as the "see-through building" and the "Beirut building."

Developer Dana Crawford took a chance on the mill, however, and found public and private funding to turn it into the Flour Mill Lofts. After figuring out structural quirks and mucking out years of debris, the developer and architects created units that gravitate toward either the mill end or the silo end, wresting unusual spaces from an unlikely building. At the same time, the city developed a "yard" for the lofts, in the form of Cuernavaca Park. In 2000, the old industrial building gained a neighbor in the form of a complementary loft building.
National Register

19 Jack Kerouac Lofts
3100 Huron Street
JG Johnson Architects, 2005

The live/work spaces of the Kerouac Lofts pull from the area's industrial context, with brick and metal siding and prominent balconies that look as if they had been rusting for decades. As urban infill, the project is a quiet addition to a neighborhood that is still evolving.
AIA Colorado Merit Award, 2005; AIA Denver People's Choice Award, 2005

20 Ajax Lofts
2955 Inca Street
John Williams Architecture, with Shears + Leese Architects, 2003

This first phase of an expansive residential complex looks at home in this part of the Valley, where gritty heritage surpasses smooth Neomodernism. Upper floors are clad in shed-like metal, and the two-story base is brick, giving the impression of a factory conversion.

Highlands and Northwest

And, yes, there are several of them in this neighborhood, including the original Highland, at its birth a city competing with Denver. This area also includes Potter Highlands and Scottish Village / Highland Park.

All hark back to the 1870s, when developers sought to challenge dirty, boisterous Denver with the cleaner air and more temperate social mores in a new area (and grid) to the northwest. The area – and the sweeping views allowed by its higher elevation – was annexed by Denver in 1896.

Over the years, fine buildings have been erected throughout, which can be seen on a tour that mixes notable architecture, one of the few parks in west Denver, as well as tightly knit residential neighborhoods and commercial districts and a veritable flood of new development.

As with all of northwest Denver, the Highlands have been home to waves of merchants, laborers, immigrants, and artists, resulting in a rich stew of historic homes, sturdy commercial buildings, and distinguished schools. And, as is true of many neighborhoods close to downtown, the blocks throughout this area are seeing a renaissance in popularity and business activity, and renovations of structures into new uses.

This is a place where a mortuary has become a restaurant and had fun with its name – and neon sign – by turning the former Olinger Mortuary into Linger; the popular Root Down is fashioned out of structures including a former gas station.

This rebirth – marked by numerous Neomodern infill projects – has made Highlands and the section called LoHi (for lower Highlands) a hot neighborhood. Throughout, new restaurants and shops jostle for space with new homes, some of which appear to compete in geometric form, the use of unexpected materials and colors, and height (to wring every bit of space from remarkably narrow lots).

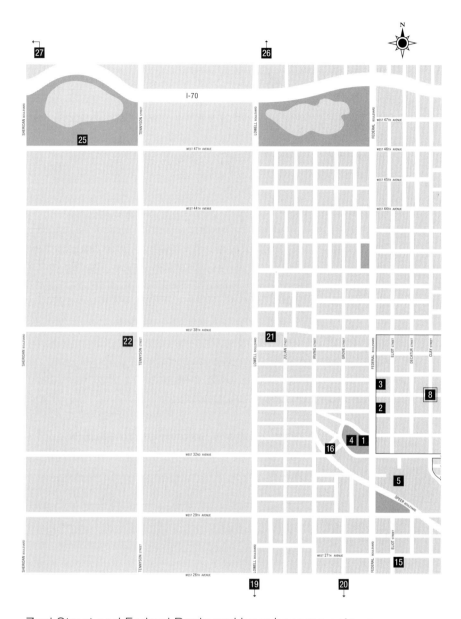

Zuni Street and Federal Boulevard have become gateway areas for development, as has LoHi, which also serves as a link to the Central Platte Valley and lower downtown. LoHi has its own landmark: the imposing Little Man Ice Cream vintage ice cream can, designed by architect Ted Schultz and built in 2008 by Western Steel and Boiler Co.

Multifamily projects along both Zuni Street and Federal Boulevard have brought new residents of many types to the neighborhood. Federal 27, affordable housing for homeless veterans, was designed by Humphries Poli Architects, and the Juan Diego Apartments, at 2449 W.

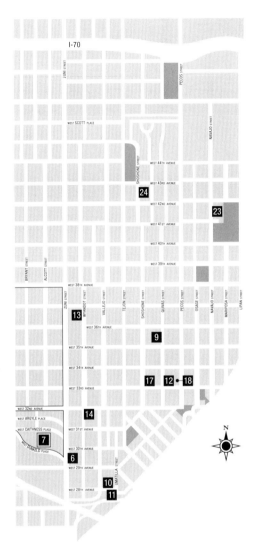

LIST OF BUILDINGS

1 Roger W. Woodbury Branch Library
2 Frank Milton House
3 Berkeley Masonic Lodge / Highlands
   Masonic Temple
4 Highland Park
5 North High School
6 Tallmadge & Boyer Block
7 Scottish Village / Scottish Highlands /
   Highland Village District
8 Potter Highlands
9 Bryant-Webster Elementary School
10 West 28th Avenue Historic District
   (Stoneman's Row)
11 2745 Umatilla Street
12 Shield House
13 Academia Ana Maria Sandoval
14 Our Merciful Savior Episcopal Church /
   Chapel of Our Merciful Savior
15 CEC Middle College
16 Anderson Mason Dale Architects
17 Green Cube
18 St. Patrick Oratory
19 Lake Middle School
20 Frederick W. Neef House
21 First Federal Savings and Loan Assn. /
   Commercial Federal Bank / Bank of
   the West
22 Elitch Theatre
23 Horace Mann Middle School
24 Smedley Elementary School
25 Smiley Branch Library
26 Regis University
27 Arvada Center for the Arts
   and Humanities

Dunkeld Place, was designed by Studio Completiva for those living with HIV and AIDS. At Zuni and 32nd, OZ Architecture designed the Zuni Townhomes, a low-scale assemblage of dwellings. Other developments along Zuni serve the neighborhood's scale, while adding contemporary flair in different levels of achievement.

The only way to really comprehend the depth of change in Highlands is to tour it and see the explosion of infill buildings that attempt to live in harmony with buildings constructed decades ago.

1 Roger W. Woodbury Branch Library
3265 Federal Boulevard
Jacques J.B. Benedict,1913; addition in 1966 by Oluf N. Nielsen, with later restoration work by David Owen Tryba Architects

On an overlook in a park setting in northwest Denver, the Woodbury branch combines sandy brick with chocolate brown trim and arched windows with a medallioned frieze. A gently hipped tile roof contrasts with the heavy decorative elements of Benedict's interpretation of a repository of learning as a Renaissance villa in Florence, a style the architect used in many residential projects. Ionic pilasters march along the entrance way, marked by gracious proportions and elaborate corner ornamentation.

Named after a businessman and member of the boards of the libraries replaced by the Denver system, Woodbury was one of several libraries in Denver constructed with Carnegie grant money.
Denver Landmark

2 Frank Milton House
3400 Federal Boulevard
Glen W. Huntington, 1916

Glen Huntington worked in the Prairie style for this home, an unusual tack to take in a part of town known more for elaborate Victorian detailing (and now, tall, narrow contemporary residences). The Milton House is a study in horizontality interpreted in stone facing, with deep, broad eaves and overhangs challenged by various vertical elements.

3 Berkeley Masonic Lodge / Highlands Masonic Temple
3550 Federal Boulevard
Merrill Hoyt, 1926

For a building rich in the symbolism of its host fraternal organization, Merrill Hoyt turned to a Neoclassical Revival style. The structure's almost unassuming tan brick and T-shaped plan are rendered monumental by an imposing entrance flanked by two massive Ionic columns. Terra-cotta trim and moldings are strong elements, as are iron grilles.

4 Highland Park

Though some historic districts in the area have turned into "Highlands," this park, first developed between 1907 and 1910, has stuck with the older, singular version of the name that referred to the earlier city there. This older version has made a reappearance throughout the area, since some residents fear that people might confuse Highlands with Highlands Ranch far to the south. (Not likely.)

Bounded by Federal Boulevard and a loop of residential streets, the park serves as an anchor to the western part of the neighborhood as it slopes down to

Federal Boulevard to the east. As with many early parks, an important structure – in this case Jacques J.B. Benedict's Roger Woodbury Branch Library – was set there, on high ground in a prominent site. The park also serves to mark the nearby entry of Speer Boulevard into the neighborhood, a vital link to downtown Denver.

5 North High School
2960 N. Speer Boulevard, at Federal Boulevard
David Dryden, 1908; addition of gymnasium, pool, and classrooms by
Charles Gordon Lee, 1959, with an auditorium, cafeteria, and classroom
addition by Haller & Larson, 1983, and 1993 classroom addition by
OZ Architecture; a new master plan addressing North's future was crafted
by Humphries Poli Architects and klipp to guide the school's rehab and restoration

Over the years, school architect David Dryden's Beaux Arts beauty – one of the city's four important "compass point" schools – has been subjected to several additions with varying degrees of success.

The recessed arches of Dryden's original entryway on Speer Boulevard are augmented by Ionic columns and a rooftop balustrade. Yet his detailing is difficult to appreciate now because the school's "front" has been relegated to almost back-wall status. Factors include the confluence of high-traffic roads and the setting of parking to the rear with a sort of "welcome" arch. There, the various additions clash in terms of style, as well as how successfully they interpreted and built on Dryden's intent.
Denver Landmark

6 Tallmadge & Boyer Block
2926–42 Zuni Street 1891

The fortunes of this commercial block have wavered over the years. But a massive rehabilitation in the early 1990s by Lantz-Boggio Architects netted more than attention. The project, sponsored by the Del Norte Neighborhood Development Corp., turned the structure into housing and breathed life back into the building's fine lines and elaborate Victorian detailing. It serves as a fine foil to the nearby Romeo Block on Zuni Street.
National Register, Denver Landmark

7 Scottish Village / Scottish Highlands / Highland Village District
Bounded by Zuni, Dunkeld, and Clay Streets and West 32nd Avenue

Laid out in 1874 by Dr. William Alexander Bell and General William Jackson Palmer, this "romantic" suburb managed to accomplish two feats: It alluded to the Scottish roots of early settlers – with street names such as Argyle Place and Fife Court – while accentuating Victorian style. Most of the homes are small, on "lanes" that follow the contour of the hillside. It is a rare instance in which a part of the city went completely off the grid – rather than invent a new one – as the original Highland had.
National Register District, Denver Landmark District

8 Potter Highlands

Potter Highlands is bounded by West 38th Avenue, Zuni Street, West 32nd Avenue and Federal Boulevard.

Temperance leaders and upstanding citizens, including Horatio Bearce and the Reverend Walter McDuffie Potter, laid out this serene neighborhood in 1871 as a centerpiece of Highlands. Bars and liquor stores were discouraged by the imposition of high licensing fees, and activities considered evidence of bad morals were forbidden.

National Register District, Denver Landmark District

9 Bryant-Webster Elementary School

3635 Quivas Street
Musick and Musick, 1930, with a classroom addition by
JH/P Architects (SethRosenman project architect), 1993

Named for the earlier Bryant and Webster Schools, the resulting Bryant-Webster School celebrated the brick. The architects created three-dimensional designs that recall American Indian beadwork and basketry, soar like plumes, and drip like jeweled pendants. The design also includes sunbursts and other vernacular elements incised into the building, reflecting influences from Navajo, Hopi, and Pima cultures. And bricks with an opalescent glaze make the building shimmer in the sun.

National Register, Denver Landmark

10 West 28th Avenue Historic District (Stoneman's Row)

2112, 2118, 2122, 2128, 2132, 2136, and 2140 W. 28th Avenue, and the
former 2753 Umatilla (now gone); built 1889–1893
Baerresen Brothers, 2122 W. 28th; J.H. Barnes, 2128 W. 28th

Three prominent stonemasons – or stonemen – built the eight intriguing homes that originally made up one of the city's smallest historic districts: William Toohey, Simon Rabjohns, and Robert Russell.

These men worked their magic in sandstone, limestone, and rhyolite facades, using brick in side and back walls. What is so apparent in these homes – some of which are single family, while others were duplexes from the beginning – is that the elaborate stonework on cornices, archways, brackets, and swags is of the type found in the city's grander mansions. The stonemen who did that work on a large scale for Denver's wealthy turned their talents to their own small Romanesque homes on Stoneman's Row.

Looking at the homes on Stoneman's Row is like reading a mason's primer. Of note: on 2122 W. 28th, one of the two credited to an architect, a bay window; on 2128 W. 28th, a cornice and bracket arrangement around a Palladian window. The home at what was 2753 Umatilla has been replaced by a contemporary home with a bright facade.

National Register District, Denver Landmark District

11 2745 Umatilla Street
Real Architecture, 2010

After several presentations before the Denver Landmark Preservation Commission, a new home was allowed to replace an old structure that formed the end piece to Stoneman's Row. And what a home: A green grid fronts this ultra-contemporary structure, with flashes on the side (viewable from Speer Boulevard) of numerous materials and geometric forms. Though this home appears skinny – as do many of the new residences throughout the Highlands – it is deeper than one might expect. Call this unusual design a study in contrast in terms of the venerable stone homes just around the corner.

12 Shield House
1735 W. 33rd Avenue
Studio H:T, 2009

This new tall, narrow home is distinguished from other new tall, narrow homes by a dramatic curved side wall of wood and metal. While appearing to "shield" the home from elements, this feature also houses interior circulation space inside the home and offers privacy from neighbors. The sweep of gleaming wood extends to the lower portion of the first level, grounding the home and adding continuity. The architects of Studio H:T have built a reputation on their design of striking contemporary homes in Denver and Boulder.

13 Academia Ana Maria Sandoval
3655 Wyandot Street
Anderson Mason Dale Architects, 2007

This dual-language Denver Public Schools magnet school works to pull the community into its style of teaching and learning within a Montessori framework. Its home is a polychromatic red brick building with two wing-type sections that meet in the middle in a glass-walled atrium that brings light – and lightness – to the structure. The addition of solar panels on the gabled spine, and pervious paving, has helped the Academia set a standard for its neighborhood.

14 Our Merciful Savior Episcopal Church / Chapel of Our Merciful Savior
2222 W. 32nd Avenue
James Murdoch, 1890

The mission congregation and community center housed in this gracious stone structure has operated under several names, including the one it took on almost a century after the Episcopal church was built. The church is marked by a soaring steeple, large stained glass rose window, woven red brick accents, and an imposing stone arch at its entry.
Denver Landmark

15 CEC Middle College
2650 Eliot Street
*Rogers, Nagel, Langhart (now RNL Design), 1976; addition and renovation
by Larson Incitti, 2006*

This campus covers more than one city block, with the original buff brick building marked by circular tower-like structures. The addition houses the Middle College's culinary arts school and cafe, an angular red brick building that has a distinct glass and metal entryway/atrium.

16 Anderson Mason Dale Architects
3198 N. Speer Boulevard
Renovated by Anderson Mason Dale, 2007

The architects purchased this former car dealership in 2007, then cleaned it up and reconfigured it to create space for support services, public spaces, and an open studio space. A cornice element was added at the front to conceal the curved roof line, with the addition of colorful infill panels that set off the dark brick. Inside, the space continues to read as a bowstring truss building with a bright and elegant wood ceiling. Windows were enlarged and a red metal frame installed to mark the entry. The building was constructed in the 1920s and 1930s.

17 Green Cube
3310 Shoshone Street
Architectural Workshop, 2011

The acid green grid that marks the facade of this home recalls the new home at the end of Stoneman's Row, which also sports a similar green grid. Though just as eye catching, the Green Cube is more compact and settled in the surrounding neighborhood. It has achieved LEED Platinum certification.

18 St. Patrick Oratory
3301 Pecos Street
Wagner and Manning, 1910

The first Roman Catholic parish west of the South Platte River (1881), St. Patricks constructed its current building in the Spanish Mission Revival style found in historic churches throughout the Southwest and California. Its red clay tile roofs, low, overhanging eaves, and twin towers shelter a group of buildings marked by arches, gables, and arcades. Some changes have been made over the century in terms of building elements, with the inclusion of a monastery, even as the church has served different waves of immigrants in the Highlands area. But this gathering of buildings has retained its original character, even as what began as a religious institution on the edge of Denver is now close to its core.
National Register, Denver Landmark

19 Lake Middle School
1820 Lowell Boulevard
Merrill and Burnham Hoyt, 1926

The Hoyts took advantage of a lofty site near Sloans Lake to build a sprawling Tudor castle with elaborate brickwork and detailing. Two copper cupolas mark the entrance, and regal ornamentation is evident throughout. The school has been expanded to add classrooms, a technology center, and support facilities.
Denver Landmark

20 Frederick W. Neef House
2143 Grove Street
Architect not known, 1886

The owner of the Neef Brothers Brewery chose a combination of Eastlake and Queen Anne architecture for his home. Stepped gables, elaborate bargeboard, a trellised half-moon entrance canopy, an oriel window topped by a dentilled gable: The Neef house is a swirl of decoration and rhythms entirely befitting the home of a merchant of the era.
National Register, Denver Landmark

21 First Federal Savings and Loan Assn. / Commercial Federal Bank / Bank of the West
3460 W. 38th Avenue
W. C. Muchow Associates, 1958, enlarged 1960

Bill Muchow worked to create a long and low complex building featuring an exposed steel frame, with an exterior in which black steel beams worked with beige brick and broad expanses of glass. The expansion was designed in a similar vein. Both portions of this project appear to float on a platform and retain their structural power even though the project is located in a busy commercial strip.
AIA Merit Award, 1964; American Institute of Steel Construction Award of Excellence, 1961

22 Elitch Theatre
Tennyson Street at West 38th Avenue
Charles Herbert Lee and Rudolph Liden, 1890; rehabilitation and renovation of theater exterior, OZ Architecture, 2007

One of the original buildings erected when John and Mary Elitch turned an apple orchard in northwest Denver into Elitch Gardens, the theater began as an open-sided affair with a tent-like roof.

Within two years, the theater was enclosed, although the verandahs were retained. The wood drop siding covers an octagonal building that is loved as much for its history as for its look. As an example of resort architecture, the theater is pure fantasy, appropriate to an amusement park and playground.

Those days are over, however. As of the mid-1990s, the amusement park moved and left the theater behind. The Gurtler family, Elitch's contemporary owners, decided to shift the enterprise to the then-growing Central Platte Valley, where a new, and nowhere near as charming, park was built. The theater has remained on the old site to become part of a housing project being developed according to New Urbanist tenets.

Formation of the Historic Elitch Theatre Foundation led to fund-raising that began in 2002. The first step was restoration of the Carousel Pavilion and creation of a grassy plaza linking the theater and the pavilion. Later, the exterior of the theater was in essence rebuilt, replacing rotten boards, and repainted dark green with white trim and topped with a soft gray roof. Urban wildlife was chased out of the interior, which last was a working theater in 1987, and work was begun to ready the historic structure for Act II.
National Register, Denver Landmark

23 Horace Mann Middle School
4130 Navajo Street
Temple H. Buell, 1931, with 1956 addition by Buell and 1993 classroom addition by Hoover, Berg, Desmond

Before Temple Buell turned to development, he designed some of the most exuberantly decorated buildings in Denver. His forte was brickwork that exploded in plumes and elaborate parapets, and Horace Mann is no exception. Here, Buell worked in blond and dark brick to create a school building marked by fanciful fillips and Art Deco lines.
Denver Landmark

24 Smedley Elementary School
4250 Shoshone Street
David W. Dryden, 1902, with 1911 north addition by Dryden, 1952; east addition by Earl C. Morris, and 1994 addition by Ramon F. Martinez

This little red brick schoolhouse may have started out little, but how it grew beyond its Neoclassical lines. The 1990s addition, connected by glass to the building's front, was commissioned after Denver Public Schools heard parents' pleas and kept Smedley open. The school is named for Dr. William Smedley, a pioneer school board member.
Denver Landmark

25 Smiley Branch Library
4501 W. 46th Avenue
Mountjoy, French, and Frewan, 1918, with 1994 renovation by David Owen Tryba Architects

Another of the eight Carnegie-funded branch libraries built in Denver, Smiley sits like a small English cottage at the side of Berkeley Park. The L-shaped bungalow-like structure is crafted of blond brick with a zigzag pattern. Accents

are stone. The renovation of Smiley, named for William H. Smiley, a Denver school superintendent, included reorientation of the reading wings toward large windows and restoration of fixtures.
Denver Landmark

26 Regis University
Regis Boulevard (W. 50th Avenue) at Lowell Boulevard
Alexander Cazin and Henry Dozier, 1888, with 1922 adjunct by
Harry J. Manning; later buildings by various architects

When the College of the Sacred Heart moved from New Mexico to Denver, the Jesuit educational institution began as most late 19th-century academic enterprises did: with the all-purpose, houses-everything Old Main.

That held true with this school, renamed Regis College in the 1920s, and now Regis University. But this Old Main had more color than most of the Richardsonian Romanesque structures lumbering across the country. Sacred Heart/Regis was built of red and buff sandstone, with a hall that was massive but not as heavy as other schools of the era. A tower tops its central bay, flanked by wings in which fourth-floor windows are styled in a mansard roofline. Other buildings have joined the campus, from Modern to Historicist, but Old Main still stands as an administration building and a symbol of the school's beginnings.

27 Arvada Center for the Arts and Humanities
6901 Wadsworth Boulevard, Arvada
Perkins & Will / Seracuse Lawler, 1976 with additions by Barker-Rinker-
Seacat + Partners in 1992, and by Fentress Bradburn Architects in 2006

In the 1970s, the city of Arvada stood out from the pack of municipalities ringing Denver by funding an arts center with space for galleries, classes, and performances. The original building was a suburban pacesetter, a Modernist structure with clearly delineated spaces. It included a bonus. An outdoor amphitheater was sited so that audiences had not only a view of performers but also a sweeping vista of lights to the east and south.

The 59,000-square-foot addition constructed 15 years later contributed color, curves, and a ration of light and openness to the center, though adding a Postmodern sensibility that somewhat diminished the building's formal tone.

Public art installed as part of the addition includes Vito Acconci's glass-covered dirt wall, which forms the spine of the new gallery/office space, and Clarice Dreyer's silvery metal trellis. The latter covers the really distracting part of the project: A new outdoor stage house in jarring shades of blue replaced the amphitheater, blocking the audience's view of the sky and the passersby's view of the center.

The center marked its 30th anniversary with the opening of a new 200-seat black box theater, expanded storage, a larger history museum space, and an additional banquet room. The expansion was a scaled-down version of the center's original wish list/master plan, a major remake (and addition of 100,000 square feet) that would have cost $69 million. That plan, too, was created by Fentress Bradburn Architects.

Five Points & Curtis Park

As the earliest settlement in Denver's lower downtown began to shift from residential to commercial development, the city's growing population spread to the north and east.

Thus began a wave of construction, between the early 1870s and early 1890s, of homes both extravagant and humble – brick and frame residences that attracted members of the city's merchant class. The prevailing design of the day was Victorian, with a predominance of Queen Anne and Italianate structures popping up in what would become, a century later, a neighborhood of historic districts. That includes the evolving Curtis Park Historic District, which has continued to grow to protect some 500 homes.

If the Curtis Park area attracted the white population, neighboring blocks that became known as Five Points served as home to the city's African American residents. Over the decades, Denver's laws concerning where people could live and where mortgages were available began to allow all people to purchase property more freely. But the early years of the city's residential development were segregated, producing separate communities that nevertheless matched each other on the health and activity of commerce and design.

Now, the clusters of historic homes and commercial buildings stand out as survivors from an age defined by recognized and popular architectural styles and standards. Many of the structures in this district have withstood the region's traditionally roller-coaster economy to carry a history lesson for all, while witnessing the inclusion of contemporary, but complementary, infill residential properties.

LIST OF BUILDINGS

1   Enterprise Hill / Centennial Hill /
      Clements Historic District
1.1 Clements Rowhouse
1.2 St. Andrew's Memorial Chapel
2   Ebert Elementary School
3   East Village / Benedict Park Place
4   Glenarm Place Historic District
5   Blair-Caldwell African-American Research Library
6   Baxter Hotel / Rossonian
7   Curtis Park Historic District
7.1 Kinneavy Terrace
7.2 Mathews-Gotthelf House
7.3 Walters House
7.4 David Crowell House
7.5 Scobey / William A. West House
7.6 Merchants Row Brownstones
8   San Rafael District
9   New Terrace
10 Lafayette Street Historic District
10.1 Foster LeNeve Cathcart House

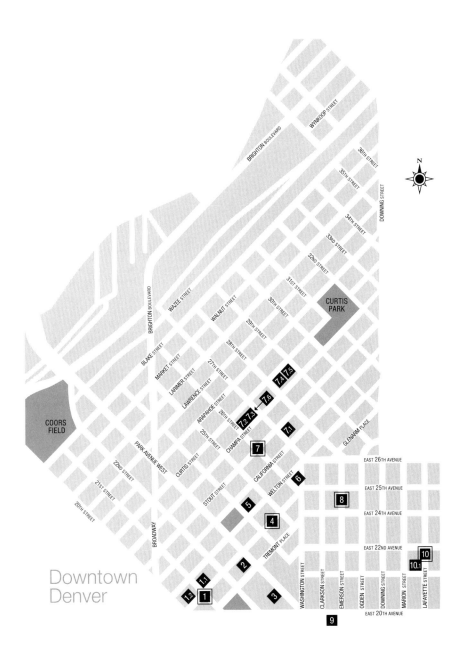

Downtown
Denver

1 Enterprise Hill / Centennial Hill / Clements Historic District

One of the many tiny historic enclaves in this area, Clements is bounded by 21st and 22nd Streets, Glenarm Place, and Tremont Place. Among Denver's oldest residential areas, it is part of Alfred Clements's Denver addition. Most of the homes were built between 1871 and 1890 for prominent residents of the day. *National Register, Denver Landmark District*

Buildings that stand out include:

1.1 – Clements Rowhouse, 2201–17 Glenarm Place, Architect not known, 1884: Elegant High Victorian styling with Italianate flair is key to this row of townhomes, which sports a lofty cornice that stretches toward being a mansard roof. Two-story bays and tall, slim windows with prominent caps extend the homes' vertical sensibilities.

1.2 – St. Andrew's Memorial Chapel, 2015 Glenarm Place, Ralph Adams Cram, 1909: In what may be his only work here, East Coast architect Ralph Adams Cram worked in late Gothic Revival for this small church. Commissioned as a memorial by a grieving widower, St. Andrews displays a sober appearance, with dark red brick trimmed with limestone. The interior is more elaborate, though no less formal. Design of the adjacent parish house is attributed to Jacques J.B. Benedict.

2 Ebert Elementary School
410 23rd Street
Montjoy and Frewan, 1924; classroom, library, and lunchroom addition, Murata Outland, 1993

At one time called Crofton-Ebert, this buff brick school is in line with Montjoy and Frewan's other Beaux Arts–influenced buildings, such as Park Hill Elementary School. Ebert's innate symmetry is set off by Neoclassical detailing at the roofline. A later addition strives for simplicity.

3 East Village / Benedict Park Place
Various locations along Park Avenue West Various architects, including Humphries Poli Architects, Studio Completiva, Chris Carvell Architects, and B+Y Architects, 2005–continuing

The former East Village housing development, constructed to house the press during the never-happened 1976 Olympic Games in Colorado, over the years sank into a state of disrepair and malaise. Built so the city grid was interrupted, East Village eventually became a project under the wing of the Denver Housing Authority using Hope VI federal funding. The street grid was reintroduced, and buildings were located so that they front right on the street. The architects chosen for these projects to a large extent chose a contemporary approach to the variety of housing types found in this mix of affordable and market rate residences. Some projects are more successful than others (the blue dots on 290 Park Avenue West are a real stretch), but this up-grade in housing quality has made a difference in a neighborhood with urban appeal.

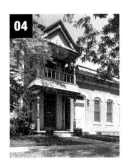

4 Glenarm Place Historic District
2417–62 Glenarm Place

Like the much larger Curtis Park Historic District, Glenarm Place explores a range of styles, though most of the homes on this block were built between 1880 and 1893. That means a concentration of Italianate, Second Empire, Queen Anne, Carpenter Gothic, and Victorian Eclectic. The Glenarm District includes homes built by prosperous merchants as well as Denver's hardworking middle class.
National Register

5 Blair-Caldwell African-American Research Library
2401 Welton Street
OZ Architects, with Harold Massop Associates and Wenk Associates, 2003

This gently Neoclassical design reflects an intent to tie into both the neighborhood context and the continuing hopes for development of an area designated the Welton Street Commercial Corridor Cultural District. Named for Omar Blair, the first African American elected president of the Denver School Board, and Elvin Caldwell, the first black to be elected to the Denver City Council, this spacious library serves as a gateway to the area and, with a $16 million price tag, a significant investment.

The brick structure is a symmetrical facade built around a tall archway and semicircular windows. On either side are large, rectangular niches that hold bronze and mosaic panels by Thomas Jay Warren, public art commissioned by the city's Percent for Art Program. A similar Classical arch appears on the building's side facing downtown (with a strong view available at the top of the staircase). The building's base is precast – a nod to the future, say the architects – and the generous windows are set in heavy metal frames. The interior includes the usual library resources, as well as exhibition space and areas that spotlight historic events. Finishes include Venetian plaster walls and granite floors – durable materials that reflect respect for the community.

6 Baxter Hotel / The Rossonian
2650 Welton Street
George Bettcher, 1911

Located at the intersection that defines Five Points – Welton Street, 27th Street, and Washington Street – this blond brick building comes to a point and claims its site like a proud ship pulling into harbor. Built as the Baxter Hotel, the structure became the site of the Rossonian, a noted jazz club, restaurant, and community gathering place. The Rossonian continues to await implementation of a new redevelopment plan, a new life for a stately Neoclassical commercial building that once was a social and economic hub in this traditionally black neighborhood. The Welton Street corridor continues to seek ways to revitalize properties and attract viable businesses.
National Register

7   Curtis Park Historic District

Much of the area within this district's boundaries was developed by 1887, less than 30 years after the city itself began. After the 2011 landmark designation of the eighth section of the neighborhood, the protected area is bounded by the alley between Lawrence and Larimer Streets, Park Avenue West, the alley between California and Welton Streets, and Downing Street. The process of assembling this district was a long campaign by homeowners, who have toiled to renovate historic structures while welcoming select infill development. In the process of connecting hundreds of homes in this district, residents have faced and overcome conflicting zoning issues, civic disinterest, and the push-pull of economic booms and busts.

The architectural styles in the district mirror those found in earlier downtown residential development. The businessmen, teachers, politicians and professional types who moved to this inner-ring neighborhood preferred the many variations of Victorian architecture: Italianate, Gothic and Carpenter Gothic, Queen Anne, and elaborate Eclectic offshoots.

The homes here are among the city's most historic, though some continue to show the ravages of time and economic neglect. By the time Capitol Hill emerged as the city's society oasis, Curtis and Champa Streets (and environs) were facing challenges, including homes being split into boarding houses and even early demolition. Now, Curtis Park is a lure for contemporary infill, much of it distinguished.
National Register, Denver Landmark Districts

Many fine examples of the district's heyday remain, including:

7.1 – Kinneavy Terrace, 2700–2714 Stout Street, John J. Huddart, 1888:
The five bays that front this row of apartments alternate in shape and window treatment, with some arched and others rectangular. Decorative brickwork and woodwork abound. Each of the units was lighted by a courtyard, with a turret at one end of the complex and the middle section of bays topped by a mansard-type roof. High Victorian meets Queen Anne in a stately stone building that looks as elegant today as it did during more than a century ago.

7.2 – Mathews-Gotthelf House, 2601 Champa Street, 1880; rehabilitation
SLATERPAULL Architects: Through efforts by Colorado Preservation Inc., which bought the house in 2007, other preservation groups, and private interests, this high-style Victorian mansion is being returned to its one-time glory. Built by ore and bullion broker James F. Mathews and bought a decade later by banker and rancher Isaac Gotthelf, this imposing structure eventually was chopped up into tiny living spaces, with the addition of an unsympathetic 1920 annex. Surprisingly, many of the interior details and finishes remained intact. Exterior work has entailed restoring the old slate roof, repairing wooden cornices, and replacing the original porch, which had been replaced by an awkward concrete deck and stoop.

7.3 – Walters House, 2663 Champa Street, Frederick Eberley, circa 1888:
Queen Anne style predominates in a two-story brick home with a center front gable covered in shingles and marked by elaborate window treatment. Dentils, fancy brick courses, and Eastlake-style ornamentation on the porch are among details on this home.

7.4 – David Crowell House, 2816 Curtis Street, architect not known, circa 1873:
Size does not equate lack of attention to detail. In a neighborhood defined by wide variations in house size, the frame Crowell House is pure-and-simple small, but made grand by a Federal-style window on the main facade.

7.5 – Scobey / William A. West House, 2826 Curtis Street, circa 1884:
This compact brick home appears to separate into two parts: the smaller one-story section, next to a two-story bay, in which the second floor is an impressive mansard roof containing a single arched window. It reflects ingenious Victorian brought down to earth.

And there is the new:

7.6 – Merchants Row Brownstones, 2665 Champa Street, in situ DESIGN, 2006:
This groundbreaking six-unit, three-story project has set the standard for the Neomodern infill residential projects that now dot the Curtis Park Historic District. Merchants Row grew out of an earlier project that had spurred investment from district residents. When in situ DESIGN's principals undertook Merchants Row, the same funding model – and sense of community ownership – came into play. Merchants Row stands out for its generous bay windows (in a contemporary interpretation), its accent on verticality (in sync with the massing of historic neighbors), and its use of honest materials, all linked by good proportions and attention to detail.
AIA Colorado Honor Award, 2008, AIA Denver Merit Award, 2006

 San Rafael District
Bounded by Washington and Downing Streets, and East 26th and East 20th Avenues, San Rafael is the fourth historic district to fit under the Five Points / Curtis Park umbrella.

Development here began as six additions to the city were platted in the early 1870s. The area is another prototypical Victorian residential neighborhood, though a few commercial buildings were part of the development. A heavy concentration of hospitals and medical facilities has marked San Rafael and part of neighboring City Park West – a long-standing fact of life that has led to demolition of some old structures and the Modernist gem, the Boettcher School. The district supposedly takes its name from San Rafael, California, the hometown of developer Henry A. Dubois Jr. Along with fine Queen Anne and other Eclectic styles of the period, the district saw the rise of churches that served the city's African American community.
National Register

9 New Terrace
900–14 E. 20th Avenue (and 1954–1958 Emerson Street)
Architect not known, 1889

This heavily decorated two-story Queen Anne–style residential project is a significant structure in the neighborhood. As with Kinneavy Terrace and other late 19th-century multifamily housing, New Terrace managed to mix the high style and elegance of the era with a more affordable type of residence. In its L-shaped format, this series of row houses serves as a terminus as Emerson Street jogs a block over at East 20th Avenue. It is notable for elaborate millwork.
National Register of Historic Places

10 Lafayette Street Historic District

The homes in the 2100 block of Lafayette Street were designed by several of the founding members of the Colorado American Institute of Architects, including William Lang, Henry Dozier, the Baerresen Brothers, and James Murdock. The final historic district in the neighborhood again reflects the Victorian design trend of detailing applied to prevailing design guidelines of the era.
National Register, Denver Landmark District

The district includes:

10.1 – Foster LeNeve Cathcart House, 2105 Lafayette Street, William Lang, 1890: This Queen Anne–style residence is marked by shingle-style detailing and ornate carving and moldings. One of the developers of the area, Thomas Cathcart, lived at several locations, including this home that reflects architect William Lang's talent.
National Register of Historic Places

Capitol Hill

Henry C. Brown's "Brown's Bluff" – home to the Colorado State Capitol and perched above downtown – proved an early magnet for the wealthy and powerful of Denver. Grand homes were built on Capitol Hill, which more than a century later retains much of the gracious attitude of the time.

Yet the city's economic shudders are woven through the neighborhood. In some parts of Capitol Hill, apartment buildings were constructed early on. This trend of multifamily buildings pushed some of the city's social arbiters to claim a southern section as "Quality Hill," where only mansions would be constructed.

In styles ranging from Victorian to Queen Anne, Georgian to Neoclassical, construction proceeded apace in Capitol Hill until the Silver Crash of 1893. Then many residents turned their attention to more simple designs, usually the Foursquare style that locally has become known as the Denver Square.

Still, the grand homes were built, and, by the 1920s, many of them were demolished or cut up into apartment buildings or rooming houses. Later, hard-to-maintain mansions became offices, and developers looked to high-rise technology for new residential properties. The density of the neighborhood has resulted in few infill projects.

Over the years, Capitol Hill has become home to the governor, social lions, elegant churches, and, for a period, hippie communes. Divided by East Colfax Avenue, Capitol Hill, and North Capitol Hill have struggled with economic fluctuations, absentee landlords, and general disinterest as Denver's population fled to the suburbs. Now, old facilities have been converted to events centers, while a rush by some to live closer to downtown has exerted new development pressures to turn apartments into condominiums, driving out longtime residents in the process. Still, the old buildings survive, many of them carefully tended and conserved. Historic districts include Swallow Hill, in North Capitol Hill, and Quality Hill and Sherman-Grant in blocks south of Colfax.

For those who appreciate the ability to see a wide spectrum of design, however, the district is a veritable architectural candy store, where High Gothic and Modernism, Victorian, and Neoclassicism share treelined streets in abundance.

LIST OF BUILDINGS

1	Trinity United Methodist Church	21	Dunning-Benedict Mansion
2	St. Mark's Parish Church	22	Croke-Patterson-Campbell Mansion
3	Rocky Mountain Masonic Consistory	23	Sayre's Alhambra
4	Central Presbyterian Church	24	Cheesman-Boettcher Mansion /
5	George Schleier Mansion		Colorado Governor's Residence
6	Old Capitol Life Insurance Building	25	Penn VII
7	Silver State Savings and Loan	26	Grant-Humphreys Mansion
8	Dennis Sheedy Mansion	27	Malo Mansion
9	Poets Row Apartments	28	Wood-Morris-Bonfils House /
10	Crawford Hill Mansion		Encore Apartments
11	DPS Administration Building	29	Adolph Zang Mansion
12	Capitol Heights Apartments	30	St. John's Episcopal Cathedral
13	Logan Street Trio	31	Morey Middle School
13.1	John L. McNeil House	32	William Lang Homes
13.2	Fred A. Thompson / John Allen House	32.1	1532 Emerson Street House
13.3	Campbell / McKinley Mansion	32.2	1624 and 1626 Washington Street House
14	Plested / Baker House	32.3	1648 Washington Street House
15	First Church of Christ Scientist	33	Perrenoud Apartments
16	Cathedral of the Immaculate Conception	34	Edbrooke House
17	William G. Fisher House /	35	Cornwall Apartments
	International House / Tryba Architects	36	Emerson School
18	Temple Emanuel / Temple Events Center	37	Dora Moore School
19	Vance Kirkland Studio / Kirkland	38	Bailey Mansion
	Museum of Fine and Decorative Arts	39	Grafton Apartments /
20	Molly Brown House		The Aldine Family Hotel

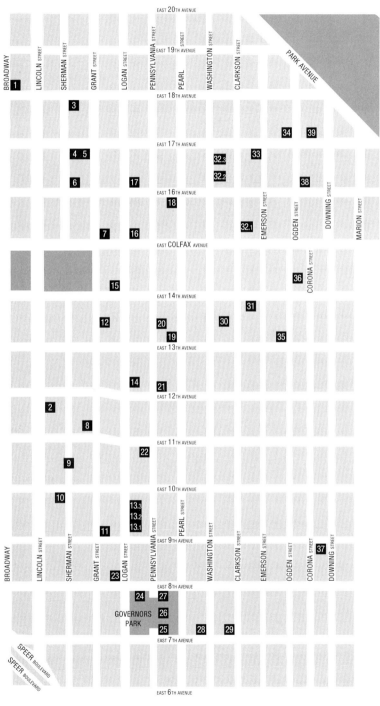

 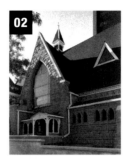 

1   **Trinity United Methodist Church**
1820 Broadway
Robert Roeschlaub, 1888

Colorado's first registered architect selected native mottled gray rhyolite for this High Victorian Gothic church, which is marked by a Tiffany stained glass rose window and a spire that soars more than 180 feet. Constructed under Pastor Henry A. Buchtel, later chancellor of the University of Denver and governor of Colorado, Trinity has been at the center of the downtown action for years: It is a worthy view terminus at the bend of Tremont Street as well as an institution that spurred change in the early 1980s by selling its development rights to a Toronto developer. The resulting building constructed (one of two planned) includes a glass wall designed to showcase the reflection of this church. (Two buildings had been planned, but the other was not realized, meaning the Cosmopolitan Hotel was demolished to no good end.) Solid but not stolid, Trinity includes an interior rich in woodwork. It was renovated in the 1980s by SLP Architects.
National Register, Denver Landmark

2   **St. Mark's Parish Church**
1160 Lincoln Street
Lang and Pugh, 1890

In the 1950s, the crenelated bell tower of this stone church was removed, but that did not really diminish the power inherent in a building that can be considered small compared to some of its more elaborate Capitol Hill peers. The architects worked in a Victorian Gothic style on the compact structure, whose interior is noted for its ceiling beams and slender stained glass windows. In 1990, the church was vacated by a dwindling congregation, and a few years later emerged as a nightclub fittingly called The Church.
National Register, Denver Landmark

3   **Rocky Mountain Masonic Consistory / 1770 Sherman Street Events Center**
1770 Sherman Street
Baerreson Brothers, 1907

For years, the former El Jebel Shrine Temple was a mystery, open only to the fraternal organization that built it. First available for public view in 1996 when the Masons sold it to a local theater company, the consistory can best be described as a Moorish confection. The architects drew on all the symbolism – real and imagined – of the Middle East when they designed the place for the Ancient Arabic Order Nobles of the Mystic Shrine, from a minaret-like tower outside to calligraphic decorative motifs inside. But the Baerresen Brothers of Denver cloaked the place in the solid red brick that held together Denver's urban fabric of the era.

After the theater company moved out, the consistory became an events center. Its interior remains rich in woodwork and includes a fanciful ballroom where the ceiling looks like a Persian carpet and the walls are painted in Arabic characters – including the sly inclusion of the architects' names.

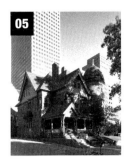

4 **Central Presbyterian Church**
1680 Sherman Street
Frank E. Edbrooke, with Willis Marean, 1892

The rich red sandstone of Central Pres may have weathered over the years, but the Romanesque Revival design with Eclectic touches at the windows has worn well. Built in a simple cruciform plan with crossing gables and four towers, this structure gave an old congregation a new home (the story goes that they had been meeting in an old theater downtown). An education building was added in the 1950s.
National Register, Denver Landmark

5 **George Schleier Mansion**
1665 Grant Street
Frank E. Edbrooke, circa 1880

An intricate roofline marks Frank Edbrooke's Queen Anne–style design for what was for years a private residence. A welter of gables seems to find simple resolution in an onion dome topping a corner turret. Later a social services center and an office building, the Schleier Mansion claims its site with graciousness as well as weight.
National Register

6 **Old Capitol Life Insurance Building**
1600 Sherman Street
Harry James Manning, 1924

In marble and granite trimmed in terra-cotta, Harry James Manning honed the fine art of detailing for a roaring '20s office building in the Classical Revival style. (He was one of more than a dozen architects to compete for the project.) A lacy filigree appears to top the cornice, while floral carvings surround the front door. In the early 1960s, Edwin A. Francis designed a tower addition, and the interior of the original building was restored in the early 1990s. The building now houses the Colorado Trust.
National Register

7 **Silver State Savings and Loan**
1500 Grant Street
William C. Muchow Associates, 1964

The prolific Bill Muchow offered a mature International Style statement for Silver State, employing precast panels, exposed concrete, and ribbon windows to claim a horizontal presence on a busy corner. In the 1990s, this distinctive building was gently restored to become the Colorado Education Association headquarters.

8   Dennis Sheedy Mansion
1115 Grant Street
E.T. Carr and William Feth, 1892

Grant Street once was home to dozens of mansions, a millionaire's row lost in the 20th century to boarding houses and demolition. Through it all, the Queen Anne–style Sheedy Mansion has survived as an office building. The home's broad curving porch at the front features a tower above and a gallery leading to another gable-topped portion of the home. Elaborate woodwork survives. Though perhaps not the grandest of the city's spectacular old homes, the Sheedy Mansion offers a lesson in how stone and brick can work together to produce a harmonious whole. The building was remodeled by Daniel J. Havekost.
National Register, Denver Landmark

9   Poets Row Apartments
1000 block of Sherman Street
Most attributed to Charles D. Strong, 1931 through 1938

A literary lair with Deco and, later, Moderne touches, the buildings lining one block of Sherman Street stand out for their clever appellations as much as their cohesive design. The earliest two – the Robert Frost and Louisa May Alcott, dating from 1931 – both had different names before construction continued on the nearby Robert Browning, Thomas Carlyle, Mark Twain, and others honoring men and women of letters. Metal and glass entries feature ceramic brick surrounds, horizontal banding, and terra-cotta decorative elements.
Poets Row anchors the small Sherman Grant Historic District

10   Crawford Hill Mansion
150 E. 10th Avenue
Theodore Boal and Frederick Harnois, 1906

The "Sacred 36" of long-ago social arbiter Mrs. Crawford Hill seems like an idea out of another universe these days, but the elegant mansion still stands as a reminder. Just barely: Boal and Harnois's French Renaissance Revival design – with ample porches, elaborate quoining and detailing, and ornate iron doors – was almost demolished in the late 1980s. The owners, the now-defunct Town Club, wanted to sell the property and other parcels of land to pay off their debt. A struggle ensued over saving and landmarking the property, which claims a noble spot on the Hill as offices. Renovation by Peter Dominick.
National Register, Denver Landmark

11   DPS Administration Building
900 Grant Street
William C. Muchow, 1970

Originally constructed for business purposes, Muchow's elegant Modernist structure was purchased by the Denver Public Schools in 1974. Though on a prominent site on a busy street, the administration building appears at home here, with an

almost oblique entrance and a stark, simple presence. The rectangular volume of the upper floors seems dropped into a first floor in which columns and walls are turned at an angle, creating motion at the street level and concept of corner offices floating free over the sidewalk. DPS's desire to move its administrative offices to another location presents an unknown future for this building.

12 Capitol Heights Apartments
1350 Grant Street
Studio Completiva, 2001

One of the rare infill projects in Capitol Hill turned a forlorn empty lot into a forward-thinking Modernist apartment block – after much neighborhood discussion. Bright colors and clean lines mark this eight-story sort-of-Neomodern project, which stands out from its historic context yet somehow seems right at home.

13 Logan Street Trio

Developer Fred A. Thompson built four spec houses in the 900 block of Logan Street, of which three were designed by Lester Varian and Frederick Sterner, or Sterner alone. They are Denver Landmarks.

13.1 – John L. McNeil House, 930 Logan Street, Varian & Sterner, 1890: Banker McNeil bought this home in 1891, a building marked by elegant windows and a restrained semicircular entry portico. Victorian influences remain, though the overall effect hints at a shift toward more eclectic design for the upper-crust, including touches of Georgian Revival.

13.2 – Fred A. Thompson / John Allen House, 940 Logan Street, Varian & Sterner, 1890: An imposing two-story Neoclassical Revival porch gives this home the look of a Greek temple perched in the middle of Capitol Hill. Corinthian columns front the home, with details including a fanlight at the entry.

13.3 – Campbell / McKinley Mansion, 950 Logan Street, Frederick Sterner, various dates given (1891–1896): Some sources claim this is the last of four speculative homes built by Thompson and designed by the same architects (the fourth, at 900 Logan Street, has been attributed to Grable and Weber). Lafayette Campbell purchased the Georgian Revival home, which features an assertive semicircular portico at the front entry and elaborate keystoned windows on the second floor.

14 Plested / Baker House
1208 Logan Street
Architect not known, 1886

This Victorian structure is credited with being the last frame house on Capitol Hill, though some preservationists point out that the bay window is not original to the structure. A simply decorated gable finds counterpoint in more elaborate second-story shingles and brackets.
Denver Landmark

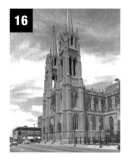

15 First Church of Christ Scientist
1401 Logan Street
Varian & Sterner, 1906

These busy architects again turned to Neoclassical Revival style for this beautiful church, constructed of white lava stone from Salida. A skylighted dome-shaped roof and portico complete the elegant picture of a religious institution nestled into a residential neighborhood.

16 Cathedral of the Immaculate Conception
1570 Logan Street
Leon Coquard; completed by Aaron Gove and Thomas Walsh, 1902–12

As befitting a structure that in the late 1900s would become a minor basilica, Leon Coquard and the architects that finished this protracted project aimed to make an impression.

They accomplished their goal in a Gothic Revival style with French influences, including buttresses and 200-foot-tall twin spires adorned with rows of bud-like crockets. Dressed Indiana limestone sheathes the exterior, while the sanctuary, altar, and side altars are made of Carrara marble. Three dozen stained glass windows by the Royal Bavarian Institute of Munich light up the inside (especially since a protective coating was cleaned in the early 1990s anticipating a 1993 visit here by Pope John Paul II).

A renovation in the 1970s by Seracuse Lawler Architects was followed by a general cleanup in 1993; a 1997 lightning strike that damaged one of the spires was repaired within months. In 2008, a multiphased interior project included the design of a new altar, modifications that restored some elements changed in the 1970s, and the introduction of new furniture.
National Register, Denver Landmark

17 William G. Fisher House / International House / Tryba Architects
1600 Logan Street
Frank E. Edbrooke and Willis Marean, 1896

A dressed lava stone facade added elegance to a home that mixed solid stylistic elements – a lofty portico, Greek columns and wraparound trim – with more practical Classical Revival style befitting post–Silver Crash Denver. The owner was the Fisher of Daniels & Fisher Department Store. In 1998, architect David Tryba added office space to the mansion and renovated the complex into a combination of spacious studio for his firm and home for his family.
National Register, AIA Denver Merit Award, 2001

18 Temple Emanuel / Temple Events Center
1595 Pearl Street
John J. Humphreys, 1899, with a major addition in 1924

This Moorish-flavored building served the Temple Emanuel congregation until the 1950s, when the temple moved to the Hilltop neighborhood. After that, John J. Humphreys's building housed several churches before being turned into an events center in the 1980s. An addition in the 1920s virtually doubled its size, adding another vault and a third tower that is in the same spirit as the original two but does not mimic them. A second front door also is more simple than the first, which features an arch and columns. About 1,500 people can be seated in the spacious vaulted interior, which features stained glass windows and intricate ceiling tracery.
National Register, Denver Landmark

19 Vance Kirkland Studio / Kirkland Museum of Fine and Decorative Arts
1311 Pearl Street
Maurice Biscoe and Henry Hewitt, 1911; addition by Melick Associates Inc., 2000

Painter Vance Kirkland's influence has moved far beyond the University of Denver, where he taught, and this region; the Ohio-born artist has found recognition around the country. After Kirkland's death in 1981, longtime friend Hugh Grant established a foundation and museum to promote the artist's legacy in an Arts and Crafts–style home in which Kirkland had worked. (He lived in a Denver Square at 817 Pearl Street.)

Grant purchased the building next door – a defunct and deteriorating former fried chicken store – and commissioned a building that is striking in its attempt to emulate the Biscoe and Hewitt structure. Both share the same color brick (a huge undertaking by Grant) and are united by similar rounded pediments. The new building features tile insets, raised brickwork, and an enclosed courtyard, a draw for visitors to this unusual museum, which showcases Kirkland's work as well as Modernist furniture, extensive ceramic pieces, and works by Colorado artists.

20 Molly Brown House
1340 Pennsylvania Street
William A. Lang, 1889–1890

The somewhat flamboyant Margaret (Molly) Brown and her miner husband bought the house in 1894, and though she is long gone, her spirit has helped make the home as much a survivor as she was. The house faced demolition in the 1960s (the fate that befell its neighbor to the north, the Monti House) but was rescued when Historic Denver, Inc. purchased Brown's home in the 1970s and turned it into a successful museum. Visitors to the House of Lions (for the stone beasts flanking the door) see a mix of Queen Anne elegance with Romanesque strength in terms of Victorian detailing mixed with more solid elements.
National Register, Denver Landmark

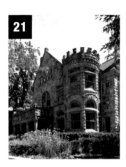  

21 Dunning-Benedict Mansion
1200 Pennsylvania Street
William A Lang, 1889

Businessman Walter Dunning built this Richardsonian Romanesque home, which later was purchased by state supreme court justice Mitchell Benedict. In this building, Lang and his crew demonstrated the architect's gift for working magic in stone. Both circular and angled towers accent this imposing rusticated gray stone structure, which features a variety of window styles.
National Register, Denver Landmark

22 Croke-Patterson-Campbell Mansion
428–430 E. 11th Avenue
Isaac Hodgson, 1890

Architect Isaac Hodgson interpreted a French chateau in red sandstone for merchant and teacher Thomas Croke, who later sold the house to politician and publisher Thomas Patterson. In turn, Patterson's daughter married Richard Crawford Campbell a few years later. The home reflects this social lineage: It oozes wealth, with walls decorated with elaborate friezes and stone coursings. The high, hipped slate roof is punctuated by a tower on the main house as well as two more on the adjoining carriage house – plus a variety of prominent parapets in alternating shapes. The three-story mansion appears to ramble, with an irregular floor plan and lush detailing. It is a good example of the movement to establish a Quality Hill part of Capitol Hill, where mansions and elegance would be the rule, as opposed to the mix of single-family homes and multifamily residences elsewhere in the district. It is now operated as a hotel.
National Re, Denver Landmark

23 Sayre's Alhambra
801 Logan Street
Architect not known, 1892

For all its flair, the home of miner, engineer, and Indian fighter (as in Sand Creek Massacre) Hall Sayre at heart has a simple bone structure. A trip to Spain supposedly inspired Sayre and his wife to import an exotic vision of Spanish and Moorish architecture. Arches, an arcaded front porch, exaggerated brackets, and protruding windows combine to add flair to a basic box. If the Rocky Mountain Masonic Consistory has a residential cousin in Denver, the Alhambra is it.

24 Cheesman-Boettcher Mansion / Colorado Governor's Residence
400 E. 8th Avenue
Marean & Norton, 1908

Though early business tycoon Walter Cheesman commissioned a different firm to design his grand home, he died before the designs were complete; his widow turned to another firm for the commission (the same firm that designed the Pavilion a year later in what became Cheesman Park). Cheesman's daughter and her husband, son of Governor John Evans, lived there until the 1920s, when the home was purchased by Claude Boettcher. In the 1950s, the Boettcher Foundation offered the home to the state as a governor's residence.

Since then, several repair and restoration projects have been proposed in conjunction with the house, beginning with a 1964 committee headed by architect James Sudler to study its preservation. In the early 1980s, an analysis was done of needed repairs, and in 1999, about half a million dollars was spent on updating the private portions of the house. As befits such a massive part public–part private structure, work continues.

The exterior is wood and brick, the interior elaborate (at least on the ground floor), with an all-white Palm Room conservatory and furnishings of the period in European styles. Though the home faces East Eighth Avenue, the four facades all carry weight, sharing design elements such as dentiled eaves, Ionic columns and pilasters, and gabled dormers.
National Register, Denver Landmark

25 Penn VII
700 Pennsylvania Street
Donald R. Roark, 1963

Donald Roark constructed this apartment building on a piece of the Humphreys estate nearby. Balconies in perforated, colored brick stand out on what was one of the first high-rises built in Capitol Hill, and still one of the most distinctive.
AIA Western Mountain Region Honor Award, 1963

26 Grant-Humphreys Mansion
770 Pennsylvania Street
Theodore Boal, 1900–1902

Built by Governor James B. Grant and purchased by iron and oil baron Albert E. Humphreys in 1917, this blond brick home was left to the state of Colorado in the 1970s. The grounds serve as a Denver park, while the state uses the home as an events center. A Colonial Revival design with heavy Georgian influences, Grant-Humphreys features a columned portico, a banistered roof garden, and a pergola to one side. Terra-cotta was used extensively in window surrounds, columns, and balustrades. The facility was renovated in the 1980s by Olson-Pellechia Architects.
National Register, Denver Landmark

27 Malo Mansion
500 E. 8th Avenue
Jacques J.B. Benedict and Harry J. Manning, 1921

This home, built for flour magnate Oscar L. Malo and his wife, Edith, illustrated a growing interest in Spanish Colonial Revival architecture. Designed with a horizontal plan, the Malo Mansion features stucco walls, a tile roof, and a triple arched entry arcade. Cast concrete is found in some detailing, with tile insets and wrought-iron balconettes on the second floor. Highly decorated window and door surrounds do not clutter up its basic elegance.
Denver Landmark

28 Wood-Morris-Bonfils House / Encore Apartments
707 Washington Street
Biscoe & Hewitt, 1909–11

Where the Malo Mansion stresses Spanish influences, the Wood-Morris-Bonfils home turned to both Spain and France for inspiration. Stucco terraces, arched doorways, tile roof, wrought-iron details, and lunette windows share space with elaborate terra-cotta swags and garlands over the windows and on the exterior wall of the main fireplace. A sweeping glass canopy announces the front door. A 1987 remodel and addition by Daniel J. Havekost converted the home into condos and offices.
National Register, Denver Landmark

29 Adolph Zang Mansion
709 Clarkson Street
Frederick C. Eberley,1903

Built by Adolph Zang, son of the founder of Zang Brewery, this home features towering columns that support a two-story portico, with a balcony that opens to an imposing dormer. The portico is echoed on the south side by a one-story circular bay, part of the Neoclassical charm of a home built in brick and sandstone. This is one of two Zang Mansions found in Capitol Hill; the other, earlier home is at 1532 Emerson Street. The family also was known for its involvement in real estate, insurance, and mining.
National Register, Denver Landmark

30 St. John's Episcopal Cathedral
1313 Clarkson Street
Tracy & Swarthout, chapter house built in 1904, cathedral completed in 1911

Eighteen firms submitted a bid to design this project; the job went to the architect who later designed the main Denver Post Office at 18th and Stout Streets. As with the Cathedral of the Immaculate Conception, Indiana limestone was the material of choice, but the style of St. John's leaned more toward late Gothic Revival and a more sleek profile.

Chartered in 1861 as the parish of St. John's in the Wilderness, the Episcopal cathedral included new features, such as a center bay with a soaring window over a three-part entrance. But the old was not forgotten: several freestanding wood reredos, carved by Josef Mayr, had been saved from the old cathedral, which had been damaged by fire. As building progressed, plans also changed, and only the nave, not nave and transept, was built from Tracy and Swarthout's plans.
Over the years, the cathedral has been subject to a series of changes and additions. They include:

St. Martin's Chapel, built in 1927, was designed by Merrill and Burnham Hoyt, and the Dean Paul Roberts Building in 1956 by Fisher and Fisher. In 1979, the Cathedral Plaza was dedicated across East 14th Avenue. Artwork, including pieces by Edgar Britton and Mina Conant, was added to the complex. A ramping system was joined to the main entry, along with reconfiguration of the columbarium, the Roberts Building, and various windows, accomplished to a plan by Arch 7 Architects.
National Register, Denver Landmark

31 Morey Middle School
840 E. 14th Avenue
Fisher & Fisher, 1921

One of Denver's premier architectural firms approached the commission for this school with an eye for elegance, producing a spacious building in an Italian Renaissance style. The building was named after cattleman and businessman Chester S. Morey.
Denver Landmark

32 William Lang Homes
Four townhomes by Denver master residential architect William Lang remain in the North Capitol Hill area. One is on Emerson Street near East Colfax Avenue, while three more are in the 1600 block of Washington Street (two others were demolished in the 1960s). All were built between 1889 and 1891.

32.1 – 1532 Emerson Street: Known as the Zang Mansion (the first one) or the Gargoyle House, this unusual stone dwelling featured a gargoyle on the steeply sloped gable, and a turret that shifts into an oriel window. The gargoyle has occasionally disappeared from its perch. *National Register*

32.2 – 1624 and 1626 Washington Street: The first home is marked by a steeply sloped gable roof, with an oriel window on the second floor and a mix of smooth and rusticated stone. The second home features a stepped gable with a facade crafted in smooth stone with some evidence of carving. Lang lived at 1626 Washington Street, where the windows feature Gothic arches on the first floor but five perfect rectangles on the second.
National Register

32.3 – 1648 Washington Street: In this townhome, architect Lang worked in massive Richardsonian Romanesque arches to match the solid rusticated stone with which he was so adept.

33 Perrenoud Apartments
836 E. 17th Avenue
Frank S. Snell, 1901

Though not an architect, Frank Snell interpreted the wishes of his clients, a trio of sisters that wanted to create a building more at home in New York than Denver. In red brick with white wooden columns (Doric at the entry, composite above), Snell's apartment building for the Perrenoud sisters hews to a Neoclassical style. The building is laid out in the same format as the Equitable Building downtown, forming back-to-back "E's," so that light wells provide natural light to every room. The restrained facade hides an interior lobby of mosaic floor tiles, mirrored and marble walls, and a four-story atrium topped by a skylight in stained and painted glass.

The Perrenoud is one of the fine examples of Victorian, Queen Anne, Eclectic, and Neoclassical buildings that fill the Swallow Hill Historic District, which is listed, in varying formats, on both the National Register and as a Denver Landmark.

34 Edbrooke House
931 E. 17th Avenue
Frank Edbrooke, 1888

Known for commercial buildings around the city (Brown Palace Hotel, Oxford Hotel, Denver Dry), Frank Edbrooke turned to residential design in several homes in this block of East 17th Avenue. For his own use, he referenced the popular Queen Anne style, in brick and stone, with arched windows and the usual hallmarks of that category of composition. His home and its neighbors were typical of the impressive but not huge homes of the city's professional class at that time.
Denver Landmark

35 Cornwall Apartments
1317 Ogden Street
Walter E. Rice, 1901

The multi-faceted Walter Rice designed this apartment building for developer W.T. Cornwall, weaving Spanish Colonial elements into sprightly facades filled with cast plaster decorations. A central area is flanked by towers, with a profusion of variety in balcony detailing. In the mid-1970s, it was converted to condominiums, and has gone through a restoration process in which paint has been stripped to reveal buff-colored brick, with stucco repainted a rich gold.
National Register, Denver Landmark

36 Emerson School
1420 Ogden Street
Robert Roeschlaub, 1885; upgrades and restoration, SlaterPaull, 2012

Robert Roeschlaub's earliest remaining school project in Colorado is part of his legacy as both the state's first architect and a designer who designed dozens of fine educational buildings here. In the 1980s, the sturdy but elegant brick and

sandstone building was converted to a neighborhood center (eventually, the Frank B. McGlone Center). The school remains guarded by a giant gnomon that tracked the sun's path on the front facade.

Some 125 years after Emerson opened its doors to Denver students, the operator of the community center gave the property to the National Trust for Historic Preservation, which proceeded with a project that had two goals: to show an historic structure can be remade into a symbol of sustainability, and to bring the area's preservation organizations together under one roof. Installation of a geothermal heating and cooling system, efficient lighting, and repairs to the original windows and doors put the project on track to achieve LEED Gold certification. *National Register, Denver Landmark*

37 Dora Moore School
846 Corona Street
Robert Roeschlaub, 1889; additions by David Dryden and Pouw & Associates

Denver's first "school architect" began this project with a brick and sandstone structure that featured imposing towers and intricate terra-cotta trim. (It was then Corona School, renamed years later for a longtime principal.) Twenty years later, David Dryden responded in brick, adding color in a classroom building whose exterior sported a greenish glaze but more simple lines. In 1992, the Denver Public Schools decided to update the two, hiring Pouw & Associates to design a gymnasium and a glass bridge building that links Roeschlaub's lofty structure and Dryden's companion piece. Neighborhood efforts over the years have raised money for improvements and well-deserved appreciation of the school. *Denver Landmark*

38 Bailey Mansion
1600 Ogden Street
Lang and Pugh, 1889

A generous turret, imposing bargeboards, balconies, and projecting bays – the architects pulled out all the styles in this rhyolite and sandstone Queen Anne home built for George W. Bailey. The building since has become offices. Detailing is key to Lang and Pugh's design – a three-story structure that claims its corner with style. *National Register*

39 Grafton Apartments / The Aldine Family Hotel
1001–21 E. 17th Avenue
James Murdock, 1890

Built as the Aldine Family Hotel, James Murdock's interpretation of Queen Anne design in these six attached row houses was renamed the Grafton when it was turned into apartments. Eclectic elements survive in a double entryway, terra-cotta panels, conical roofs, and a strong rhythm between bays on the facade. *National Register*

City Park & City Park West

An assortment of notable buildings rings the city's premier park, including ornate residences, sleek commercial structures, and one of Denver's fine "compass point" schools.

City Park's fortunes have mirrored those of Denver, with ups and downs that have affected the conditions of its buildings and the attention paid to the overall neighborhood. Yet this imposing recreational oasis long has been a fitting home to two of the city's major cultural attractions, which just keep growing: the Denver Zoo and the Denver Museum of Nature & Science.

Though it has become somewhat of a cliché, one of the best views mixing park ambiance, modern construction, civic tradition, and mountain majesty is found in City Park: stand on the western steps of the Denver Museum of Nature & Science, or head up to the top floor of the museum's light-filled Leprino Family Atrium, and look west.

With the rebirth of the City Park Pavilion, extensive repairs to the park's monumental entryways, and the continuing influx of renovation-minded residents, City Park and City Park West again are showing off natural beauty marked by a tradition of elegance, whether a memorable moderne office building or a cottage that has been renovated into a museum.

LIST OF BUILDINGS

1   American Woodman's
    Life Building /
    Humphries Poli Architects
2   Mullen Building
3   Pearce-McAllister Cottage
4   Denver Skin Clinic
5   2190 East 17th Street
6   Schlessinger House
7   Raymond House /
    Castle Marne
8   East High School and
    Esplanade
9   Miller House
10 Eastside Human
    Services Building
11 Salvation Army Red
    Shield Corps and
    Community Center
12 Clayton College for Boys /
    Clayton Early Learning
13 City Park
14 Denver Zoo
15 Denver Museum of
    Nature & Science

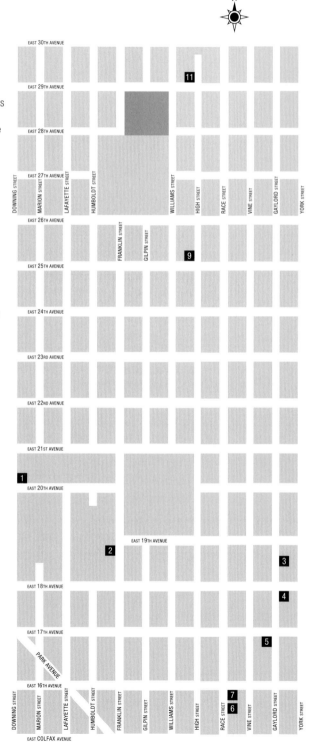

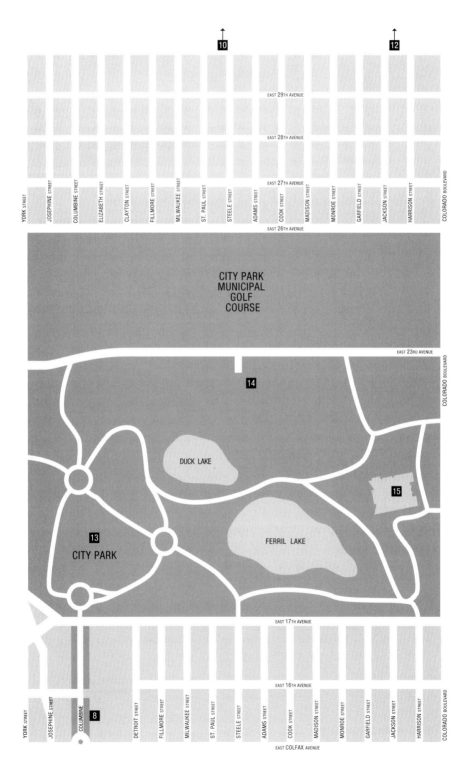

1 **American Woodman's Life Building / Humphries Poli Architects**
2100 Downing Street
Gordon D. White, 1950

Now home to an architecture firm, this sleek example of restrained Moderne design was built to house a fraternal organization and insurance company that served the city area's black community. White terra-cotta wraps around most of the building, with pale aqua decoration emphasizing horizontal strips and a modified Greek key design. The architect's light touch does not negate the sense that this building, influenced by the International Style, anchors its part of the neighborhood. The new owners worked to restore and improve the building while turning it into a contemporary office.
Denver Landmark

2 **Mullen Building**
Franklin Street at East 19th Avenue
Temple Hoyne Buell, 1932

The nurse's home at St. Joseph Hospital, named in memory of Catherine Mullen, wife of philanthropist John Mullen, adds Art Deco whimsy to an eclectic hospital district. Temple Buell's love of elaborate brickwork resulted here in exuberant plumes of dark brown masonry marching along the roofline and atop the entry bay. The fancy brickwork between windows adds to the building's strong sense of verticality, allowing it to maintain its importance as the hospital district has evolved over the years.
Denver Landmark

3 **Pearce-McAllister Cottage**
1880 Gaylord Street
Frederick J. Sterner, 1899

This turn-of-the-century cottage mingled Victorian Eclectic design elements with the vaguely countrified air contributed by frame construction. Three dormers punctuate the home's generous gambrel roof, all set off by a broad veranda. The home was built for Harold Pearce, general manager of the Argo Smelter, then sold to Henry McAllister, general counsel for the Denver and Rio Grande Railroad. It now is home of the Denver Museum of Miniatures, Dolls, and Toys.
Denver Landmark

4 **Denver Skin Clinic**
2200 E. 18th Avenue
Victor Hornbein, circa 1951

A preponderance of hospitals that began to fill the neighborhood bred related services such as clinics, pharmacies and other medical facilities. This is one of the most appealing: a red brick building that plays off horizontal planes and windows to reflect Victor Hornbein's mastery of Modernism, emphasizing the massing and architectural vocabulary of the Usonian Style.

5 **2190 East 17th Street**
*Henry Caldwell Toll, 1955; renovations include adaptation by
Root Rosenman Architects into office space, 2003*

This pharmacy with the floating butterfly–style folded roof picked up the name "Thebus" because of a nearby bus stop. The architect's generous use of glass at the front and on the sides welcomed light into a long, thin building that recedes into the background (and is much larger than it appears). A 2003 renovation into an office for architects added interior color, open volumes, and a sense of design that brought the old pharmacy to life. Since then, the building has housed other tenants.

6 **Schlessinger House**
*1544 Race Street
William Lang, 1888*

"Restraint" is not a word associated with this home, one of many designed in that era by the talented residential architect William Lang. The brick and limestone facade is inherently intricate, deeply Victorian–made even more so by elaborate millwork around the second-story porch and balcony. The porch is an arched Palladian style.
National Register

7 **Raymond House / Castle Marne**
*1572 Race Street
William Lang, 1890*

Another home by William Lang, though conceived on a grander scale. Lang worked in a heavy Richardsonian Romanesque style and creamy limestone, experimenting with several window forms to add movement to the imposing structure. A Palladian window faces south, a stained glass window north, and at the front is an arched opening supported by a center post. Built as the home of banker Wilbur S. Raymond, this elaborate confection is now a well-known bed-and-breakfast.
National Register, Denver Landmark

8 **East High School and Esplanade**
*East Colfax Avenue at City Park Esplanade, or 1545 Detroit Street
George H. Williamson, 1925. Addition by Murrin, Kahn, Mountain, Zeller, 1975
with a new gymnasium designed by Mountain Kasch Associates, 1981*

George Williamson worked in the Jacobean style, a Neoclassical form of architecture popular in 17th-century England. Three arched entryways and windows placed in sets of three accentuate a sense of symmetry enhanced by two window parapets and a clock tower topped by a cupola. Gray Ozark marble was used in the main lobby.

The two-block Esplanade that fronts East High was built and planted between 1905 and 1918. It serves as a link to City Park to the north via the Sullivan Memorial Gateway. In conjunction, the Esplanade incorporates an earlier fountain in a shell and dolphin motif, as well as the Thatcher Memorial Fountain, installed in 1918 (figures sculpted by Lorado Taft). The school's connection to City Park via the Esplanade has been marred somewhat by the encroachment of parking, but East High still sits like a minor urban castle up against the park.

9 Miller House
2501 High Street
Robert Russell, 1902

Essentially a large cube, this Romanesque house was home to banker and Realtor Byron L. Miller, until it was sold in the late 1940s to a railroad worker and eventually repurposed as a boarding house. Now home again to one family, the Miller House is notable for its elaborate stonework, setting red sandstone details such as window surrounds against rusticated gray limestone walls. Imposing and unusual, this home stands out for its corner location and its well-crafted architectural elements.

10 Eastside Human Services Building
3815 Steele Street
RNL Design, 2011

An emphasis on horizontal form is enlivened by soaring rooflines noting entryways. Built of white metal panels with dashes of orange, RNL included numerous windows to lighten up a building that houses services for people who need help, from food assistance to Medicaid. Built to achieve LEED Gold certification, the new human services building stands out in a residential neighborhood for its stylish lines and colorful accents.
AIA Denver Honor Award, 2012

11 Salvation Army Red Shield Corps and Community Center
2915 High Street
RNL Design, 2009 addition

In a similar vein, RNL used glass and contemporary design to bring light into an addition that relies on honest, simple materials for its strength and neighborhood impact. The addition serves as a link between two other sections of the complex, which is resolved by careful massing and volumes.

12 Clayton College for Boys / Clayton Early Learning
3801 E. 32nd Avenue
Maurice Biscoe and Henry Hewitt, 1909–1911; cottages built in 1959 by Dudley Smith and Casper Hegner; Educare Center wings, RDG Planning and Design of Omaha, 2007; Northeast Dormitory, Buchanan Yonushewski Group, 2007

Philanthropist George Washington Clayton established a trust in the waning years of the 19th century for the care of orphaned boys. The earliest buildings on the campus are predominantly red sandstone, though brick appears, too, in structures that mix Richardsonian Romanesque solidity with Neoclassical detailing. Later, Modernists Smith and Hegner constructed several cottages marked by brick and block construction and clerestory windows. In the late 1980s, the complex began an evolution that has transformed this campus into a center for early learning as well as other nonprofit and educational services. A 2005 master plan by Buchanan Yonushewski Group led to RDG's bright "wings" that flow from the old Power Plant (Educare Center) as well as BYG's renovation of the Northeast Dormitory into Clayton Early Learning's administrative offices. The dairy farm that served the needy boys is now Park Hill Golf Course.

13 City Park
York Street to Colorado Boulevard, East 23rd Avenue to East 17th Avenue

The city of Denver acquired much of the land on this site in 1880. The first design of the park was by city engineer Henry F. Meryweather. As the years progressed, plantings increased and evolved, many of them through popular efforts. In addition the park's recreational uses began to separate into different zones: active to the north (including a zoo and neighboring golf course), more passive to the south. Also over the years, different designers worked on City Park, including Reinhard Schuetze and S.R. DeBoer.

A gift from John Clarke Mitchell in memory of Dennis Sullivan, the Sullivan Memorial Gateway includes tall pylons designed in 1917 by Edward Herbert Bennett. Atop the shafts and columns along each pier are cast concrete statues of pioneer women and men, representing, respectively, agriculture and mining. (The figures were sculpted by Leo Lentelli.)

The Sullivan gateway was restored in the 1990s, along with three other entryways. The red sandstone Sopris Gateway, at East 17th Avenue and Fillmore Street, was designed in 1911 by Frank E. Edbrooke in memory of former Denver mayor Richard Sopris. The McLellan Gateway, designed in gray granite by Edwin H. Moorman was installed first in 1903 at the park's west entrance but moved to its current location at East 21st Avenue in the 1950s. And the Monti Gateway at the intersection of Montview and Colorado Boulevards was designed by Richard Phillip in pink granite as a 1917 gift from Joshua Monti. The gateways are notable for more than stone, however; they incorporate artwork, metalwork, and lighting to add a gracious note to the park approach.

Buildings and artwork also dot the park's interior, including an Italian Renaissance–style pavilion (designed in 1929 by William E. Fisher and John J. Humpnreys) and Grant W. Stevens's bronze statue of Robert Burns, plus various gardens and lakes. One attraction, the Electric Fountain, has been renovated and re-electrified so that the lights and bursts of water again play over Big Lake. An elaborate Martin Luther King Jr. memorial by Denver sculptor Ed Dwight replaced a late 1970s sculpture of the slain civil rights leader, incorporating African American history and accomplishments into the mini-plaza.

14 **Denver Zoo**
East 23rd Avenue between York Street and Colorado Boulevard

The story goes that the Denver Zoo began in 1896 with a black bear named Billy Bryan. In the century-plus since, this major Denver cultural attraction has grown dramatically, eventually soothing frayed neighbors' nerves by constructing a multilevel underground parking structure.

In 1918, zoo superintendent Victor Borchert built Bear Mountain, a project that was part of the "habitat zoo" movement. The concrete was cast from molds of rock outcroppings from the hogback west of Denver, with terraced pits and an overhang – all designed to provide a more natural home for the animals.

Over the years the zoo has added numerous modern structures that share space with relics of an earlier era, again working to create the sense of natural habitat and place an emphasis on species preservation. In the process, several designers have contributed their skills to major exhibitions and an education center:

• Tropical Discovery was designed by Anderson Mason Dale in conjunction with Ron Abo Architects.

• The Gates Wildlife Conservation Education Center is the work of Barker, Rinker, Seacat & Partners.

• Predator Ridge and the new multibuilding Toyota Elephant Passage were designed by CLR of Philadelphia. The palace for pachyderms (and hippos and rhinos) was funded by a $62.5 million bond issue approved by voters in 1999.

15 **Denver Museum of Nature & Science**
2001 Colorado Boulevard.East wing (completed in 1903) and central wing (for 1908 opening) by Frederick J. Sterner; 1939 Phipps Auditorium and 1948 wings by Roland L. Linder; 1986 additions by Stearns-Roger; Leprino Family Atrium, 2002, Hardy Holzman Pfeiffer Associates of Los Angeles, with HLM Design of Denver; North Loading Dock, Humphries Poli Architects, 2012. Collections and Education Facility, estimated completion 2014, klipp

The small Neoclassical museum that crowned the eastern boundary of City Park has grown over the years to become an imposing presence in Denver, adding several wings, an auditorium, additional exhibition space, a light-filled atrium, and most recently a space for science education and proper collections storage and processing.

The institution doubled in size in the late 1980s with the addition of two clunky new wings and atria that add little to the exterior appearance and that shifted the building's orientation to a side-door situation. Inside, it's another story, as the spacious atria form a buffer around the old central building and allow light to wash through the museum. The 2002 atrium addition, facing west, brought several stories of windows and expanded views of City Park, downtown, and the mountains, while adding interior color and form. The Collections and Education Facility, on the museum's south side, will present a contemporary face to busy East 17th Avenue, and was funded by $30 million in Better Denver Bonds and private contributions.

At the museum's western – back – door, note the 1930 bronze *The Grizzly's Last Stand*, the Louis Paul Jonas sculpture that for years served as a symbol of the museum.
AIA Denver Honor Award, loading dock, 2012

Congress Park & Cheesman Park

Land that began as Congress Park – a government gift to the city of Denver – was renamed to reflect the Cheesman family's generosity. Around this great green lawn have grown two of Denver's most respected and gracious residential neighborhoods: Cheesman Park and Congress Park.

Earlier, a portion of the park had been used as a city cemetery – now long gone, though the occasional reminder still surfaces. Shortly after the death of businessman Walter Cheesman, upon his family's donation of funds for a memorial there, much of the park gained its new name.

The boundaries for the Cheesman Park neighborhood are East 6th Avenue to East Colfax Avenue, between Downing and York streets; the boundaries for the Congress Park neighborhood are East 6th Avenue to East Colfax Avenue, between York Street and Colorado Boulevard. What remains of Congress Park lies to the east of York Street.

Special highlights of the Congress Park and Cheesman Park neighborhoods include engrossing historic residential enclaves such as Humboldt Island and Morgan's Addition, as well as cultural facilities such as the Denver Botanic Gardens complex and what is now called the Colfax Culture Complex (still Bonfils / Lowenstein Theater to many here).

Also important in these adjacent neighborhoods are the far-reaching Wyman Historic District and the elongated 7th Avenue Historic District, both created in 1993. The latter entity – hundreds of homes along East 6th, 7th and 8th Avenues – was created with an eye toward noting the architectural diversity and excellence of east Denver.

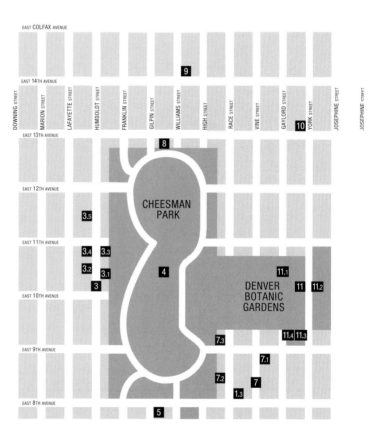

As in other parts of Denver, the impact of the Silver Crash of 1893 was felt throughout these neighborhoods, leading to more simple design and construction and a proliferation of sturdy Foursquare homes. A few infill projects have pushed evolution of the neighborhoods' architecture into the late 20th century and beyond.

In all, this predominantly residential area is a strong reminder of a period in Denver in which style – not just flash – took an honored place in the development of civic aesthetics.

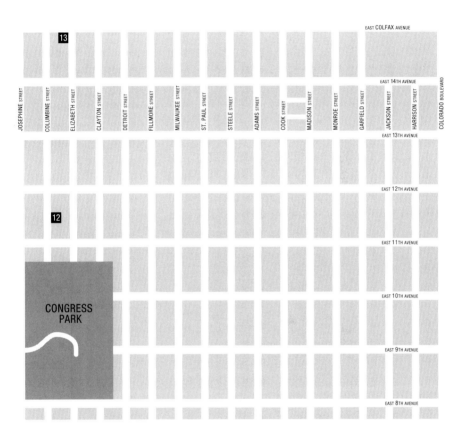

LIST OF BUILDINGS

1 Jacques J.B. Benedict Homes
1.1 Brown Garrey House
1.2 Kerr House
1.3 M. Samuel Radetsky House
2 John Doud House
3 Humboldt Island Historic District
3.1 Stoiber-Reed-Humphreys Mansion
3.2 Harry H. Tammen House
3.3 Thompson-Henry House
3.4 Sweet-Miller House
3.5 Denckla-Walker House
4 Cheesman Park, formerly Congress Park
5 Gilpin Street Residences
6 7th Avenue Parkway /
    7th Avenue Historic District
7 Morgan's Addition / Morgan's Subdivision
7.1 Daniel A. Millet House

7.2 L. Ward and Helen Bannister House
7.3 Livermore House
8 One Cheesman Place
9 Divine Science Church / Brook Center
    for the Arts
10 Owen Lefevre House
11 Denver Botanic Gardens
11.1 The Boettcher Conservatory
11.2 Denver Botanic Gardens Parking
    Complex and Bonfils-Stanton Visitors
    Center
11.3 Richard Crawford Campbell House /
    Botanic Gardens House
11.4 James Waring House
12 Stevens Elementary School
13 Bonfils Memorial Theatre / Lowenstein
    Theatre / Colfax Culture Complex (also
    referred to as Lowenstein CulturePlex
14 UMB Bank

1   Jacques J.B. Benedict Homes

Denver architect Jacques J.B. Benedict earned a reputation for many things – including a flamboyant personality – but what we appreciate now is his talent at residential architecture. The Denver architect was a master of applying Eclectic elements to the bones of Classical design, playing with symmetry and lush materials in the process, as demonstrated by these homes in the neighborhood:

1.1 – Brown Garrey House, *1300 E. 7th Avenue, 1921:* Benedict's design applies French details to a long, narrow home tailored to fit a long, narrow site. But then few frills were needed in this home marked by elegant simplicity, among the many Benedict designed in the Seventh Avenue Historic District.
Denver Landmark

1.2 – Kerr House, *1900 E. 7th Avenue, 1925:* This example of Benedict's elongated designs was built for John G. Kerr, who operated a stone and marble quarry. From Kerr's operation came the travertine used as trim on this house, in which the door is placed in a way that nudges symmetry. A carved cartouche tops the doorway of this elaborately detailed Mediterranean Revival mansion.

1.3 – M. Samuel Radetsky House, *800 Race Street, 1920:* Benedict moved away from the more slender, horizontal form of other projects to create a home in which wings flair out from a huge central turret. The entryway is topped by an intricate iron balcony, while windows on the lower floors of the wings feature soaring arched surrounds and keystones.

2   John Doud House
750 Lafayette Street
Edwin Moorman, 1905

This basic Foursquare – known in these parts as the Denver Square – managed to grab a bit of history. The family of Mamie Doud, who married the soon-to-be military hero and president Dwight D. Eisenhower, had purchased this home shortly after its construction. The buff brick two-story home features simple porch columns in front and a carriage house in back. Since converted into office space, that small structure housed Secret Service men when Eisenhower used this home as his western White House. Woodwork and fireplace surrounds are fine, and there are stained glass accents. But in layout and style, the Doud House is a Denver Square at heart.

3   Humboldt Island Historic District
Humboldt Street between East 10th and East 12th Avenues. Homes built between 1895–1920. Architects: the leading designers of the day in Denver

The beautifully designed homes of what has come to be called Humboldt Island were never intended to be as flashy as the mansions of Capitol Hill. Instead, this was a society oasis, where the rich and powerful could seek seclusion, where apartment houses could not intrude (until a home was demolished in the 1960s

to build a high-rise), where front lawns were deep, and where nearby Cheesman Park offered a cooling buffer against development.

The evolution of the park also served to prod development along Humboldt, as moneyed Denverites continued moving east. Almost two dozen of the old residences remain today, although in the early 1980s, a home was moved out of the district to save it.

This post-Victorian enclave reflected the popular designs of the day, from the expanded Denver Square to Georgian Revival to Colonial Revival. The city's top architects contributed to the neighborhood, although there also are several homes for which no architects have been credited. A sampling is detailed below. *National Register Historic District, Denver Historic District*

3.1 – Stoiber-Reed-Humphreys Mansion, 1022 Humboldt Street, Marean & Norton, 1907: Built on nine lots, this Renaissance Revival style home is made of tan pressed brick with a truncated hipped slate roof. Mining magnate Edward G. Stoiber died before the house was completed, and his widow called it Stoiberhof as a memorial. Later, it was sold to oilman Verner Reed, then to A.E. Humphreys Jr. Of note: substantial quoined corners and an iron and glass hood over the central entrance (not seen: a basement swimming pool).

3.2 – Harry H. Tammen House, 1061 Humboldt Street, Edwin H. Moorman, 1909: In dark green glazed brick, with trim in cream and white tile, the Tammen House has experienced several additions and modifications. A two-story brick porch was added five years after its completion, then enclosed for a solarium. In 1929, a copper Tudor-style balcony was added to serve as a hallway for rooms over the porte cochere, and part of the front porch was enclosed.

3.3 – Thompson-Henry House, 1070 Humboldt Street, Baerresen Brothers, 1905: Realtor Alonzo H. Thompson's home reflects the Georgian Revival style, with a grand semicircular portico topped by a rounded balcony, a structural conceit repeated as a crown for the third story. The light brick is a pale backdrop for six fluted columns, Palladian windows, and, on the north side of the house, more columns and an entablature with balusters. The National Register nomination says this home is reputed to be the first built with steel-beam construction in Denver.

3.4 – Sweet-Miller House, 1075 Humboldt Street, Sterner & Williamson, 1906: Home of Governor William Sweet, this Georgian Revival structure in red brick features a broad front porch with brick pillars and a balustraded roof with frieze, an arched front door with mullioned sidelights, and several Palladian design elements, including a window at the end gable and another at the center of the second story.

3.5 – Denckla-Walker House, 1151 Humboldt Street, H.T.E. Wendell, circa 1895: Another Georgian Revival home, this residence was built in brick, with a symmetrical facade and a semicircular arch supported by engaged columns at its front entrance. The end gable roof has an eyebrow dormer at its center. First-floor windows have voussoired lintels.

4   **Cheesman Park, formerly Congress Park**
    East 8th Avenue to East 12th Avenue, between Franklin and High Streets

One of Denver's most beautiful parks began as Denver's Mount Prospect
Cemetery in 1858. Platted for park use in the late 1860s, the land actually was
developed much later, with the 1892 design and planting of the park by Reinhard
Schuetze. The 80-plus-acre park basically was completed in 1898, though some
changes have occurred over the years – including the regular reconfiguration of
the roads around and through the park.
National Register

Additional amenities add a Classical air to the park, which took on two names
after Mrs. Walter S. Cheesman and daughter Gladys Evans Cheesman offered
to fund a memorial to the tycoon. Now divided by York Street, the parks are
Cheesman to the west, and Congress to the east.

The Esplanade, basically an entryway into the park, runs for about a block, and
is bounded by Williams Street, High Street, and East 7th and 8th Avenues. In this
small space, credited to landscape architect S.R. DeBoer, are a replication of a
meadow, strong plantings, and terraced land that showcases the entire composition.
A recent master plan and repair work included the installation of concrete walks
through the park, and elements that control speed on the roadways.
National Register

The Cheesman Memorial Pavilion was built in 1909 to a design by Marean &
Norton. Constructed of Colorado Yule marble, the pavilion is Classical in nature,
and rectangular in shape with square pillars and Tuscan columns. Though
parking and plantings have changed over the years, the pavilion remains a
popular destination.
Denver Landmark

Also notable is a structure that serves as a counterpoint to the pavilion: the
building called the Japanese Tea House, to the park's north, which includes
wooden supports and is often described as rustic.

As Don Etter, historian and former Denver parks codirector, noted in his
nomination of the city's parks system to the National Register, "Cheesman Park
was, and is, a classic work of art."

5   **Gilpin Street Residences**
    780 and 790 Gilpin Street
    OZ Architecture, 1992

Though infill in these neighborhoods has not been frequent, these early 1990s
homes show that new construction can be sympathetic to historic neighbors. A
cogent integration of the two homes on a compact site, and intelligent treatments
of walls in terms of color and detailing prevent the residences from resembling
ships lost as they steam along the street.

6   7th Avenue Parkway / 7th Avenue Historic District

The parkway, which extends for more than 20 blocks through the neighborhoods east of Milwaukee Street to Colorado Boulevard, was built on land paid for in 1912 by creation of an improvement district.

With organization and plantings credited to S.R. DeBoer, this lush strip serves as spine for the 7th Avenue Historic District. A few blocks to the south, the shorter and more compact Williams Street Parkway is attributed to the Olmsteds. Both are Denver Landmarks.

The district from Logan Street nearly to Colorado Boulevard includes almost a thousand homes. Research by historian Nancy Widmann turned up structures designed by more than 30 noted architects who worked in Denver between 1890 and 1942. Generally, corner lots feature larger homes, with more moderate structures in between. Along a portion of East 7th Avenue to the west of the district, homes actually face 7th, in many cases in long, narrow configurations.
National Register Historic District

7   Morgan's Addition / Morgan's Subdivision

This compact historic district developed on land purchased in 1887 by Samuel P. Morgan from the Catholic Church. In the process, former cemetery land again was brought back to life.

Most of the four dozen homes homes were built between 1910 and 1930. The stylish structures in Morgan's Addition feature work by prominent architects eager to please those moving east from Capitol Hill. The addition generally is bounded by East 8th Avenue, the Denver Botanic Gardens, and York Street, with a varying line along Race and High Streets. Many of the homes reflect the elegance of the City Beautiful era as interpreted in Classical substance with an occasional French and Spanish twist.
Denver Landmark District

7.1 – Daniel A. Millett House, 860 Vine Street, Fisher and Fisher, 1925: The Fishers turned to Georgian Revival for their design of a home for New England businessman Millett and his wife, adding a carved cornucopia as the major decorative element.

7.2 – L. Ward and Helen Bannister House, 849 Race Street, Maurice Biscoe, 1912: Alternately described as English country or vernacular design, Maurice Biscoe's home for the Bannisters included prominent eaves and a generous porch, with abundant windows, that dressed up a basically simple two-story structure.

7.3 – Livermore House, 901 Race Street, Biscoe & Hewitt, 1910: Then-partners Biscoe and Hewitt focused purely on Colonial Revival for this home for retired Captain Richard L. Livermore and his wife. Attic dormers cap a solid two-story home that features a balustrade on its coping but little other decoration.

8 One Cheesman Place
East 13th Avenue and Williams Street
Charles Sink and Associates, 1968

One Cheesman Place is the most successful of the high-rise apartment buildings built around Cheesman Park. Although 20 stories tall, its balconies manage to exert enough horizontal pull to keep the strong vertical thrust in check. The reenforced concrete construction has been well maintained, adding to the classic status of this thoroughly Modern building.

9 Divine Science Church / Brooks Center for the Arts
1400 Williams Street
Jacques J.B. Benedict, 1921–22

The metaphysical views of the Divine Science Church were promulgated by founder Nona Brooks, who has been called Denver's first woman minister. (She arrived here in the 1870s as a girl.) Jacques J.B. Benedict made a Greek temple for the congregants, with marble columns and a covered portico. The terra-cotta detailing is among the most elaborate in Denver, with a plethora of animals and symbols paying homage to a purely Classical design.

10 The Owen Lefevre House
1311 York Street
Kirchner & Kirchner, 1891

The home of a judge in the Arapahoe County, later Denver County, court system, the imposing three-story red brick building has served various substance abuse support groups. (Slightly ironic: More than a century ago this was the scene of parties given by the judge's wife, philanthropist and socialite Eva French Lefevre.) Of note: the sweeping veranda and the striking leaded, beveled glass in window treatments and at the entrance.
National Register, Wyman District contributing structure

11 Denver Botanic Gardens

Major structures at the Denver Botanic Gardens easily combine the feeling of sumptuous traditional luxury with the stylistic challenge of Modern design. The Gardens, built on the site of part of the old city cemetery, was founded in the early 1950s after years of discussion and planning. Graves were moved and land dedicated for construction of a complex devoted to gardens and botanical pursuits.

11.1 – The Boettcher Conservatory, 1005 York Street, Victor Hornbein and Edward D. White Jr., dedicated early 1966: The Modernist concrete and plexiglass conservatory carries a geometric pattern built on the principle of an inverted catenary curve. The reinforced concrete ribs soar, much like some of the specimens the building shelters. The entry to the complex has an almost

Wrightian feel, with horizontal motifs offering a subtle counterpoint to what lies ahead. Dedicated to Mr. and Mrs. Claude Boettcher, the building was funded by the Boettcher Foundation and family and Ideal Cement.

11.2 – Denver Botanic Gardens Parking Complex and Bonfils-Stanton Visitors Center, Tryba Architects, 2009:
The addition of this mound-like parking structure between York and Josephine Streets helped solve the problem of too many visitors for a small surface lot. Topped by the Mordecai Children's Garden, and sporting a sculptural installation by artist Osman Akan (the colorful *Albedo*), the garage brings a touch of green across York. The visitor center, however, when viewed from York, seems out of place with its red sandstone walls, even though its Neomodern lines complement the garden's entry. The face the visitors center presents inside is much more compatible in color and materials.
Parking Complex: AIA Denver Honor Award, 2010; Visitors Center AIA Denver Merit Award, 2011

11.3 – Richard Crawford Campbell House / Botanic Gardens House, 909 York Street, Jacques J.B. Benedict, 1926:
Serving as a complement to the Hornbein-White conservatory, the garden offices are housed in a mix of Beaux Arts and Tudor styles, an example of Benedict's feel for weaving disparate elements together to create a fine home. The rectangular structure, with one wing slanted slightly to the rear of the grounds, is of brick and stucco with cut stone trim. Green tile covers the irregular set of roof shapes, including hipped and gabled. (Historians say this is one of the first homes here built with central heating.) In 1958, Mrs. James J. Waring bought the home and gave it to the Gardens in memory of her father, Henry M. Porter. The library includes a collection of volumes on botany and horticulture.
National Register, Denver Landmark

11.4 – James Waring House, 910 Gaylord Street, Jacques J.B. Benedict, 1922:
Benedict's Beaux Arts tendencies came to the fore for this home, with its remarkable detailing – from finials, a near-Tudor oriel window, graceful paired arched windows, and his dramatic use of stone.

12 Stevens Elementary School
1140 Columbine Street
Robert Roeschlaub, 1901

The authors of *Robert S. Roeschlaub: Architect of the Emerging West* note that this was the designer's last documented public school in Denver. Turning from his usual red brick to a tan palette, Roeschlaub nonetheless again worked with a massive roof profile to produce a school more stolid than many amassed in his portfolio as Denver's school architect. Built as Clayton School, the building was renamed in the late 1920s after its principal, Eugene C. Stevens. Converted to condominiums in the early 1990s, the building's interior still contains many of the signs of a century-old school.
Denver Landmark

13 Bonfils Memorial Theatre / Lowenstein Theatre / Colfax Culture Complex (also referred to as Lowenstein CulturePlex)

East Colfax Avenue at Elizabeth Street
John K. Monroe, 1953; Josh Comfort, addition, 2006, Semple Brown Design retail interiors, 2006

Built by philanthropist and theater lover Helen Bonfils, the original complex housed the popular Denver Civic Theatre and was the precursor to the huge Denver Center theater complex built downtown more than two decades later. John K. Monroe's Art Moderne style infuses a contemporary building of pale brick and peach-colored marble with sweep and grandeur – especially the glass-grid entry on Elizabeth Street. Renamed the Lowenstein Theatre in 1985, after veteran producer Henry Lowenstein, the theater closed in 1986 and was used for occasional production work and offices.

Then it sat vacant from 1989 until developer Charles Woolley took the plunge and remade the existing building as a home for the Tattered Cover Book Store (which moved out of Cherry Creek North) and other retail. A compatible, but much more simple addition houses other shops and restaurant space, as well as the Denver Film Society, which moved in after a cinema closed.

The inclusion of parking bolsters this complex, which has had a strong positive effect on that stretch of East Colfax Avenue. Old and new sections of the complex are linked by a walkway sometimes referred to as a mini-esplanade, a nod to the City Park Esplanade nearby. Of note in the bookstore, now housed in the old theater auditorium: The railings and stairs inside may not be quite 1930s cruise ship quality but exhibit a fine sense of line.

AIA Colorado Merit Award, AIA Denver Honor Award, both 2007 (Semple Brown Design)
National Register, Denver Landmark

14 UMB Bank

707 Colorado Boulevard
RNL Design, 2002

The former site of a fast-food restaurant became home to a classy bank branch office through a design that stresses the interplay of angularity and curve. An asymmetrical glass and metal grid entry, upper-level curved wall, and mini-mast mark this compact building, home of a bank whose upper management is known for its support for the arts.

Park Hill

One of Denver's historic suburbs, Park Hill boasts a large collection of homes, schools, parkways, and civic and religious structures built on high land east of both City Park and the at-one-time magic dividing line of Colorado Boulevard.

Not magic in the usual sense of the word. Park Hill had begun as an unusually gracious collection of homes, with adjoining areas filled with smaller residences. But it became Ground Zero when integration of housing and schools became a major issue in Denver in the 1960s and 1970s. Denver's African American residents had not been allowed to move east of Colorado Boulevard, but many Park Hill residents decided to change that, as all people were invited to live in a cluster of neighborhoods that gathered under the Park Hill umbrella.

Park Hill was another neighborhood born when a dreamer came to Colorado and envisioned a real estate fortune. Just as Baron Walter von Richthofen foresaw a health spa lifestyle in Montclair, Baron Allois von Winkler pronounced that he would build an upscale residential subdivision – with a racetrack. The latter never materialized, but Park Hill became a magnet for people tired of the growing density of Capitol Hill and other close-in neighborhoods.

Today, the area's parkways especially are lined with large homes in Spanish Colonial, Mediterranean, and Tudor styles, along with the rich landscaping that parkway development encouraged. Like other established neighborhoods, Park Hill has faced development pressure, including contemporary infill and pop-tops. But the neighborhood has retained its sense of stability and elegance.

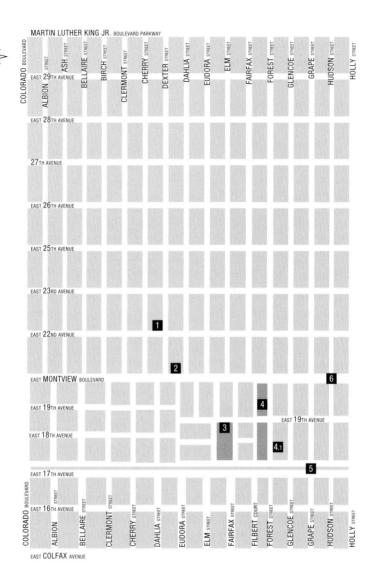

This district includes information on one church, a neighborhood library, two very different schools, the three parkways that connect Park Hill, and a scattering of homes. Also described are several buildings that represent a longtime Park Hill neighbor: the old Colorado Women's College, which was repurposed several years ago as a campus for a school devoted to the culinary arts and hospitality.

MARTIN LUTHER KING JR. BOULEVARD PARKWAY

EAST 29TH AVENUE
EAST 28TH AVENUE
EAST 27TH AVENUE
EAST 26TH AVENUE
EAST 25TH AVENUE
EAST 23RD AVENUE
EAST 22ND AVENUE
EAST MONTVIEW BOULEVARD
EAST 19TH AVENUE
EAST 18TH AVENUE
EAST 17TH AVENUE
EAST BATAVIA PLACE
EAST 16TH AVENUE
EAST COLFAX AVENUE

HOLLY STREET
IVANHOE STREET
IVY STREET
JASMINE STREET
KEARNEY STREET
KRAMERIA STREET
LEYDEN STREET
LOCUST STREET
MONACO PARKWAY
MONACO PARKWAY
MAGNOLIA STREET
NIAGARA STREET
NEWPORT STREET
ONEIDA STREET
OLIVE STREET
PONTIAC STREET
POPLAR STREET
QUEBEC STREET

7
9
8
8.1
8.2
8.3
8.4

LIST OF BUILDINGS

1 St. Thomas Episcopal Church
2 Park Hill Branch Library
3 Park Hill Elementary School
4 Forest Street Parkway
4.1 1730 Forest Street
5 East 17th Avenue Parkway
5.1 Fox/Kittleson Residence
6 Montview Boulevard
7 Smiley Middle School

8 Colorado Women's College /
Johnson & Wales University
8.1 Treat Hall
8.2 Whatley Chapel
8.3 Permelia Curtis Porter Library
8.4 Porter Memorial Hall
9 Houston Fine Arts Center / Lamont School
of Music / Denver School of the Arts

1   St. Thomas Episcopal Church
2201 Dexter Street
Harry J. Manning, 1908

One of the most notable entryways in all of Denver marks this church, which mixes elements of Spanish Baroque and Spanish Colonial Revival. Harry J. Manning worked in tile and stucco for his compact building, with a loggia at one side of the courtyard. For the entrance, though, he used intricately carved stone, rising through a carved doorway to the window surround above. The bell tower of St. Thomas may be taller, but it is Manning's entry, in a style termed Churrigueresque (after late 17th-, early 18th-century architect Jose Benito Churriguera), that draws the eye.
Denver Landmark

2   Park Hill Branch Library
4705 Montview Boulevard
Burnham Hoyt, 1920, with renovation by Smith and Thorson, 1964, and
a restoration and addition by David Owen Tryba Architects, 1992

One of the eight branch libraries funded by flinty philanthropist Andrew Carnegie, Park Hill was an instance in which Burnham Hoyt worked in a more Historicist vein. The later Modernist chose Spanish Renaissance design for this structure, which features warm cream-colored stucco topped by a hipped, red tile roof. Acanthus-motif pilasters frame leaded glass windows and define the building's edges. An unsympathetic renovation in 1964 added a small structure to the entry that was known as a dog house and that covered the library's name plaque. The first was removed and the second repaired in a 1990s project that remade the library's community room and added a courtyard.
Denver Landmark

3   Park Hill Elementary School
5050 E. 19th Avenue
Frederick E. Mountjoy and Frank W. Frewan, 1901 (though Denver Public
School records also show input by David W. Dryden); additions by Mountjoy and
Frewan, 1912 and 1928, plus additions by Phillips, Carter, Reister, 1952 and 1969

An early entry into the neighborhood, the school featured the lush stucco and tile of Mediterranean Revival design, marked by prominent arches and frieze, with elaborate terra-cotta detailing. Additions have been respectful to the building, which helps set the tone for the rest of Park Hill.
Denver Landmark

THE PARKWAYS AND BOULEVARD

4 Forest Street Parkway
Links Montview Boulevard and E. 17th Avenue

This two-block stretch of trees and various plantings was designed at some point after 1913. It is attributed to the Olmsted Brothers of Massachusetts, and features a symmetry reflective of that firm's plans for East 17th Avenue Parkway.
National Register, Denver Landmark

Notable residences include:

4.1 – 1730 Forest Street, Burnham Hoyt, 1923: This mini-manse is an instance in which Burnham Hoyt worked in brick in a subtle Tudor vocabulary. The sprawling home features turned, twin chimneys as well as a massive bay window at one end.

5 East 17th Avenue Parkway
Between Colorado Boulevard and Monaco Street Parkway

The right-of-way for this parkway was acquired in 1909, and over the years residents taxed themselves to fund grading and planting. Parks historian Don Etter attributes the design of this parkway to the Olmsted Brothers, with influences from Denver parks planner S.R. DeBoer in some sections of this lengthy stretch of East 17th Avenue.
National Register, Denver Landmark

5.1 – Fox / Kittleson Residence, 5730 E. 17th Avenue, Robert Louis Fox, 1920: This Mediterranean Revival home features two wings emanating from a central section. Robert Louis Fox worked in stucco and topped his home with a Ludowici green tile roof. An iron gate and other details mark this home, where Fox installed an early outdoor swimming pool.

6 Montview Boulevard
Between Colorado Boulevard and Monaco Street Parkway

Montview was an early parkway, with the street laid out in 1892 and calls for development several years before. An improvement district was formed to fund design and plantings, which parks historian Don Etter says may have been developed by city park draftsman Frederick W. Ameter. Another extensive and important thoroughfare, Montview serves as open space for residents and as a scenic link for commuters.
National Register, Denver Landmark

7 **Smiley Middle School**
2540 Holly Street
George H. Williamson, 1928, with additions by Raymond Harry Ervin, 1953
and 1958, an addition by Piel, Slater, Small, Spenst, 1964

Full-blown Tudor in red brick was the style George H. Williamson chose for what began as Holly Street Junior High and Park Hill Junior High. This impressive building, in the northern portion of Park Hill, later was renamed for Denver school superintendent William H. Smiley. The design includes a crenelated roofline, with a huge entry arch and quatrefoil details – pre-Depression grandeur in an educational setting.

8 **Colorado Women's College / Johnson & Wales University**
Bounded by E. 17th Avenue and Montview Boulevard, and Oneida
and Quebec Streets

This campus grew in fits and starts, beginning as Colorado Woman's College, and, at one point became Temple Buell College when school officials established a relationship in the 1960s with architect-philanthropist Buell.

Founded as a Baptist educational institution, the school had incorporated in 1888 but didn't open until 1909. Eventually, financial troubles led to CWC's 1982 sale to the University of Denver. On what became known as the University of Denver's Park Hill campus, DU developed the Lowell Thomas School of Law and found a home for the one-time Lamont School of Music in the Houston Fine Arts Center, which later was transformed into the Denver School of the Arts. To continue the CWC legacy, the Women's College opened in its own home at DU in 2004.

In 1999, a portion of the campus was acquired by Johnson & Wales University, a school devoted to business and the culinary arts. In fall 2000, the school began holding classes in the eclectic mix of buildings that take some historic cues from old Treat Hall but include fine Modern, even exotic touches.

Buildings include:

8.1 – Treat Hall, Poplar Street between E. 18th and 19th Avenues, Frank H. Jackson, cornerstone laid 1890, completed 1909: The first building on campus housed the entire school for several years and was named after the school's first president. Frank H. Jackson worked in a Richardsonian Romanesque style, yet in a less massive way than many of the initial buildings at educational institutions in that era. The entrance features a rounded voussoire and decorated keystone, with the arch echoed in doors within the entryway. Horizontal banding is notable.
National Register, Denver Landmark

8.2 – Whatley Chapel, E. 18th Avenue at Oneida Street, Stanley E. Morse, 1962: The architect found inspiration in the Modern and the Gothic to create this complex, which includes the buff brick chapel, an amphitheater to the south, and a carillon. Probably most impressive are the chapel's more than three dozen stained glass windows made by Gabriel Loire of Chartres, France.

8.3 – Permelia Curtis Porter Library, E. 18th Avenue between Olive and Pontiac Streets, Victor Hornbein and Edward D. White Jr., 1963: Longtime CWC supporters, the Porter family was remembered in several ways on campus. Among them was Hornbein and White's design for a library that, as with the chapel, mixed influences – in this case medieval interpreted in Modern materials.

8.4 – Porter Memorial Hall, E. 18th Avenue at Poplar Street, S. Arthur Axtens, 1939: Simplicity marks the architect's design in brick and stone for Porter Hall, which turns a corner in three segments to show a welcoming sensibility.

9 **Houston Fine Arts Center / Lamont School of Music / Denver School of the Arts**
7111 Montview Boulevard
Stanley E. Morse (Morse, Dion, and Champion), 1968; Klipp Colussy Jenks Dubois Architects, renovation and addition, 2003

This magnet school had several homes before Denver Public Schools purchased the old Houston Fine Arts Center, a striking Modernist building designed in such a way by architect Stanley E. Morse that the fly tower read as one of several volumes in brick. A renovation of the older building and completion of a new one introduced metal panels, curving surfaces, and a windows set in a glass and metal grid. Sophisticated and yet welcoming, the Denver School of the Arts reveals a dramatic presence on the predominantly residential Montview Boulevard.

Montclair

The West has been the proverbial magnet for dreamers and schemers, and Denver is no exception. One of the city's more colorful visionaries was Baron Walter Von Richthofen, who in the late 1870s arrived in Colorado and for the next decade worked hard to make money and a name. By the late 1880s, he had platted the land and was selling shares in the model suburb-cum-health farm named Montclair.

Though Richthofen's total plan for Montclair never came to be – he died in 1898 – Denver residents interested in a bucolic, healthy lifestyle away from the city's messy core took note of his work in east Denver. There, residents eventually shaped a neighborhood centered around the Baron's castle and the Molkery, where the milk cure promised good cheer, and where TB houses offered the ailing clean air and comfort.

The castle and Molkery survive today (the former as a private home, the latter as a community center), while the larger farmhouses and more compact TB houses have been joined by other structures.

The homes of several of Richthofen's close associates, such as Dennis Tirsway, remain. The contractor built several TB homes in the neighborhood with developer Charles Kittredge, featuring sleeping porches that since have been enclosed or absorbed into the house. Kittredge's imposing stone home has been demolished (Kittredge Park stands testimony to it on East 8th Avenue at Oneida Street). But Tirsway's Victorian residence – sunburst pediment and all – remains at 1433 Olive Street. Tirsway served as a Montclair official, as did Matthias Cochrane. The town's first mayor after its incorporation in 1888, Cochrane is survived by a brick and stone estate at 1304 Olive Street. And Richthofen's attorney, John H. Denison, lived in a brick and shingle home still standing at 1006 Olive Street.

Two of Denver's finest modern architects made Montclair their home. Known for residential design in the Hilltop and Crestmoor neighborhoods, Joseph and Louise Marlow built their own home at 1196 Oneida Street, while the multi-faceted Victor Hornbein's low-slung home fills the lot at 714 Pontiac Street, though it has suffered from an unsympathetic upper-level addition. Both original structures date from the late 1940s.

Over the years, the peaceful enclave of Montclair gained an airport and air force base as neighbors. Over the past decade, Stapleton International Airport and Lowry AFB have evolved into large developments devoted to residential, retail, and commercial uses, making Montclair's architectural heritage even more apparent.

Montclair was absorbed into Denver in 1902, and Denver mayor Robert Speer created the broad street – Richthofen Parkway – that keeps alive the name of one of the city's most memorable developers.

The Denver Landmark District – basically Newport, Oneida, Olive, and Pontiac streets between East 7th and 12th Avenues – includes one short parkway, two parks, and a monument, all sited just to the east of the bustling Monaco Street Parkway.

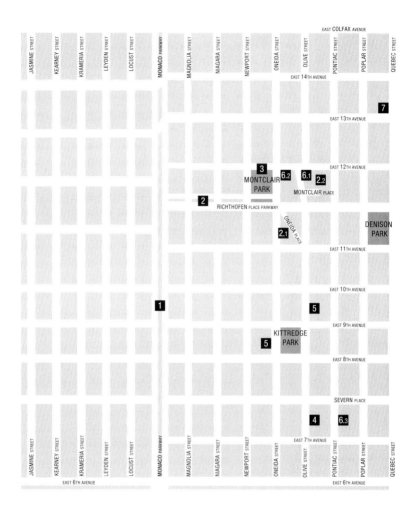

LIST OF BUILDINGS

1 Monaco Street Parkway
2 Richthofen Place Parkway
2.1 Richthofen Fountain / Monument
2.2 Richthofen Castle
3 Molkery / Montclair Civic Building
4 Thomas House
5 Tuberculosis Homes
6 Key Modern Homes
6.1 Buka House
6.2 Marlow House
6.3 Hornbein House
7 Stanley School / Montclair School /
Stanley British Primary School /
Paddington Station Preschool

1   Monaco Street Parkway

The stretch of this parkway that runs directly west of Montclair is a particularly telling amenity. The broad, well-planted median in that area was conceived during the tenure of city landscape architect S.R. DeBoer, with plantings of elms and evergreens beginning in about 1907 and completion by 1911. Like all parkways in Denver, drought and spotty maintenance have dimmed the initial promise.
National Register

2   Richthofen Place Parkway

Though only about one-quarter mile in length, this gracious stretch of roadway between E. 11th and E. 12th Avenues provides a formal entry into Montclair as well as a link between the neighborhood's unusual historic structures and the community at large. Influential landscape architect S.R. DeBoer in this instance focused on evergreens, in a mini-forest that leads to Montclair Park to the north, the Richthofen Monument to the south and east, and, further on, the Richtofen Castle itself.
National Register

2.1 – Richthofen Fountain/Monument, Richthofen Parkway at Oneida Street, Harlan Thomas, 1901: Built originally to provide a trough for animals and a fountain for people, the granite structure mounted by granite stairs eventually became a large-scale flower box. Developer Baron Walter von Richthofen's widow contributed to the project as a memorial to her late husband. Her own ashes were interred there.

2.2 – Richthofen Castle, 7020 E. 12th Avenue, Alexander Cazin, 1887, with heavy renovation in the 1910s by Maurice Biscoe and Henry Hewitt, and a 1924 addition by Jacques J.B. Benedict: Though modified over the years from a stark but heavy stone castle with crenelated towers into a more subtle Tudor style, Richthofen's "castle" remains an imposing, if less medieval, structure. Attended by a gatehouse at 1177 Pontiac Street, the castle passed into the hands of manufacturing tycoon Edwin Hendrie and his heirs, who changed its appearance. Though still grand, the capacious castle now is more in tune with larger more elegant homes in the neighborhood. Richthofen's Castle remains a private home and carries the singular status of being a European-based stimulus for an all-American suburb.
Denver Landmark, National Register

3 **Molkery / Montclair Civic Building**
6820 E. 12th Avenue
Architect not known, though it has been attributed to Alexander Cazin, 1888;
restoration SlaterPaull Architects, 2004

After more than 100 years, the Molkery, or milk house, underwent a restoration project that involved rebuilding its tower and turning it into an events venue and community center. With hints of Swiss chalet and French country home style, the building that claims center stage in Montclair Park began as a health center for TB patients who were considered potential residents of the emerging neighborhood. At one point, the Molkery served as an asylum before passing to the city of Denver for use as a community center. Though its open-air porches have been closed or altered, the Molkery still has a sturdy rustic charm, with a mix of brick and stone trimmed in wood and the air of a rural retreat in an active neighborhood setting.
Denver Landmark
AIA Colorado Citation Award, 2005

4 **Thomas House**
740 Olive Street
Harlan Thomas, 1897

Architect (and one-time Montclair mayor) Harlan Thomas donated his services for the charming Richthofen Monument, but for himself he had more grand plans. His rusticated sandstone mini-castle features a tower, bay windows, and the kind of overall detailing more at home in downtown Denver's upscale neighborhoods. Thomas worked in the Queen Anne style, though much design of the late 1890s had moved in more simple directions.

5 **Tuberculosis Homes**
928 Olive, 940 Olive, and 956 Olive Street
Credited to Frank H. Panadice Jr., developed by Charles M. Kittredge and
Dennis Tirsway, circa 1906–07

Each of these homes has a different appearance and level of complexity of detail, but all were built for their ability to provide access to the clean air of Montclair. The TB houses that dot the neighborhood – including these three notable examples – generally were simple in layout, with an entry hall and groupings of rooms to either side. Side sleeping porches over the years often were enclosed or integrated into the home as the concept of the TB house faded from popularity in Denver.

6   Key Modern Homes

Montclair may be known by many for its rich history and the buildings that reflect that. But in a compact area, five homes demonstrate how architects worked with site and location to express the fundamentals of Usonian and Second Phase International Style design. Several of these were the architects' own homes, and reflected an investment in a neighborhood that welcomed the future as much as it honored the past.

6.1 – Buka House, 1180 Olive Street, Victor Hornbein, 1953: Victor Hornbein's status as a civic architect was rivaled by the talent he displayed in residential design. For this project, he focused on two levels linked by an overhang that emphasized the sense of a receding ground level. Broad eaves – a Usonian hallmark – mark this home, as does an unerring sense of proportion. Next door, the Kobey House (1170 Olive Street, Alan Gass, 1955) works on multiple levels. Creating a home that is fully integrated with a street-level garage recedes into the volume of the home, respecting the integrity of the design.

6.2 – Marlow House, 1190 Oneida Street, Joseph and Louise Marlow, 1948: The Marlows were known for their residential design, including their own home in Montclair. Expanses of windows link this distinctive design project with its surroundings, connecting to the outdoors and the neighborhood. The nearby Kloverstrom House (1184 Oneida Street, Carl Kloverstrom, 1953) emphasizes a sense of horizontal movement, elevated by an upper bank of clerestory windows that connect with the home's surroundings. Kloverstrom was known for his work designing schools in the region.

6.3 – Hornbein House, 714 Pontiac Street, Victor Hornbein, 1948: Horizontal planes and the strategic placement of windows define the architect's personal residence, which has long been a landmark in the neighborhood. Recent unsympathetic additions have marred the sweeping horizontal character of the home, and changes in fenestration have diminished the integrity of the original design.

7   Stanley School / Montclair School / Stanley British Primary School / Paddington Station Preschool
1301 Quebec Street
John J. Huddart, 1890, with addition by David Owen Tryba Architects, 1991

Marked by fine detailing – including basket-weave brickwork, dentils, and arched windows – this former Denver school first was named after British explorer Henry Stanley. It became Montclair School in 1902, then Montclair Annex in the early 1940s. Since 1978 (Historic Denver, Inc. won a fight against demolition), the elaborately crafted building has been used for private educational purposes by various organizations.
Denver Landmark, National Register

Hilltop & Hale

One of Denver's true "Modern" neighborhoods, Hilltop includes a wide array of residential styles.

Along these tree-shaded blocks, it is possible to see everything from imposing Tudor estates to (a few remaining) vernacular cottages, from fanciful designs on the fancifully named Shangri-La Drive, to bold, timeless Modernist homes that reflect the tenets of the International Style and Frank Lloyd Wright's Prairie vision. Over the past few decades, however, fine design has been forced to share space with faux stucco starter castles, where Postmodern pastiche meets bloated Romanticism. The scrape-off mania in Denver has torn through Hilltop, in most cases replacing gracious residential structures with boastful trophies. Still, in recent years, as Neomodern design has begun to define contemporary residential architecture in some parts of the metro area, Hilltop has seen its share of gems emerge. And empty lots.

Free of restrictive covenants found in other neighborhoods, Hilltop at mid-century proved a haven for Denver's Jewish community. Adventurous residents responded by commissioning homes in groundbreaking designs, as well as a fine synagogue whose congregation relocated in the late 1950s from its home in Capitol Hill.

Platted in 1886, Hilltop also still boasts a few of the original Victorian dwellings. But this architecturally diverse neighborhood perhaps is best known for its generous lots, which began to spark controversy in the late 1990s as developers sought to scrape existing homes off expansive properties in order to squeeze in additional (and huge) dwellings. Still, green space is a hallmark of the neighborhood – including Robinson Park, an open area salvaged from a former yard for material to make bricks.

One of the most generous pieces of property serves as a frame for the former home of George Cranmer, at 200 Cherry St. This gracious 1921 manse with Italian and Spanish elements claims a park as its front yard: Cranmer, a developer and later head of the city's parks department, bought property where he learned a park might be located. For his buffer from the world – not to mention high ground that provided excellent mountain views – Cranmer chose to build near what would become Inspiration Park. Later named Mountain View Park, and, finally, Cranmer Park, this lovely swath of green is anchored by a sandstone platform and a large sundial.

Time certainly has not stood still in the ever-evolving Hilltop, but the outsized dial has become almost a symbol of the neighborhood, one of the prime places in Denver that has become threatened by those who profess to love it.

To the north of Hilltop, the Hale neighborhood for years was defined by the University of Colorado Health Sciences Center, a giant complex of hospital, laboratory, and office structures on a cramped site in the city. The decision more than a decade ago to move the center to a former army post in Aurora left many historic, Modernist, and contemporary medical buildings in danger of demolition.

While the new University of Denver Anschutz Medical Campus to the east has followed design guidelines that call for sleek contemporary buildings in compatible materials, the now nearly vacant health center in Denver has seen plans dissolve and reappear, buffeted by a bad economy and facing a murky, blighted future.

LIST OF BUILDINGS

1 Shangri-La / Harry Huffman Residence / Hirschfeld Residence
2 Gerarden-Razee House
3 D.C. Burns Park
4 Steck Elementary School
5 East 6th Avenue Parkway
5.1 Lewin Residence
6 Touff-Bershof House
7 Groves House
8 Sandler House
9 Kohn-Neusteter House
10 Millman House
11 Joshel House
12 Rothenberg House
13 Marvin Hatami House
14 The George Cranmer House and Cranmer Park
15 Graland Country Day School / Anschutz Commons
16 Temple Emanuel
17 Law House
18 Hannah Evans House
19 Four Mile House

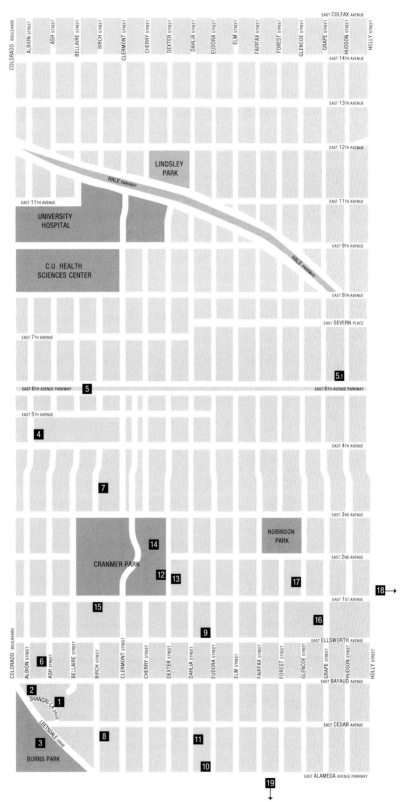

1 **Shangri-La / Harry Huffman Residence / Hirschfeld Residence**
150 S. Bellaire Street
Raymond Harry Ervin, 1937

Even the most gracious neighborhood can have a gimmick, and Shangri-La was supposed to serve as a lure for development in Hilltop. The story goes that theater magnate Harry Huffman became entranced by the Deco/Moderne structure that formed the centerpiece for the cosmic movie tale "Lost Horizon," released in 1937.

The home indeed sports similar Deco motifs (such as chevron shapes) and does include a striking hemicycle with thick columns and deep eaves. But it's hardly a dead ringer for the lamasery in which Ronald Coleman and a band of troubled travelers sought refuge after their plane crashed in the Himalayas. And the home's design by the prolific Raymond Harry Ervin undoubtedly began before the movie was shown in theaters.

This American Shangri-La features the conflation of broad overhangs that stress a horizontal feel, with tall shoots of fretwork emphasizing verticality. A thoroughly square second floor wing tops a semicircular columned room. Whether or not Hollywood played a part in Shangri-La's birth, this remains one of Denver's most unusual homes, fantastical in design yet rooted in its neighborhood.

2 **Gerarden-Razee House**
4141 Shangri-La Drive
Charles A. Haertling, 1970

This rare Denver example of Charles Haertling's work offers a brisk lesson in Modernism. The Boulder architect worked in cast and grooved concrete, in volumes arranged in layers that appear to serve as platforms for a roof and living spaces. Though the material is brutal, Haertling's arrangement of walls and horizontal elements produces a compact presentation of geometric form, a late 20th century interpretation of a Mayan temple, though one now hidden by a huge fence.

3 **D.C. Burns Park**
Bounded by Colorado Boulevard, Leetsdale Drive, and
East Alameda Avenue, 1968

For an unprecedented sculpture symposium in June 1968, nine artists gathered in the tiny park bounded by busy thoroughfares to create what was supposed to be temporary work for a major sculptural symposium in Denver. (The park was named for Daniel C. Burns, whose estate conveyed the land to the city in 1940.)

The nine artists – Dean Fleming, Peter Forakis, Anthony Magar, Robert Mangold, Robert Morris, Richard Van Buren, Wilbert Verhelst, Roger Kotoske, and Angelo DiBenedetto – worked in plywood and other materials. Their creations were supposedly only going to remain on view for a few months.

But over the years, Denver residents began to feel protective of the pieces, created as striking geometric elements in strong colors. Most residents, anyway. Slowly, because of inadequate maintenance and persistent vandalism, sculpture after sculpture was lost. A turning point came in the mid-1990s, when the city demolished Dean Fleming's *Magic Cube* because it was deemed a hazard; then Kotoske's work was set on fire, though later reconstructed with insurance money.

As a result, a group of private citizens calling themselves the Friends of Burns Park began to raise money for repairs and new pieces of sculpture. The remaining works have been restored – a boon to the city and all who drive by this pocket park. (Works by DiBenedetto, Magar, and Verhelst were refurbished, while the Kotoske piece was replicated and fire-proofed.)

After a competition, one new piece was commissioned, and installed in 1999 – but Barbara Baer's *Jazz*,' sited along Colorado Boulevard, is too small and incompatible in form to make an impact in the space and to compete with the earlier, bolder work. In 2010, a 1968 sculpture by Magar, long sited at the Joshel House, was installed in Burns Park, a donation by the late Suzanne W. Joshel. The work adds an angular yellow and gray form to the assemblage, and reaffirms the standard of excellence set by the original sculptural program in the park.

4   Steck Elementary School
425 Ash Street
S. Arthur Axtens, 1929; additions in 1942 by Axtens and in 1994 by Hans Kahn

Buff and brown brick serve as the main mode of decoration for this school, which is marked by horizontal banding, windows that stress verticality, and a soaring entry arch topped by a massive keystone. S. Arthur Axtens's design was amplified by wings added in 1942, when he played off the polychromed brick courses while changing to a more subdued window treatment. In 1994, several classrooms were added. The school is named after Amos Steck, a pioneer Denver resident who served as mayor, judge, and school board member. (Nearby, at 451 Clermont Street, is Hill Middle School, a Modernist 1954 design by Raymond Harry Ervin, with Robert D. Laramey and Alfred H. Piel Associates.)

5   East 6th Avenue Parkway

This boulevard, between Colorado Boulevard and Quebec Street, has been described as the longest east-west stretch in the city's system of parks and parkways. Developed between 1909 and 1912, the plantings and median composition were planned by S.R. DeBoer, though influenced by Olmsted. By the mid-1880s, Baron Walter Von Richthofen had urged the creation of treelined parkways to lead to his development in Montclair. The response on East 6th Avenue helped define east Denver and set a standard for development, landscaping, and generous open spaces.
National Register

Numerous residences along East 6th Avenue Parkway display distinctive architectural elements, from Tudor to Modernist. The Lewin Residence is among them.

5.1 – Lewin Residence, 5435 E. 6th Avenue, Earl Chester Morris, 1941: One of several architects in the Morris family, the designer of this pre war residence utilized red brick and a golden yellow brick to set off various volumes. Wooden trim adds horizontal movement to a building that adopts the International Style belief that material can be its own decoration.

6 Touff-Bershof House
47 S. Ash Street
Victor Hornbein, 1958; renovation by Oz Architecture, 1995

Compact in scale and harmonious in proportions, this residence stresses the horizontal planes popular in the era in which Victor Hornbein worked. Clerestory windows that wrap one end of the building allow for illumination, while overhangs help protect the interior with shade.

7 Groves House
330 Birch Street
Eugene G. Groves, 1938

Architect Eugene G. Groves mixed traditional residential design with a bent for Modernism in residential and commercial work that often incorporated poured and cast concrete. His home is a stellar example of his use of this material: Fluted columns, a bay window on the semicircular front room, a tile-surrounded dome, and curvy balusters on the exterior staircase are among the notable details found in this quirky home.

8 Sandler House
220 S. Birch Street
Joseph Marlow, 1954

Joseph Marlow and his wife, Louise, gained fame in the area for their compact Modernist residences, and the mid-1950s Sandler House shows why. A glass box for living is elevated over lower-level service and entry space. The upper deck provides both a wrap for the box and an impression of greater size through an extended horizontal line.

9 Kohn-Neusteter House
1 Eudora Street
Victor Hornbein, 1947

This heavily landscaped home is also a presence on E. Ellsworth Avenue, and its distinguished lines continue on all visible sides. A bold roofline and

expansive windows mark this Victor Hornbein project, which stands out for its elegant proportions.

10 Millman House
275 S. Eudora Street
Aaron G. Green, 1955

San Francisco–based architect Aaron G. Green worked in the long, low ranch style that dots the neighborhood. Fronted by stone entry piers, the most striking characteristic of his design is a horizontal row of seven generous windows to one side, in effect stretching the building visually as well as in form.

11 Joshel House
220 S. Dahlia Street
Joseph and Louise Marlow, 1950

A carport and roof appear to wrap around this home's lower level, constructed of pale brick, but an exterior glass and louvered wall to the south adds light and a spacious air to the design, which produced one of the top International Style residences in Denver. After the owner's death, a large-scale sculpture by Anthony Magar was moved to Burns Park for installation.
Denver Landmark, National Register

12 Rothenberg House
145 Dexter Street
Ream, Quinn, and Associates, 1967

In a heavily wooded setting, the Rothenberg House stands out for its play of horizontal and vertical elements – especially the latter, emphasized by wood siding as well as a variety of windows and porches. In some respects, the home is a cross between a chalet and the 1960s spin on Modernism.

13 Marvin Hatami House
142 Dexter Street
Marvin Hatami, 1991

Built in the 1950s, this home 40 years later was completely remade by architect Marvin Hatami. The home was a pioneering effort: Not only did the architect choose to proceed with a severe interpretation of planes, vertical forms (especially the striking "canopy"), and window grids, he also used synthetic stucco, not yet in as wide a currency as today. It's an update that holds its own.

14 The George Cranmer House and Cranmer Park
200 Cherry Street
Jacques J.B. Benedict, 1917

Jacques Benedict's design skills were almost like a stylistically eclectic grabbag, since he drew on French and Tudor elements in some projects, Italian and Spanish in others. For the Cranmer house, Benedict produced an Italian Renaissance Revival mansion with Spanish touches. The floor plan uses a long gallery hall to link major rooms – the dining room to the north, a sun room to the south – and to open onto a back courtyard. (Upstairs, the rooms are in more of a maze, with varying ceiling heights calculated to fit the proportions of the room.)

The stucco exterior, topped by a low, hipped tile roof, includes decorations such as a cartouche-topped doorframe and Classical arches. To one side of the entry is an open arcade, to the other a Palladian window.

The house fronts on what is now called Cranmer Park, testament to the original owner's role as head of the city's parks system. Mrs. Cranmer was active with the city's orchestra, and musicians often practiced in the home's high-ceilinged music/living room. The park, anchored by a large stone sundial, is a landmark in the Hilltop neighborhood.
National Register, Denver Landmark

15 Graland Country Day School / Anschutz Commons
30 Birch Street
Various architects, including Victor Hornbein; Anschutz Commons,
Semple Brown Design, 2010

This prestigious private K–8 school began in the mid-1920s on a campus that grew to be as gracious and well-designed as the homes that lined Cranmer Park just to the north. Although the community lost the original building, designed by Jacques Benedict, newer buildings have attempted to find compatibility with his mix of late Beaux Arts elegance and the American-born Prairie style. Among the most successful is the Anschutz Commons building, which houses a dining hall and student areas. Notable features are a south wall featuring expansive areas of glass and broad overhangs that integrate the structure into the overall campus aesthetic. The building is slated for LEED Gold certification.

16 Temple Emanuel
51 Grape Street
Percival Goodman, 1959, addition by Barker Rinker Seacat, 1990

When Denver's Jewish community began its move to east Denver, religious institutions followed. Among them was the congregation of Temple Emanuel, which left its Moorish building on Capitol Hill for a brick and stone complex whose most notable feature is a crown-shaped roof inset with stunning stained glass and topped by a smaller crown.

New York architect Percival Goodman used stone to lend a regional sensibility to the building and serve as an almost neutral backdrop for the colorful glass

purchased in Europe. An addition shortly after construction stressed the International Style in its design. A 1990 addition employed dark red brick in a diamond pattern with vertical windows to both refer to the older structure and differentiate itself from it.

17 Law House
139 Glencoe Street
Steve Chucovich, 2011

Many infill projects in Hilltop (and other Denver neighborhoods) strive for the clean lines of Neomodernism, only to lose that goal in a welter of fussiness and badly integrated materials. That is not the case with this long, low home in which horizontal forms, and the contrast between light and dark materials (stone, metal, glass), come together in a harmonious whole. This serene residence serves as a model of restraint, resulting in an intriguing composition that is as honest as it is elegant.

18 Hannah Evans House
60 Kearney Street
OZ Architecture, 2003

Another example of discipline in design, the Evans home is a beacon in the Crestmoor neighborhood to the east of Hilltop. Strong geometric forms, telling window details, and practical aspects come together to produce a winning example of Neomodernism.
Colorado AIA Merit Award, 2002

19 Four Mile House
715 S. Forest Street
Vernacular architecture, begun in 1859

Travelers to the early settlement of Denver moved slowly, and needed sustenance along the way. Four Mile House, now part of a larger park open to the public, helps today's residents and visitors get an idea of what life was like on a frontier in the process of turning into an urban center. The Brantner Brothers' operation was in a remote location in those days, but is now part of the fabric of east Denver. The city purchased the home in the mid-1970s, restored it, and opened the historic site to the public in 1978.
National Register, Denver Landmark

Cherry Creek

The old town of Harman is merely a memory, recalled by a former city hall that has been returned to its original brick appearance but turned into a residence enhanced by a sensitive contemporary addition. Most of the remaining "old" Cherry Creek neighborhood, however, is now long gone.

Much hand-wringing and debate accompanied the changes and challenges that Cherry Creek North faced over the past two decades. Yet this convenient mix of retail and residential has spurred some well-designed developments and homes. True, some of the cottages were scraped to be replaced by faux chalets and pseudo-Tuscan villas. But a Neomodernist spirit lives here, in prominent buildings on East 1st Avenue and several private residences that stand out for their commitment to fine design. Like the Highlands neighborhood, Cherry Creek has changed, but without the damaging scars that growing pains have left on other neighborhoods, such as Hilltop.

The change really began when architect and developer Temple Buell decided to turn a Denver city dump into a shopping center. In the late 1940s, the construction of Cherry Creek Shopping Center propelled the construction of a pedestrian-friendly, human-scale shopping district to the north. The move brought retail and commercial services to the many blocks of tidy brick cottages.

After completion of a new and expanded Cherry Creek Shopping Center in 1990, a boom economy produced a new wave of development and new plans that recognized the neighborhood as an area of change – and a desirable one at that. Cottages disappeared, some replaced by mega-townhomes and residential clusters. Though many small retail concerns remain, and several new stores show adventurous design, other structures – such as Buell's fine Modernist Sears store – were renovated into bland, could-be-anywhere buildings. New development continues, this time seeking to push up, not out, with proposals for new high-rises in contrast to the neighborhood's prevailing scale.

The old neighborhood by the dump has become a place for which the word "posh" was coined, and where change has become a constant for residents and visitors alike.

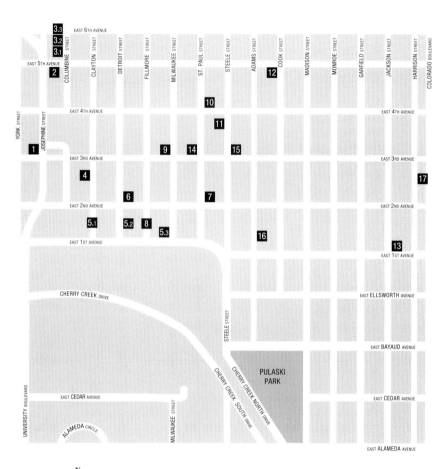

LIST OF BUILDINGS

1	Hillstone Restaurant	**10**	Harman Hall
2	The Carriage Houses	**11**	375 Steele Street
3	Columbine Street Homes	**12**	Yale Residence
3.1	Poli House	**13**	100 Jackson
3.2	557 Columbine Street	**14**	The Shops
3.3	Ooms House	**15**	3201 E. 3rd Avenue
4	255 Clayton Street	**16**	Monigle Associates
5	East 1st Avenue Developments	**17**	Harrison Townhomes
5.1	Clayton Lane development		
5.2	North Creek		
5.3	Pura Vida / One Fillmore Place		
6	Room and Board Remodel		
7	Cherry Creek Medical Building		
8	Cherry Creek North Streetscape and Fillmore Plaza Updates		
9	Ross Cherry Creek Branch Library		

1 Hillstone Restaurant
303 Josephine Street
Frederick Fisher and Partners of Los Angeles, with William J. Hinkley
Architects of Aurora, 2009

Los Angeles–based Frederick Fisher and Partners has completed several restaurant designs for the Hillstone Restaurant Group, and the one in Denver hews to the contemporary aesthetic taking hold in Cherry Creek North. Serving as somewhat of a link between residential and commercial aspects of the neighborhood, the design is rooted in the interplay of wood and glass, fronted by a louvered screen made of perforated copper panels. The restaurant's open sensibility and mix of horizontal and vertical planes aims for the sophistication that marks the best of new design in the neighborhood.

2 The Carriage Houses
450 Josephine Street, 2450 E. 5th Avenue, and 449 Columbine Street
Donald Roark, 1974

Long before the wave of townhome construction in Cherry Creek, architect Donald Roark designed these Carriage Houses, which put their front doors on the street in an arrangement that rounds a block near Bromwell School. Roark mixed brick, wood, and concrete for his low-rise units, and in a tradeoff with the city, was allowed to build more densely because he dedicated some of the block to open space. After 35 years, his low-key design remains timeless.

3 Columbine Street Homes
Subtle yet distinctive contemporary design is evident in a trio of homes on the 500 block of Columbine Street.

3.1 – Poli House, 553 Columbine Street, Joseph Poli, 2004: Architect Joseph Poli used the interplay of angles and materials (including wood) to create a home that has the sense of a retreat. A canted third level accentuates the home's sense of verticality, while a pathway from sidewalk to entry stresses the impression of privacy.

3.2 – 557 Columbine Street, Bothwell Davis George, 2006: This firm's designs for residential infill have created a near template for massing and volume throughout the metro area, as shown in a home that achieves its own vertical stretch.
AIA Colorado Young Architects Honorable Mention, 2009

3.3 – Ooms House, 561 Columbine Street, Frank Ooms, 1998: Architect and architectural photographer Frank Ooms chose to give his residence the very basic form of a Monopoly game house, dominated by a huge grid window that connects it to the outdoors.

4 — 255 Clayton Street
Saiber Saiber Architecture Inc., 2005

This development fronts the street with a curtain wall of honed limestone; zinc paneling covers the other elevations, introducing an unusual, even playful mix of materials into the Cherry Creek landscape. The firm's offices are located here, as is the penthouse-style home of the head of the firm.

5 — East 1st Avenue Developments

Another trio of buildings also raised the bar for design in Cherry Creek North, anchoring a prominent stretch of busy East 1st Avenue. The placement of each project helps link the avenue to East 2nd Avenue and bring interest to the cross streets.

5.1 – Clayton Lane development, Tryba Architects, RNL Design, studioINSITE, 2005: Urbanity was the goal of this mixed-use and multistructure project, which brings together a hotel, retail, residential, and office space – all clustered around a new, narrow, one-lane stretch of what is now called Clayton Lane. In replacing a parking lot, the Clayton Lane development also filled in the city street grid in this part of the neighborhood. As with the other buildings in this row, the materials utilized in Clayton Lane are, for the most part, honest, and wisely used as counterpoints and accents to bring Neomodern design into the most visible part of the neighborhood. Careful massing creates a connection to the updated (but not improved) Sears store, and incorporates a large parking structure; *AIA Colorado Merit Award, 2004 (RNL Design, Clayton Lane Parking Structure). AIA Denver Honor Award, 2007 (Tryba Architects, Clayton Lane)*

5.2 – North Creek, 100 Detroit Street, Humphries Poli Architects, E. 1st Avenue at Detroit Street, 2009: Another mixed-use project, and the middle entry in this trifecta, North Creek concentrates on various types of high-end residential and retail, sparked by the imaginative use of sandstone and glass. The residential block features prominent balconies and open space, while the retail offers a dramatically designed street-level element that resembles a hemicycle. In a sense, it plays off the west facade of the development, a sweeping curve of windows set in a broad, metal grid.

5.3 – Pura Vida / One Fillmore Place, 2955 E. 1st Avenue, Gensler, with Semple Brown Design, 2008: For years the stodgy mid-rise building at this location was remarkable only for being the home of the main Tattered Cover (apparently in an earlier life, it was a Modernist landmark that suffered from an unsympathetic renovation in the 1970s). Through the work of Gensler, and interior design by Semple Brown, the building lives again, through a new curtain wall of glass panels that make it one of the sleekest structures in town. *AIA Colorado Citation Award, 2009; AIA Denver Merit Award, 2009 (Gensler, One Fillmore Place)*

6 Room and Board Remodel
222 Detroit Street
Roth Sheppard Architects, 2001

This upgrade and reconfiguration was designed as more than a new coat for a longtime Cherry Creek retail outlet; Roth Sheppard, known for its talent at creating clean lines and using interesting mixes of materials, produced an exterior that speaks to the personality of the furnishings and accessories sold inside. The store appears to be built around a cube, with plentiful glass, stone, zinc, and elements (wood columns and deep overhangs) that give the building a Prairie flavor. A general opening up of the building helped set a tone for later commercial design in the district, where light and air speak as firmly as traditional brick and concrete.

7 Cherry Creek Medical Building
215 St. Paul Street
Sexton Lawton Architecture, 2011

Rather than a predictable scrape-off and infill project, Sexton Lawton instead renovated an existing 1980s three-story brick office building into a model of transparency. This unexpected side street building includes a glass fin window system of different opacities of glass. A glass tower marks the building's penthouse area and is lighted at night, adding to the drama of a hidden gem in the district.
AIA Colorado Honor Award, 2011; AIA Denver Merit Award, 2011

8 Cherry Creek Streetscape and Fillmore Plaza Updates
Fillmore Street between East 1st and East 2nd Avenues
Design Workshop, Communications Arts, 2011

After years of discussion, many meetings, and a fair share of disagreement, Fillmore Plaza was reconfigured from pure pedestrian mall to a mix that accommodates those on foot and those driving. With a rich mix of colors used in cobblestone-like pavers, little grass, and a generous number of planters, this one-block plaza has become the front yard for updated and upgraded buildings and retail operations. The streetscape improvements brought new street signs, banners, directories, and street furniture that send the message that the wealthy are, indeed, different from you and me. The $18.5 million district-wide streetscape renovation – motto: The New North – was paid for by members of the Cherry Creek North Business Improvement District through the sale of bonds.

9 Ross Cherry Creek Branch Library
305 Milwaukee Street
Michael Brendle Associates,1993, renovation, Studiotrope, 2010
(original building: Paul Reddy, 1961)

Paul Reddy's Modernist cube gave way to Postmodernism and a whiff of Deconstruction during a renovation and addition designed by Michael Brendle Associates. Glass brick walls, exposed ornamental trusses, bold dashes of color, and references to complicated grid systems added a jazzy touch to the neighborhood.

A serene box became an art piece during the process of enlarging this branch library. *AIA Colorado Design Award, 1993; Western Mountain Region Award for excellence, 1994*

10 Harman Hall
400 St. Paul Street
Historic building attributed to Kidder and Humphreys, 1890;
addition Semple Brown Design, 2009

Built in 1890 as the town hall of the town of Harman (soon annexed by the city of Denver), the structure served various uses until it became the Lawrence N. Greenleaf Masonic Temple in the 1930s. At some point, the brick structure was stuccoed, had its windows altered, and underwent interior changes. When the Masons decided to sell the building, some feared that whoever bought the old Harman Hall would scrape it for development. Instead, a sympathetic developer purchased the property, with plans to turn the site into two townhomes, to a plan by Semple Brown Design that stripped off the stucco and added a portion that relied heavily on glass and clean, contemporary lines.

That deal fell through for legal reasons, and the building went into foreclosure. Harman Hall eventually was sold to a new owner who concentrated on turning the landmark into a single-family residence. The stucco came off, revealing a red brick building with a graceful civic presence. The additions, which expanded the structure on two sides and on top, remain the work of Semple Brown, which for the most part designed an almost recessive expansion to a rare historic structure in Cherry Creek. A predominantly glass connector links old to new, maximizing the property while leaving the old as the centerpiece – a fitting blend of the historic and the contemporary.
Denver Landmark

11 375 Steele Street
Semple Brown Design, 2005

A large corner lot gave the architects plenty of room to experiment with different materials and surface treatments in a home that accents the horizontal line. From grid windows to gray panels and buff brick, this home turns the corner, while the sense of variety and rhythm continue. Stone orbs and other sculptural objects surround the building, adding to the accumulation of aesthetic cues.

12 Yale Residence
495 Cook Street
OZ Architecture, 2005

In a neighborhood filled with angles, the architects turned toward the curve to add street interest and invite controlled light into the interior of a home designed to showcase art. A wood frame supports a masonry veneer exterior, with some stucco accents. A copper roof blends with the neutral palette chosen for the home, where two segments of curved roof approach each other in a complementary fashion.

13 100 Jackson
Bothwell Davis George, 2008

High style Neomodern volumes and clean materials mark this office building on a prominent corner lot. Here, a second story clad in metal, and marked by a floating portion of the facade, shifts its position to hang over a first floor wrapped in wood and windows. The recessed and popped-out wall planes add rhythm and interest to the composition.

14 The Shops
3033–39 E. 3rd Avenue
Roth Sheppard Architects, 1994

Small but interesting retail buildings have been a hallmark of the shopping district, and this series of shops signaled the beginning of a new way to interpret that. The architects played with a mix of materials – stucco and slate, concrete and wood – in a design that tips out a portion of the facade and employs a roofline sunbreaker to create patterns on the building's facade. Inventive yet cohesive, this solution connects diverse retail establishments while involving them in the fabric of the streetscape.

15 3201 E. 3rd Avenue
Richard Crowther, 1974

This simple office block – designed to be connected to 310 Steele Street at the rear – appears to reflect in on itself, a composition that makes a commercial property almost a bridge between the street's retail strip and its residences to the east. Decades before the term "sustainable architecture" became popular, Denver architect Richard Crowther was a proponent of putting Colorado's abundant sunlight to work in the service of Modernist design.

16 Monigle Associates
150 Adams Street
Arley Rinehart Associates, 1998

This public relations and corporate branding firm built the first phase of its complex in 1982. As business grew, so did space needs: Monigle commissioned the new structure to the south, in which a brick building appears to be encased in a heavily detailed frame. Heavy computer use and other work requirements mandated small, carefully placed windows, a need that gives part of the complex a somewhat mysterious appearance. It is linked to, yet it does not mimic the older structure.

17 Harrison Townhomes
262–268 Harrison Street
Arquitectonica, 1984

Buildings by this Miami firm brightened the Florida cityscape beginning in the late '70s, and became almost a point of reference on the old *Miami Vice* television series. For its only Denver outing, Arquitectonica (Bernardo Fort-Breschia) designed four townhomes with windows in witty shapes, from flying triangles to amoebas. Glass block and the tubular railing evoke a look popular in ocean-side resort areas. Originally, the units were two shades of green, but after some consternation in the neighborhood, the homes were painted gray, with white accents. Of note: the bow windows more than 10 feet high on the Harrison Street facades.

Belcaro and South

Belcaro and Bonnie Brae are among Denver's most charming neighborhoods, areas that were laid out with curving streets, generous lots, and easy access to small parks that help anchor both communities. As with other older neighborhoods in Denver, though, there has been pressure to scrape and rebuild, sometimes with unfortunate results – mini-mansions that do not reflect the authentic appeal of a mix of traditional and Modern residential architecture.

Farther south, the University of Denver is a strong presence in Denver, located in a busy area of residential and commercial development. DU grew free-form over the years until an ambitious – and committed – chancellor sought the services of an architect who had a vision to organize the campus, adding new buildings that are imposing but that reflect a singular style constructed out of honest materials. Since that architect left the post, the campus style has grown more traditional in nature.

LIST OF BUILDINGS

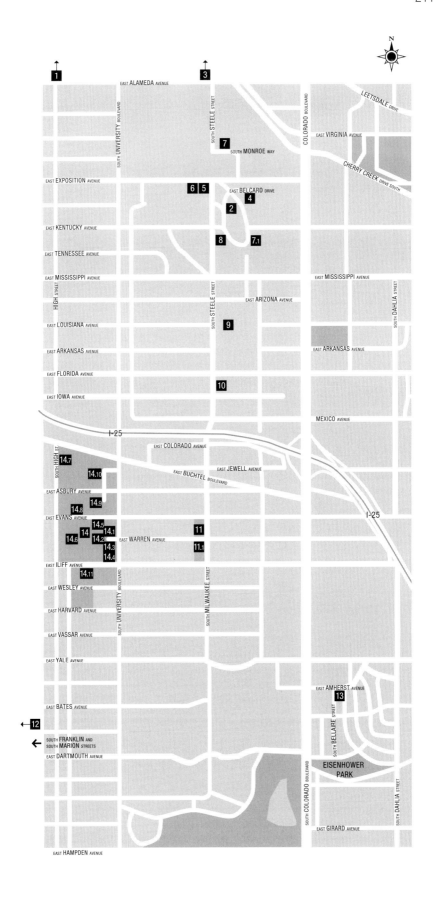

1 **The Weckbaugh Mansion**
   1701 E. Cedar Avenue
   Jacques J.B. Benedict, 1933

Constructed by Mrs. Ella Mullen Weckbaugh during the Depression era, this home wears a French Provincial veneer on its magisterial frame.

The mansion, with marble and travertine trim from Alabama, Georgia, and Italy, includes 25 rooms spread over two and a half stories. A steep slate roof ambles over a five-sided tower and around balconies, and gabled and round dormers. Four Tiffany windows are part of the assemblage. Mrs. Weckbaugh moved here from a 1908 mansion at 450 E. 9th Avenue.
National Register

2 **Paul Kobey House**
   800 S. Adams Street
   William Muchow, 1985

Architect William Muchow's hands can be detected throughout the neighborhoods south of downtown Denver, in homes that reflect a Modern sensibility while meshing with the landscape. This is true of this well-composed home, which appears as two parts: a section that references the A-frame style, with a dramatic wall of windows, and a horizontal portion that shows a Prairie influence in a roofline that seems to protect the home in more ways than one. Two windows are punched into this dramatic roof, helping to form a connection between someone disparate components.

3 **Cherry Creek Towers**
   3100 Cherry Creek Drive South
   Carl F. Groos and J. O'Neil Ford, with consultant Mardi Buell Groos, 1962

The Groos-Ford tower is the prototypical apartment high-rise, fighting to make constricted living as open as possible with sheltered, screened terraces for each apartment. The strong verticality of its aluminum window-wall construction and its linear planning in reinforced concrete combine to give the exterior an amazing sense of airiness, despite the fact that many people have enclosed their balconies to add extra year-round living space.

4 **The Phipps Mansion (Belcaro) and Tennis Pavilion**
   3400 Belcaro Drive
   Fisher and Fisher, with Charles Platt, 1932

This estate of 54 rooms on eight acres – plus a grand, armory-like tennis house – was completed in 1933 as the residence of Senator and Mrs. Lawrence C. Phipps. The late Georgian Revival mansion is clad in hand-pressed, sand-molded brick and dressed Indiana limestone.

Two subtle design tricks keep Belcaro from being outlandish: Quoined corners add a sense of restraint, and the home's front bays alternate foreground and background placement. Three windows capped by keystones top the entry bay's second story, then the house unfolds in sets of two windows per floor per bay. The central corridor is of travertine.

After Phipps died in 1958, his widow bequeathed the estate to the University of Denver for use as a conference center. In 2010, DU put the mansion and equally imposing tennis pavilion on the market. The property was purchased by an area businessman and philanthropist aiming to restore it to its original use as a private residence. Former senator Phipps platted the neighborhood through his Belcaro Realty Co. Nearby are homes of two other members of the Phipps family: the Allan R. Phipps residence, at 885 S. Garfield Street, and the Gerald H. Phipps residence, at 801 S. Adams Street. Both were designed by Lester E. Varian. *National Register, Denver Landmark*

5   Burnham Hoyt House and Studio
3130 E. Exposition Avenue
Burnham Hoyt, 1947

Architect Burnham Hoyt lived and worked in a structure that reflected the aesthetic principles he applied to other projects: proper massing and proportions, a relationship to the land and natural light, and a strong sense of the horizontal complemented by other geometric elements. Located on a busy east-west street, this residence exists as a reminder of Hoyt's expertise at finding the essence of the International Style while retaining the sense of home.

6   Arndt House
3100 E. Exposition Avenue
Thomas Moore, 1938

Next door to the Hoyt House and Studio, the Arndt House reflects design cues from an earlier decade, including architect Thomas Moore's use of glass block in a curved second floor element near the entry. Built on a slight rise off the street, the Arndt House also displays the clean lines that signal the coming of a more simple and sleek approach to domestic architecture popular in this neighborhood.

7   William Muchow House
618 S. Monroe Way
William Muchow, 1954

Architect William Muchow left an unforgettable legacy to Denver, both through his own work as a commercial and residential designer and his firm's role as an enterprise that nurtured other talent.

For his own home, in the area known as Cherry Creek South, Muchow helped define his approach to Modernism. In a style inspired by the A-frame, Muchow relied on soaring glass walls to extend the link between interior and exterior

space, with broad overhangs to provide shade. This relationship to light extends to a skyline that runs the spine of the steeply pitched roof to flood the inside with daylight. For all its openness, the home is protected by a brick wall at the front that adds interest while remaining a practical addition to the composition.

Other residential designs by William Muchow in the surrounding neighborhoods include:

7.1 – Schlaijker House / Woodward Hall House, 3446 E. East Kentucky Avenue, 1954: Like its neighbor, this home stretches across a broad lot, creating a strong, but human-scale presence in the neighborhood. A generous entry is marked by skylights; wings extend on either side for public and private spaces. Following the Usonian tradition, the home includes window walls that connect the interior to a well-landscaped yard to the rear. Farther to the south, 3112 and 3130 S. Monroe Street hail from the mid-1950s and emphasize the same design elements: horizontal lines, generous use of glass, the addition of hand-crafted elements, and abundant landscaping.

8   Wolf House
950 S. Steele Street
Steve Gale Architects, 2007

This newer entry to the neighborhood addresses how material and color can balance the concepts of contrast and harmony. With elements of blond brick, weathered metal, and deep blue-gray panels, the Wolf House explores how geometric forms can distinguish a home. The standout element may be a frosted glass balcony wall that attracts immediate attention to this home (and is reflected in the glass backboard of a basketball hoop below).

9   St. Thomas Seminary / John Paul II Center for the New Evangelization
1300 S. Steele Street 1908; St. Thomas Seminary Chapel / part of the John Paul II Center, Jacques J.B. Benedict, 1931, and the Holy Family of Nazareth Chapel of Redemptoris Mater Archdiocesan Missionary Seminary, Kiko Argüello, with Mattia del Prete and Bruce Larson, 2009

The original portion of this complex, the De Andreis House, reportedly was designed by a priest, Nicholas M.J. Steines, under the supervision of architect John J. Huddart.

Two decades later, Bishop John Henry Tihen commissioned architect Jacques Benedict to add to the complex. Among the structures Benedict designed were the chapel and the seminary, as well as the landmark Tihen Tower, a Renaissance beacon for the campus.

Benedict worked in a style termed Lombard, which draws on elements as disparate as Gothic and Romanesque. The use of multicolored and formed bricks gives the walls of this elaborate complex a mosaic effect, enhanced by numerous carvings and statues (the four 12-foot-high angels were created by Enrico Licari).

For years, St. Thomas was operated as a seminary by the Vincentian fathers, an order founded by St. Vincent de Paul. In the mid-1990s, the Archdiocese purchased the complex, renamed it in honor of Pope John Paul II, then moved the Pastoral Center there.

A decade later, Spanish architect Kiko Argüello added a new element to the campus: the octagon-shaped Holy Family of Nazareth Chapel of Redemptoris Mater Archdiocesan Missionary Seminary, which contributes a new form, but incorporates the red tile roof found campus-wide and the red brick of St. Thomas Seminary. The chapel's simple, strong lines culminate in a tower that lines up with the Tihen Tower constructed decades ago. The chapel features elaborate decoration inside built around large icons and a depiction of Christ the Pantocrator.
National Register

10 Cory Elementary School
1550 S. Steele Street
Victor Hornbein, 1952

Architect Victor Hornbein was among Denver's premier interpreters of Modern architecture, especially buildings that drew on the Prairie and International Styles. Such is true with Cory, which is a blond brick and glass assemblage of planes and overhangs, volumes that accentuate the school's horizontal appearance while not sacrificing Hornbein's compact Usonian arrangement of parts. The school was named for John J. Cory, principal of South High School and a district administrator.
Denver Landmark

11 Observatory Park
South Fillmore Street at Warren Avenue

A small open space set in the middle of a quiet neighborhood, Observatory Park serves to showcase the Chamberlin Observatory to the south. Though the park now is divided by Warren Avenue, continuity is achieved by rows of fir trees that dot both sections. Observatory Park is among several spaces set aside by early officials of the University of Denver.

11.1 – Chamberlin Observatory, 1930 E. Warren Avenue, Robert Roeschlaub, 1892: Robert Roeschlaub designed this structure for Humphrey B. Chamberlin, who gave it to the University of Denver. Though small, the building reportedly took three years to build. The architect set an iron dome atop a round red brick and rusticated stone building, then accented the silvery shape with bands of patterned brickwork at the roofline. At either end, he added small wings that offer a sense of stability. The generous entry features a stone surround with a rectangular entablature. The lens for the observatory was brought from New York by DU's then-arts and sciences dean Herbert Howe. The observatory still is operational, with public hours during astronomical events.
National Register, Denver Landmark

12 Arapahoe Acres
Bounded by East Bates and East Dartmouth Avenues, between South Marion and South Franklin Streets, Englewood
Eugene Sternberg and Edward Hawkins, 1949–1957

The nation's first 1950s residential development to be placed on the National Register is among the high points in terms of the area's architectural heritage. Postwar suburbs were supposed to be the answer to a nation's housing nightmare, but too often the promise of well-designed, well-built homes was lost to speed and greed. Not here.

Builder Edward Hawkins and architect Eugene Sternberg worked together to plot a neighborhood that eventually grew to more than 120 homes. Sternberg laid out the site and designed homes along Marion Street, but then he and Hawkins parted ways. Their planning, though, demonstrated that intelligently crafted spaces, fine materials, and flowing landscaping could unite an area and provide aesthetically pleasing housing.

Arapahoe Acres follows one typical suburban style note – it is set off the grid, on curved streets – but from there all similarity ends. Homes in Arapahoe Acres ranged in size from very small to expansive, but never lost sight of Wright's Usonian ideal involving space and composition.

Horizontal planes are accented, with rooflines that range from butterfly shaped to rectangular, often with overhangs that shelter upper levels or carports. Rather than present a fixed selection of cookie-cutter designs, the builders melded each home's footprint to the site, allowing for individual appearance as well as landscaping that continued from lot to lot. Driveways exist, but are grouped to downplay the interruption. Sun and shade both play a role, as the homes showcase both a public face and a recognition of the need for privacy.
National Register

13 Ross-University Hills Branch Library
4310 E. Amherst Avenue
Michael Brendle, 1995; reconstruction of a 1963 building by Alfred Watts Grant

Architect Michael Brendle's taste for Deconstruction, demonstrated in the explosion of the Cherry Creek Branch Library, continued at University Hills. His commission doubled the size of the existing library, while turning a busy branch in a quiet neighborhood into a colorful collision of shapes and materials.

Though the basic design of the library is a long, low structure, Brendle moved out of the box by creating a glass box and hoisting it into the air. Designed to house a conference room, the cube-like element hangs up along a bridge section of the building. The length of the library is accentuated by a red metal "prow" that comes to a point at one end. Most of the structure mixes more neutral corrugated metal and glass.

14 **The University of Denver**
   2199 S. University Boulevard

Though Colorado's first institution of higher education was founded in 1864 as Colorado Seminary, the construction of a campus along South University Boulevard did not begin until much later.

The private school with a Methodist affiliation first had to be reborn as the University of Denver. Over a century, the school grew in waves, as reflected by an incredible amount of architectural diversity on the University Park campus. Diversity? Some might say hodgepodge, since unlike the University of Colorado at Boulder, no one strong design sense took hold until decades later. Richardsonian Romanesque, Gothic, Modern, Brutalism – they're all there, represented by some buildings more distinctive than others.

Various master plans were created over the years, including one in the late 1950s in which the firm of Perkins & Will was charged with creating an integrated campus, a move that led to a somewhat consistent stylistic construction program in the mid-1960s. In the mid-1990s, school officials again looked for a plan: Under Chancellor Daniel Ritchie, architect Cabell Childress began to oversee the design of several buildings – big, elaborate structures that use materials of quality, in quantity – that will set the tone of the campus for years to come. In the year 2000, Childress took on emeritus status and was succeeded by Mark Rodgers, who has introduced more traditional elements into buildings constructed during his tenure.

14.1 – University Hall / Old Main, Robert Roeschlaub, 1890: Noted architect Robert Roeschlaub used gray-pink rhyolite for this particular all-purpose hall, with the requisite Romanesque arches and rusticated charm. The campus's debut building is topped off by an imposing tower. (To the northeast of Old Main is one of the campus's newer buildings, the 2000 Daniels College of Business, by Anderson Mason Dale Architects with Cabell Childress.)

14.2 – Mary Reed Library / Mary Reed Building, Harry J. Manning, 1932: This is arguably the most "academic" building on campus. Architect Harry Manning worked in a full-blown Collegiate Gothic style, using deep rose brick in various patterns as a backdrop for stone window surrounds and quatrefoil detailing. The building itself is reinforced concrete, a sturdiness belied by the tracery of the limestone across its broad facade.

14.3 – Iliff Hall, attributed to Frank Edbrooke, 1892: The stylistic shifts continue with the second building on the University Park campus: the bright red sandstone structure that was the first building at the Iliff School of Theology. For this religious component of the university, the architect worked in Romanesque forms with a welter of window stylings. (Iliff later split from DU, then briefly closed, and has been a separate entity since its reopening in 1910.) Now Iliff Hall, the building shows its ecclesiastical heritage with cruciform finials perched on its gables, a companion in age, if not in style, to the old University Hall.

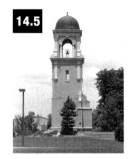

14.4 – Iliff School of Theology, Lamar Kelsey Associates, 1981: Yet another style is seen in this contemporary rendering of a religious institution. Connected to Iliff Hall by a glass walkway, the new Iliff building is a multisided structure in red brick, opened up by large circular windows. Its roof is notable for rising in the center to a spine that bisects the building.
AIA Colorado Citation, 1982

14.5 – Buchtel Tower, Thomas Barber, 1917: The remains of the Buchtel Memorial Chapel stand behind one corner of University Hall. The tower is what was saved of the Moorish Baroque structure after a fire in 1983. It has been restored, and presides over gardens nearby.

14.6 – Evans Memorial Chapel, architect not known, circa 1875–80: The Evans Memorial Chapel of Grace Methodist Church was moved to the campus in the late 1950s, around the time the University of Denver was constructing buildings near Civic Center for its short-lived downtown campus. The chapel, cleared from a corner at West 13th Avenue and Bannock Street to make room for a parking lot, had been built by John Evans in memory of his daughter. (Josephine Evans Elbert died in 1868.) The small Gothic Revival sandstone building was taken apart and then reassembled on campus and restored. It stands west of the gardens behind the Mary Reed Library/Mary Reed Building.
National Register, Denver Landmark

14.7 – Centennial Residence Tower, 1870 S. High Street, Perkins & Will Architects and Engineers, with Edwin A. Francis, 1963: From 1961–65, the university marked its centennial with a fund-raising campaign and building program. These mid-rise dorms were among the results. The architects created towers that were in a similar Modernist style but of different dimensions. Both, though, featured windows that appeared as vertical strips of glass, with broader glass insets at either end. (More expressive, perhaps, were other dorms built during that period, Francis's corrugated roof Johnson-McFarlane Residence Halls several blocks to the south.)

14.8 – William T. Driscoll Student Center, 2055 E. Evans Avenue, one block east of South Race Street, Michael Barber Architects, 1983: Architect Michael Barber built on an old residence hall to create a student center and bookstore, connected over East Evans Avenue by a stepped-up bridge clad in glass. The buildings themselves are fairly straightforward structures, designed for ease of use and an emphasis on glass walls and transparency to cut their bulk. Driscoll includes one of the few practical skybridges in Denver, since it keeps pedestrians out of harm's way on Evans Avenue below. The connection links the student center with Sturm Hall.

14.9 – Sturm Hall, 2000 E. Asbury Avenue, Perkins & Will Architects and Engineers, 1969: renovation by Root Rosenman Architects, 2000: Sturm Hall is the terminus of the bridge over East Evans Avenue from the William T. Driscoll Student Center, and a completely different style of building. This longtime classroom building depends on concrete and brick to articulate its clean, Modern

lines, adding an almost austere element to a campus that is growing increasingly complex in nature and use of materials. Sturm is a reminder of an era in which strong, simple architecture was the style favored by DU.

14.10 – Daniel L. Ritchie Center for Sports and Wellness, 2201 E. Asbury Avenue, Cabell Childress, with Davis Partnership, 1999: The buzz began
when the spire became visible on the horizon, a gold-covered steeple that signaled a massive building was about to be completed at DU. At about the same time, the school began running television commercials touting the building's materials: brick, limestone, copper, gold. It may be a first in the history of construction here.

The result is a mega-recreation and entertainment center squeezed into a space behind DU's old Shwayder Art Building. A swimming pool, several arenas, a health facility, a carillon, offices, donor amenities: The Ritchie Center is set in a complex of building shapes designed to recall an Italian village, albeit a mammoth village that can overwhelm its neighbors. Although the spire is the most notable piece of the equation – and noticeable far from campus – the architects' choice of copper for much of the skin is an intriguing element. Since completion, the metal has gained a brown, occasionally purple, patina – an odd juxtaposition with the more traditional red brick and limestone trim in other portions of the building.

14.11 – F.W. Olin Hall, 2190 E. Iliff Avenue, Cabell Childress, with Davis Partnership, 1997: University architect Cabell Childress wanted only the best
materials for buildings constructed during his term as DU's planner and designer. He also wanted each building to have a defining element that made it stand out on a campus that was growing increasingly "taller" as time went by. For Olin Hall, that element is an elliptical copper dome, using the material to link it to other new structures on the campus to the north. Olin, however, is a low-rise building that seems nestled into its site, a comfortable place that demonstrates the power of light – and lightness.

Country Club

One of Denver's most gracious neighborhoods once was home to a racetrack and recreation area designed for the delight of high rollers downtown.

But with the organization in 1901 of the actual Denver Country Club, south of East 1st Avenue, business interests looked toward turning the area to the north into a neighborhood of homes marked by elegance and taste. (The first club building, designed in 1904, is now gone, after several reconstructions and additions by various architects.)

Mayor Robert W. Speer was among those who invested in the Fourth Avenue Realty Co., which laid out and promoted Park Club Place and Country Club with an eye to Kansas City's own Country Club neighborhood. Park Club Place came first, in 1905, from Downing to Humboldt Streets, followed the next year by Country Club, from Humboldt to High Streets, then East 1st and East 4th Avenues form the north-south boundaries.

Architect William E. Fisher worked with real estate developer Frederick Ross to plat the broad streets of Country Club, and designed gateways and entrances. Fisher also was among the many architects of note in early 20th-century Denver to design homes in the district – including his own, at 110 Franklin Street. Yet there also are homes whose design cannot be traced to any architect.

Most of the homes in Country Club were built before 1940, though construction continues today, as new residents remodel and reinvigorate the fine old residences, along with the rare infill project. Many of the older homes hew to Mediterranean and Spanish Revival styles, in keeping with Fisher's choice for gateway designs. But wealthy Denverites building in Country Club looked to all corners for inspiration – French and Georgian, Tudor and chalet style, with a few modern designs woven in. Though purely residential, Country Club remains a neighborhood of architectural diversity in style, size, and density.

North of the historic district are more compact versions of the grand homes – residences designed by the Small House Bureau active here in the 1920s. The Bureau was the regional office of a national project sponsored by the American Institute of Architects; about a dozen area architects worked together during that decade to provide plans for jobs too small to engage one professional. Many of the homes are in the 400 block of Williams and Gilpin Streets.

Though not in Country Club proper, two apartment projects nearby are in sync with the refined tone of the district.

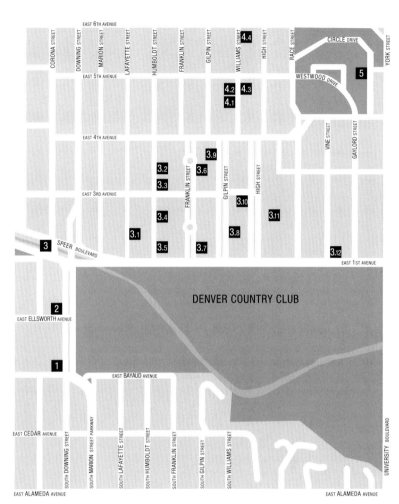

LIST OF BUILDINGS

1	Norman Apartments	**3.9**	Arthur House
2	Country Club Gardens	**3.10**	Tyson Dines–Mary Converse House
3	Speer Boulevard	**3.11**	Sudler House
3.1	McGowan House	**3.12**	McIntosh House
3.2	Biscoe / Hoover House	**4**	Williams Street Homes
3.3	Robert W. Speer House	**4.1**	457 Williams Street
3.4	Paul Atchison House	**4.2**	465 Williams Street
3.5	Charles L. Wellington House	**4.3**	464 Williams Street
3.6	Sheldon Residence	**4.4**	George P. Fackt House
3.7	William E. Fisher House	**5**	Verner Z. Reed House
3.8	Arthur Fisher House		

1   **Norman Apartments**
    99 S. Downing Street
    William Norman Bowman, 1924

This luxurious apartment building – since converted to condominiums – was named after its architect, who also designed the Colorado State Office Building near the Capitol and the old Mountain States Telephone Building downtown.

The Norman, in six stories of buff brick, manages to convey a feeling of park-side splendor, overlooking the portion of Downing Street that is a parkway through the neighborhood. The Norman's elaborate entry, flanked by glazed beige columns and touched by Colonial Revival decorative motifs, is at the south end of the facade – an asymmetrical touch to a building that sports two equally important parapets.
Denver Landmark

2   **Country Club Gardens**
    East Ellsworth Avenue between Ogden and Downing Streets
    Fisher, Fisher, and Hubbell, 1940

The Gardens complex was an experiment in modern group living: The project was financed by Denver investors, a syndicate of banks, and an FHA construction loan. In a group of five buildings spanning two city blocks, the architects strived to create modern apartments of quality design and construction.

The hallmark of the buildings is their brickwork, red and yellow-tan bands that accentuate the streamlined shapes. Although more than 60 years old, Country Club Gardens still has a futuristic feel, with clean lines and inventive angles. Also important in this complex is the inclusion of spacious courtyards and extensive landscaping – amenities that add social zest within and yet link the Gardens to its neighbors. (The project's landscape architect was M. Walter Pesman.)

As development pressure has grown in the area, however, County Club Gardens has faced proposals that could alter its landscaping and configuration, with the addition of residential towers and other challenges to the project's scale, massing, and integrity. Elaborate design guidelines were crafted in 2001 by a developer and the city's Landmark Preservation Commission, but have not yet been implemented.
Denver Landmark

3   **Speer Boulevard**
    West Colfax Avenue to Downing Street
    George Kessler and S.R. DeBoer, completed in 1918

Named after Denver mayor Robert W. Speer, the boulevard follows the Cherry Creek channel line. Conceived as a link between parks, Speer Boulevard also serves as an intelligent diagonal connector for the city, while forming an edge for various neighborhoods. Small triangles of parkland in turn give a sense of closure to the parkway, while linking it to several parks (Alamo Placita, Hungarian Freedom) to the side. Historic lampposts serve a practical as well as nostalgic role, and several bridges across Speer and Cherry Creek add functionality.
National Register District, Denver Landmark District

THE HOMES OF COUNTRY CLUB

The dozens of homes in Country Club hang together as a cohesive unit, though some in this historic district (National Register, Denver Landmark) are especially notable:

3.1 – McGowan House, 160 Lafayette Street, 1909: This Craftsman-style home has the presence of a chalet, marked by brackets and decorative wood trim.

3.2 – Biscoe / Hoover House, 320 Humboldt Street, Maurice Biscoe, 1908: Architect Maurice Biscoe followed a Mediterranean style, executed in stucco, for his own residence, which conceals its size through an L-shaped section to the rear.

3.3 – Robert W. Speer House, 300 Humboldt Street, Marean & Norton, 1912: Denver's influential mayor, neighborhood developer, and civic booster commissioned a more eclectic home, memorable for massive bandsaw brackets under the hipped roof, a generous porch, and all-seeing eyebrow windows.

3.4 – Paul Atchison House, 160 Humboldt Street, Paul Atchison, 1956: As construction in the neighborhood continued after the war, architect Paul Atchison ventured into a more Modern style, designing a home with deep eaves and a strong horizontal sensibility. A later upper-level addition is set back just far enough to harmonize with the original home.

3.5 – Charles L. Wellington House, 100 Humboldt Street, Maurice Biscoe and Henry Hewitt, 1910: Biscoe and Hewitt pursued the neighborhood's overarching Mediterranean impulse, with a slight shift. The two-story stucco home with fine detailing is anchored by a corner tower topped by a conical roof. Historians note that the L-shaped home was designed around a tree, which has not survived.

3.6 – Sheldon Residence, 350 Franklin Street, David Owen Tryba, 1995: This home stands as a sign that contemporary development reached out to Country Club. Architect David Tryba drew upon the neighborhood's reliance on fine materials and workmanship to create a home in an L-shape that conceals a courtyard between the house and nearby garage. Large expanses of glass are isolated, while the home's front facade is marked by sturdy but simple columns and a second story covered in wood shingles.
AIA Denver Citation Award for Design Excellence, 1995

3.7 – William E. Fisher House, 110 Franklin Street, William Fisher, 1910: Architect and neighborhood planner William E. Fisher designed his home to reflect an Italian style, in two stories of stucco with a red tile roof, and decorative eave brackets. The single-story porch is supported by columns and topped with a balustrade. Entry is off the driveway.

3.8 – Arthur Fisher House, 128 Gilpin Street, Arthur Fisher, 1909: Architect Arthur Fisher, brother of William E. Fisher, chose a mix of Tudor and English cottage elements for his home. Red brick quoins and trim, and half-timbering are set against stucco in a residence that plays grandeur off simplicity.

3.9 – Arthur House, 355 Gilpin Street, Jacques J.B. Benedict, 1932: Jacques J.B. Benedict worked elements of the era's popular Moderne style into a home with a simple travertine door surround but extravagant interpretations of oriel windows. The latter come to a point, balancing either side of a home whose horizontal strength is accented by a course of stone between the first and second stories.

3.10 – Tyson Dines–Mary Converse House, 195 High Street, Frederick Harnois, 1912: If the Small House Bureau lived up to its name, the Dines-Converse House aimed for grandeur. Spanish inspired, this sweeping stucco confection is marked by elaborate decoration based on the motifs of fruit and the ram's head.

3.11 – Sudler House, 180 High Street, James Sudler Associates, 1976: Known for contemporary designs including the Denver Art Museum, architect James Sudler turned his attention to residential projects for his own home and that next door. The Sudler home, with solar panels, follows a contemporary plan with Mediterranean elements in keeping with the neighborhood. The Sudler House, which has been reconstructed, is tucked behind a larger home to the front.

3.12 – McIntosh House, 100 Vine Street, Temple Hoyne Buell, 1929: Temple Buell, who distinguished himself in Denver as both an architect and a developer, worked in the French Chateau style for this manse at the entrance to Vine Street.

4 **Williams Street Homes**
West 4th Avenue Parkway

The one-block West 4th Avenue Parkway, planted before 1915, is among the many early Denver projects to extend parkland through a city facing the challenge of growing automobile traffic. As with many of the plans, it is difficult to credit any one landscape architect or park designer, though this parkway offered the familiar goal of shade from elms and pines. Eventually, detailed landscaping and mature trees throughout Country Club developed into a vital part of the ambiance.

North of East 4th Avenue, along Williams Street, the Small House Bureau made its mark in an area now known as Country Club North and the Driving Park Historic District, which turned from racing to residential development in the late 19th century. Notable residences include:

4.1 – 457 Williams Street, design attributed to Merrill and Burnham Hoyt: This well-massed stucco home has a Pueblo sensibility unusual in Denver.

4.2 – 465 Williams Street: This modest Small House Bureau design was elevated by the addition of a balustrade along the roofline. Sidelights also add interest to this compact residence.

4.3 – 464 Williams Street, design attributed to Varian & Varian: A massive tile roof anchors a stucco structure with Mediterranean aspirations.

4.4 – George P. Fackt House, 580 Williams Street, 1922: This home displays Italian Renaissance Revival stylistic elements rendered on a small scale, with arched windows and a shallow hipped roof.

05

5 **Verner Z. Reed House**
475 Circle Drive, where East 5th Avenue extends into Westwood Drive
Harry J. Manning, 1931

Though not technically part of Country Club, the sprawling Reed mansion presides over the neighborhood like the resident grande dame. As well it should. In what could be considered the most extravagant example of Tudor Revival in Denver, the Reed home is anchored by four towering chimneys that appear to float over the building's intricate tapestry brick walls. Nothing was too good for Mrs. Reed, whose beautiful home is trimmed in Indiana limestone and roofed in slate. Elaborate landscaping is attributed to the noted parks planner S.R. DeBoer.

Washington Park

Washington Park's solidly middle-class ambiance has made it one of the city's most attractive residential neighborhoods.

The anchor is Denver's most pastoral park, which teems with activity in all kinds of weather. Though Denver's parks are recognized for the quality of the structures they include, those inside Wash Park are particularly important to the neighborhood. They range from the Eugene Field House (moved there in 1930) to the sophisticated boathouse and bathhouse to stylish fire station to a more utilitarian recreation center. Mabel Landrum Torrey's statue *Wynken, Blynken and Nod,* has survived weather and vandalism since its installation in 1919 in the park.

Though homes of all sorts fill the Wash Park neighborhood, cottages and bungalows are the prevailing style, along with a few Victorians and more spacious contemporary residences. A hot economy put particular pressure on the Washington Park and Observatory Park area, leading to scrape-offs and pop-tops that threatened to destroy the character of the quiet streets and small business districts along South Pearl and South Gaylord Streets. Still, a few sensitively designed homes have been added to the mix, carefully preserving architectural integrity, scale, and neighbors' access to sunlight.

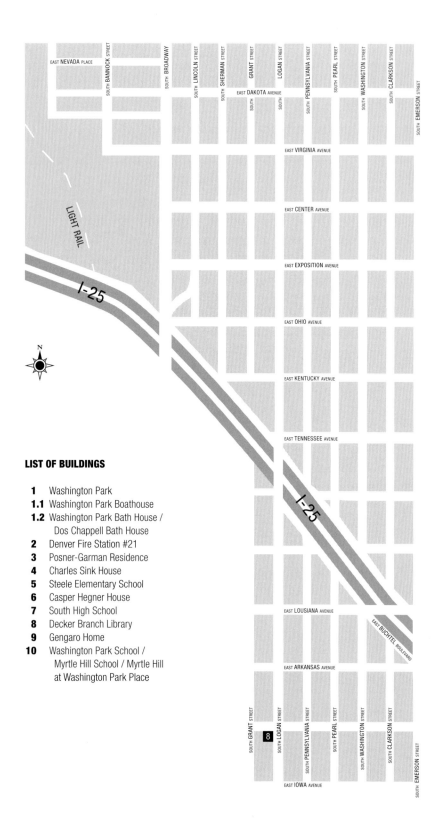

LIST OF BUILDINGS

1 Washington Park
1.1 Washington Park Boathouse
1.2 Washington Park Bath House /
Dos Chappell Bath House
2 Denver Fire Station #21
3 Posner-Garman Residence
4 Charles Sink House
5 Steele Elementary School
6 Casper Hegner House
7 South High School
8 Decker Branch Library
9 Gengaro Home
10 Washington Park School /
Myrtle Hill School / Myrtle Hill
at Washington Park Place

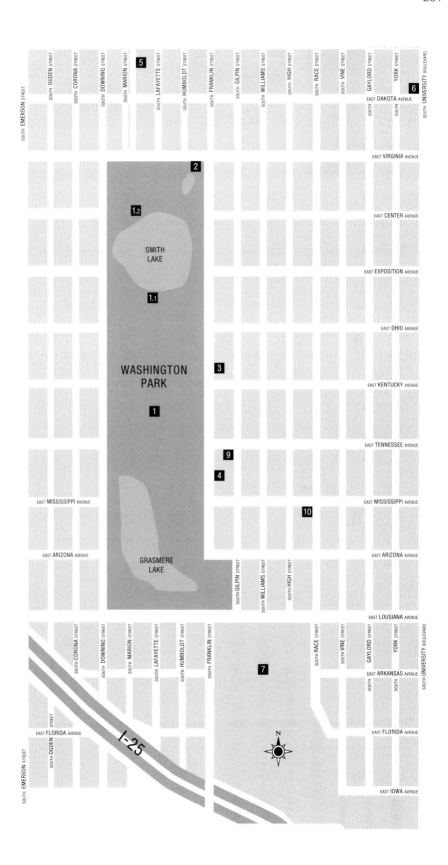

SOUTH EMERSON STREET
SOUTH OGDEN STREET
SOUTH CORONA STREET
SOUTH DOWNING STREET
SOUTH MARION STREET
SOUTH LAFAYETTE STREET
SOUTH HUMBOLDT STREET
SOUTH FRANKLIN STREET
SOUTH GILPIN STREET
SOUTH WILLIAMS STREET
SOUTH HIGH STREET
SOUTH RACE STREET
SOUTH VINE STREET
SOUTH GAYLORD STREET
SOUTH YORK STREET
SOUTH UNIVERSITY BOULEVARD

5
6

SOUTH EAST DAKOTA AVENUE
SOUTH

EAST VIRGINIA AVENUE

2

1.2

EAST CENTER AVENUE

SMITH
LAKE

EAST EXPOSITION AVENUE

1.1

EAST OHIO AVENUE

WASHINGTON
PARK

3

EAST KENTUCKY AVENUE

1

EAST TENNESSEE AVENUE

9

4

EAST MISSISSIPPI AVENUE
EAST MISSISSIPPI AVENUE

10

EAST ARIZONA AVENUE
EAST ARIZONA AVENUE

GRASMERE
LAKE

SOUTH GILPIN STREET
SOUTH WILLIAMS STREET
SOUTH HIGH STREET

EAST LOUSIANA AVENUE

SOUTH CORONA STREET
SOUTH DOWNING STREET
SOUTH MARION STREET
SOUTH LAFAYETTE STREET
SOUTH HUMBOLDT STREET
SOUTH FRANKLIN STREET
SOUTH RACE STREET
SOUTH VINE STREET
GAYLORD STREET
SOUTH YORK STREET
SOUTH UNIVERSITY BOULEVARD

7

EAST ARKANSAS AVENUE
SOUTH
SOUTH

SOUTH EMERSON STREET
SOUTH OGDEN STREET

SOUTH STREET
EAST FLORIDA AVENUE

EAST FLORIDA AVENUE

I-25

N

EAST IOWA AVENUE

1 Washington Park
Bounded by South Downing and South Franklin Streets,
between East Louisiana and East Virginia Avenues

Though platted for homes, the site was developed as a park in the late 1890s.
Two lakes are part of the park: Grasmere Lake to the south and Smith's Lake to
the north. They are joined to the much-celebrated source of the city's early growth –
the City Ditch, later Smith's Ditch, which wanders through the greensward and
meadow that dominate Washington Park and give it a certain bucolic character.
(The Ditch, surveyed and constructed between 1860 and 1867 by John W. Smith,
is both on the National Register and a Denver Landmark.)

Design of the park is attributed to Reinhard Schuetze, with input by S.R. DeBoer.
Gardens, picnic spots, and paths for joggers and cyclists take priority over the few
truncated roadways in the park. Upgrades have continued there for several years,
including reconfiguration of the running trails.
National Register

Three structures add an elegant air to the park and serve as community amenities.

1.1 – Washington Park Boathouse, Jacques J.B. Benedict, 1913: Jacques
J.B. Benedict worked in a wide array of styles to create elegant buildings throughout
Denver. In the boathouse he achieved a horizontal building that appears to hug
the south shore of Smith's Lake. Playing off the overall effect are tall, vertical
first-floor windows that reach to the water. Detailing at the cornice shows the
influence of the Arts and Crafts movement, while tile insets offer color to a
building that appears to melt into its surroundings. Restoration in the late 1980s
by Anthony Pellechia Associates helped bring the building and outdoor pavilion
back to life. Another restoration project was supported by Denver bonds and
the Denver organization the Park People.
Denver Landmark

**1.2 – Washington Park Bath House / Dos Chappell Bath House, Frederick
W. Ameter and James B. Hyder, 1911**: On the north side of the lake sits the
Bath House, which began as a place for swimmers to change, with boat storage
below. Those days are gone, and after a late 1990s renovation by Root Rosenman
Architects, the cottage-like house became offices in the newly named Dos
Chappell Bath House. The addition of restrooms and improved accessibility
was the goal of a 2011 city project with Andrews & Anderson Architects. More
work may be completed in a later phase.
Denver Landmark

2 Denver Fire Station #21
1500 E. Virginia Avenue
Arthur R. Siegried + Associates, 1974

This humanely scaled brick building with bright red doors perched at the
northeast corner of Washington Park looks more like a small church or a home
than a fire station. But that's the point: to integrate into the neighborhood a

civic building designed to handle nearby emergencies. The contextual elements of its quiet Modernist design combine to make this a building fitting for a park-like, neighborhood setting. The station's low-key design served as a template for other fire stations built during that era.

3 Posner-Garman Residence
880 S. Franklin Street
Philip and Susan Greenberg, 1980

The Greenbergs designed this residence to fit a narrow lot by building up and back. The home, in authentic stucco, sits far back on the lot to maximize views of the park across the street. The client wanted a private space to the south side of the house, while roll-up garage doors to the back allowed for easy entertaining. An upper-level row of clerestory windows atop the south wall afforded rewarding views – until a neighbor to the south added another story and made the expansive ribbon of glass appear cramped.

4 Charles Sink House
1050 S. Franklin Street
Charles Sink, 1986

Modernist architect Charles Sink also faced the challenge of a narrow city lot, a coveted piece of property facing the park. His solution was an almost geometric one, in which all aspects of the home followed the same degree of angle as the roofline – from the gate at the front to the slanted top of the chimney. Pale stucco lightens the structure. Changes since construction include the enclosure of an upper level balcony and the addition of helical stairs at one side.

5 Steele Elementary School
320 S. Marion Street
David W. Dryden, 1913; addition by Merrill and Burnham Hoyt, 1929

Among the landmarks of the Washington Park neighborhood, this school sports twin towers with festive tile decorative panels. At the roofline, brick is laid in a rick-rack pattern, while a frieze over the entry includes stylized chevrons and plumes. Dryden was the Denver Public Schools' second "school" architect, and his designs brought a spirited sensibility to the academic arena. The school is named after Robert W. Steele, a judge and territorial governor.
Denver Landmark

6   Casper Hegner House
2323 E. Dakota Avenue
Casper Hegner, 1935

Casper Hegner, a Denver architect known for the purity of his International Style designs (he was involved in City and County Annex One), took that tack when planning his own residence. Historians have suggested that this home is the first in the area to hew to the International Style. Finished in white stucco, the Hegner house is not quite stark but is devoid of applied decoration. It is lifted up and away from the street by a protective wall. Window placement accentuates the Home's wraparound horizontal design.

7   South High School
1700 E. Louisiana Avenue
Fisher and Fisher, 1926; additions by Charles Gordon Lee, 1963, and
by MCB Architects, 1988

South is probably the most exotic of the "compass point" schools, and in a way appears to be a tryout by the architects of a design used a year later in the B'nai B'rith Building at National Jewish Hospital.

For South, the Fishers worked in polychrome brick, with elaborate patterning and detailing that borrowed from Italian Renaissance and Moorish styles. The school's main building features a heavily bracketed tower and brickwork laid at the roofline in what seems to be repeated archways. Though the school is striking from any angle, the east facade is particularly imposing.

Sculptor Robert Garrison was commissioned to add artistic elements, including a rooftop griffin as well as animals and a bas relief that supposedly spoofs a faculty meeting.
Denver Landmark

8   Decker Branch Library
1501 S. Logan Street
Willis Marean and Albert Norton, 1913; renovation by David Owen Tryba
Architects, 1993

Reportedly modeled after Anne Hathaway's home in Stratford-on-Avon, the Decker Branch Library relies on brick and tile (not thatch) for its homey look. Bay windows, leaded glass, and split-beam construction give this V-shaped brick cottage a classical feel. A niched chimney wall outside is just one example of the architects' attention to detail, as is placement of the entry at the conjunction of the library's wings.

Located in James H. Platt Park, the branch library was constructed with Carnegie funds and named after Denver suffragette Sarah Platt Decker.
Denver Landmark

9 **Gengaro Home**
1001 S. Gilpin Street
Architect not known, circa 1925; addition by John Villa, 1991

Throughout the various sections of what is popularly called Wash Park, pop-tops and oversized infill has caused debate over how to preserve the scale and integrity of these charming neighborhoods. But in some cases, additions have been designed that respect the original home and its neighbors, through smart placement that renders the new living space either nearly invisible or seamlessly integrated.

That is the case with this home, a typical brick bungalow on which an addition has been placed toward the back of the roof and down the back of the home. In compatible neutral colors, the addition can be seen best from the rear of the home, which reveals new construction that was crafted with care, while doubling the living space. The lesson: Even on a small, traditional home – like a bungalow – an addition can be designed that works with the existing building, adding space without overpowering its surroundings.

10 **Washington Park School / Myrtle Hill School / Myrtle Hill at Washington Park Place**
1101 S. Race Street (Race at East Mississippi Avenue)
Harry J. Manning, 1928, as well as other additions; reconfiguration and additions, Studio K2 | Architecture, 2008

Many Washington Park residents were concerned when a developer announced plans to scrape part of historic Washington Park School to build numerous single family homes and townhomes. Although the school had been empty since owner Denver International School closed it in 2000, the remaining buildings were a landmark in the neighborhood.

After much discussion and debate, the developer and preservationists came to an agreement: The 1928 portion of the school would become lofts, and other sections would be demolished to create space for townhomes to the south; single-family homes were planned for South High Street. The result is a rejuvenated school, reconfigured for loft living while retaining the facade and many interior reminders of the school's former use. The adjoining townhomes are Neomodernist in style and materials, but hew to the verticality of the dignified remaining historic school – a solution that demonstrates that discussion and debate can pay off for developer and neighborhood alike.
Denver Landmark (as Myrtle Hill School)

Baker Neighborhood Historic District

Incorporating areas originally known as South Side and Broadway Terrace, the Baker neighborhood first emerged in the 1870s, although most of the actual development occurred from the 1880s through the 1920s.

As with many of Denver's founding fathers, one of the men who helped plat Baker had a finger in many economic pies: William Byers, who launched the now-defunct *Rocky Mountain News*, also dabbled in real estate – including this neighborhood. (It is named for a one-time principal of East High School and president of the University of Colorado who apparently never lived here but was honored by having his name affixed to a school in the district.)

Many of the houses in the large Baker Neighborhood Historic District are finely detailed Victorian and Queen Anne designs, including several by Lang and Pugh, although more sturdy architecture is abundant, too. Baker also is home to a fine Deco-era fire station and post office, as well as handsome churches and libraries. To the north of the district sits the motley campus of Denver Health and Hospitals. And across Broadway, one of the city's earliest north-south main drags, sits one of the crown jewels of the city: The Mayan survives as the city's most elaborate historic picture palace. As part of the continuing remaking of Broadway, the renovated First Avenue Hotel joins the Mayan to signal the gateway to numerous entrepreneurial enterprises that have reenergized that major thoroughfare.

Baker has not been immune to the development pressures buffeting many of Denver's close-in neighborhoods, as infill projects accompany improvements to many homes. Yet the residential fabric has remained strong here for well over a century.

The tight-knit Baker neighborhood is listed as a historic district on the National Register and by the City and County of Denver's Landmark Preservation Commission.

LIST OF BUILDINGS

1   Byers Branch Library
2   West High School / West Leadership
     Academy and West Generation Academy
3   Robert W. Speer Memorial Hospital
4   Denver General Hospital / Denver Health
     and Hospitals
5   St. Peter and St. Mary Episcopal Church
6   Denver Fire Station #11
7   Mayan Theatre
8   First Avenue Hotel
9   Ross-Broadway Branch Library
10 South Denver Post Office
11 South Broadway Christian Church
12 Red Cross Mile High Chapter Building

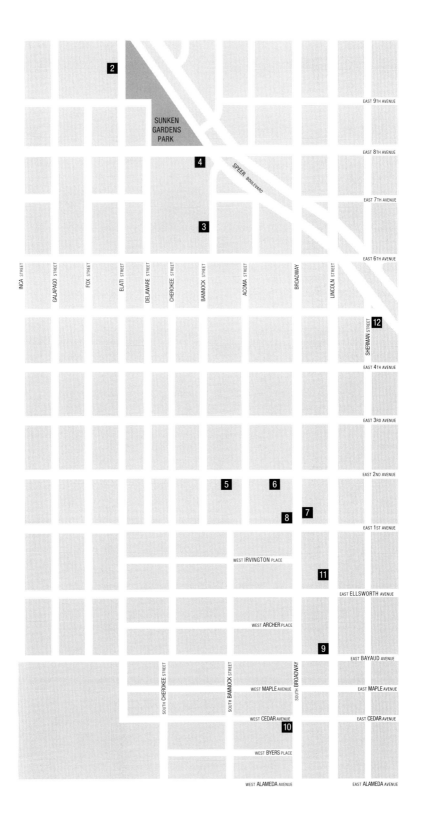

1   Byers Branch Library
675 Santa Fe Drive
Varian and Varian, 1918; early 1990s renovation by Pouw & Associates

Father-and-son architects Ernest and Lester Varian chose an Italian Renaissance style for the compact branch library, but it has enough of a Mediterranean atmosphere to make it feel right at home in the neighborhood gaining new life centered on Santa Fe Drive. Pilasters with flowery Corinthian capitols and sleek trim have maintained their integrity, aided by a renovation that was among numerous library upgrades and expansions in the early 1990s.
Denver Landmark

2   West High School / West Leadership Academy and West Generation Academy
951 Elati Street
W. Harry Edwards, 1925

W. Harry Edwards worked in the collegiate Gothic style for this often overlooked Denver "compass point" school to the west of Sunken Gardens Park. It is a building that is neither as showy nor as well known as East, North, and South. In fact, it now is not West High School: In 2012, community pressure and Denver School District review led to a change of name and purpose, with the creation of two academies within the building. Still, the building remains. The school's wings angle slightly toward the street, flanking an arched main entry over which a crenelated tower soars. Bay windows serve as a transition between the main building and wings.
Denver Landmark

3   Robert W. Speer Memorial Hospital
645 Bannock Street
Fisher, Fisher, and Hubbell, 1938

Even in an eroded state, the old Speer Memorial (built to serve sick children) proudly shows off its Moderne lines in concrete and brick. (The huge smokestack to the rear is not part of the building and no longer is in use.) The mural above the hospital's entry is by an unidentified artist, and has deteriorated to what may be the point of no return.

4   Denver General Hospital / Denver Health and Hospitals
777 Bannock Street
Eugene D. Sternberg, 1970; trauma center addition at the front in 1992 by Davis Partnership

Eugene Sternberg won the hospital commission through a competition in 1965, and in turn the design won an AIA National Award. The architect's aim was to put the offices at street level and elevate patients so they would get better exposure to the sun. This humanistic approach gives the hospital a slim profile, and the use

of butter-colored stone set off by concrete panels adds warmth. The Davis addition in rosy precast has a 1990s feel, while the colors are one step away from clashing with the original building, whose lower levels are now wrapped and obscured by the addition.

5 St. Peter and St. Mary Episcopal Church
126 W. 2nd Avenue
Boal and Harnois, 1891

The National Register inventory for the Baker district describes this building as reminiscent of an English rural church – a succinct summation, to be sure. What began as St. Peter's Church is all weighty brackets and generous overhangs, in roof areas segmented around a compact tower. Walls are rusticated limestone. A buff brick parish hall was added in the 1940s.

6 Denver Fire Station #11
40 W. 2nd Avenue
Charles F. Pillsbury, 1936

Charles Pillsbury, who designed other fire stations in Denver, relied on splashy plumes of brick for decoration on the Art Deco #11, as well as the play of horizontal and vertical in dark red-brown masonry. The station was constructed as a Works Progress Administration building.
Denver Landmark

7 Mayan Theatre
110 Broadway
Montana S. Fallis, 1930

Saved from destruction in 1984, the Mayan is all exotic verticality and Deco dazzle. It's the perfect example of the Depression-era movie house that drew on another culture's imagery for decoration – in this case Aztec and Mayan details such as zigzag strips outside and masks, jaguars, and flora inside. The terra-cotta Mayan "chief" on the marquee is a high point of the design, among the handful of such "Mayan motif" theaters remaining in the United States. In that era, Montana Fallis worked extensively in terra-cotta (the Oxford Hotel annex, for instance) and in the geometry of Art Deco or Streamline Moderne (such as the Buerger Brothers building downtown). After restoration, the Mayan resumed operation in 1987, an enduring reminder of the period and the most elaborate of Denver's old theaters to survive.
Denver Landmark

8 First Avenue Hotel
101–115 Broadway
William Quayle, 1905; renovation by Alvarez Morris Architects Studio, 2009

This solid, elegant building served as a hotel for years, close to Broadway's thriving automobile outlets, downtown, and state government activities. The ground floor was home to diverse retail, including the State Bar and Grill. But then it went off the rails, serving as an SRO and eventually left empty. An area restaurateur took a chance on it, cleaning up the lower two floors for offices, rehabilitating the exterior, and opening a street-level restaurant and wine bar. The hotel lobby is basically intact, if not fancy, though a Greek key pattern is woven through the tile floor. The building's owner has experienced financial problems and conflicts with city codes, leading to confusion over the building's future.
Denver Landmark

9 Ross-Broadway Branch Library
33 E. Bayaud Avenue
Victor Hornbein, 1951

Built in a design evocative of the Prairie style, the Ross-Broadway branch exhibits long, low lines capped by a sweeping roof with wide overhangs. Architect Victor Hornbein's emphasis on brick construction gives solidity, while clerestory windows allow light and the play of colors in the geometric grid sparked by squares of tinted glass. Mullions are wood, as is the front door – a warm, modern look in Denver's near inner city. Ross-Broadway is one of four libraries built through the bequest of Frederick R. Ross.

10 South Denver Post Office
225 S. Broadway
Louis A. Simon, circa 1935

Flashy Moderne was not in the cards for this simple, almost formalist structure. Though a red tile roof hints at the Mediterranean style popular throughout Denver, the architect added a classical touch with heavy dentil detailing around the roofline – about the only decorative touches on this building.

11 South Broadway Christian Church
23 Lincoln Street
Miller and Janisch, 1891

Oh, to be in England, where this beautifully composed modified Romanesque church finds inspiration in detailing.

Though the address is given as Lincoln Street, site of adjoining church offices, South Broadway actually fronts on Ellsworth Avenue. There sits its claim to glory: a massive square tower, with crenelated roofline, accented by a slim turret attached at one corner. An imposing arched window surround, a modest

entryway, and an elegant arcade are important elements, as is the addition of louvered belfry coverings that include a base reminiscent of a pulpit. Heavily carved finials round out the picture for a religious structure that draws strength from rusticated rhyolite walls and repeated gables.
Denver Landmark

12 Red Cross Mile High Chapter Building
444 Sherman Street
Edwin Francis, 1951

What is now the headquarters of a prominent charitable organization began as the Van Hummell Insurance Company Building, a Modernist design that relies heavily on the color, integrity, and texture of sandstone. Although it is difficult to view all four sides, a trip down an adjacent alley and parking lot reveal variety in the way Edwin Francis worked each facade. While the entry side facing Sherman Street is composed of both rusticated slabs of sandstone and stone panels, the alley side shows red slabs defined by a course of buff sandstone slabs. Elegant diversity marks this warm and welcoming building, where the weight of stone is leavened by the way the light plays off the generous windows.

West

1 **Three Stone Buildings / Denver Water Department**
1600 W. 12th Avenue
Muchow and Partners, 1983

In the middle of a parking lot in the middle of an industrial area sits one of Denver's most resourceful renovation projects. The first stone building in question was built before 1880 as the Denver City Irrigation and Water Co.'s West Side Pump Station. The second, the North Stone Building, was operating by 1880 as a pump house. And the third, the South Stone Building, was constructed in 1905 as a boiler house. The people who designed and built these structures worked in the same gray-pink mottled rhyolite, helping to link the appearance of these small but distinguished mechanical buildings.

Years later, long after Denver's competing water companies were put to rest by the Denver Water Board, the pumps were removed from buildings then turned into shops. Eventually, the Water Board decided to restore the buildings to house employee amenities and a community room.

In the process, an estimated 80 tons of rhyolite was quarried to make repairs, and the original stones were cleaned. The architects connected the North and Middle Buildings with an entry and gallery, installing a slate floor but restoring the old high wooden ceilings. Some of the original furnishings were kept in a mezzanine space, and old lamps from the parapet of Cheesman Dam were added as decorative elements. In a region where water was as precious as blood, the Three Stone Buildings tell a story of survival and community will. *AIA Western Mountain Region Design Excellence Award, 1983; AIA Colorado Citation Award, 1983*

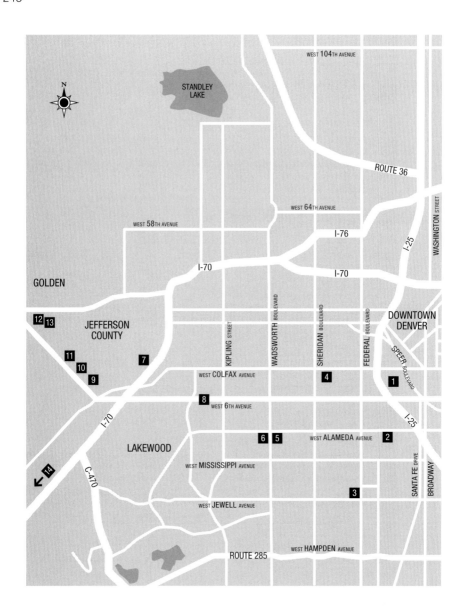

LIST OF BUILDINGS

1 Three Stone Buildings /
  Denver Water Department
2 Valverde Elementary School
3 Hadley Branch Library
4 Stuart Street Historic District
5 Belmar
6 Lakewood Public Safety Center /
  Lakewood Municipal Center
7 National Renewable Energy
  Laboratory (NREL) / Solar Energy
  Research Institute (SERI)
8 6th Avenue Bridge

9 Jefferson County Municipal Center
10 Jefferson County Justice Center and
   Detention Facility
11 Jefferson County Human Services Building
12 Marquez Hall / Colorado School of Mines
13 Golden Welcome Arch
14 The Sculptured House /
   Charles Deaton Residence

2   Valverde Elementary School
2030 W. Alameda Avenue
H.W.J. Edbrooke, 1924, with additions in 1947 by R. Ewing Stiffler, in 1951
by Burnham Hoyt, and 2000 by Yon Tanner Architecture

For this school, which replaced an earlier Valverde to the west, architect
H.W.J. Edbrooke produced a building that mixed simple lines with elaborate
ornamentation. Even a bracketed cornice was hardly a match for the school's
facade, which incorporated soaring, symmetrical arches that flank a highly
detailed multistory entrance frieze. Additions are almost invisible on the site,
a rise that showcases the original building.

3   Hadley Branch Library
1890 S. Grove Street, Smith and Thorson, 1964, with 1993 reconstruction by
OZ Architects

As part of the bond issue that produced an expanded Denver Central Library,
voters also kicked in money to remodel, restore, and reconfigure many branch
libraries. Such was the case with Hadley. From a clean-lined, if unprepossessing
1960s building, Hadley was remade into a building of many gables and a mix of
block, opaque, and gridded green glass. This brush with Postmodern design does
make the building stand out in a busy stretch of southwest Denver, though the
cursive script on the facade is more lighthearted than found on most library buildings.

4   Stuart Street Historic District
1389, 1390, 1435, 1444, and 1471 Stuart Street
William Lang and Marshall Pugh, 1888–1892

The first question to address in regards to these beautiful Victorian homes is:
How did they get here? How did Denver's Quality Hill land in the middle of a
neighborhood of more simple bungalows and cottages? The answer is a
developer and one-time state legislator named Ralph Voorhees, who commissioned
the noted residential architects Lang and Pugh to design his home and others on
Stuart Street.

Though all five homes exhibit roots in one era, each of the structures is a bit
different in detailing and its use of the stone for which Lang was famous.

Voorhees's own home, at 1471 Stuart Street, is a heavy stone Richardsonian
Romanesque mansion, with a broad porch capped at one end by an impressive
turret. The style is shared by 1435 Stuart, which includes a checkerboard-type
panel on the course of stone panel between the first and second floor and
windows on the south wall designed to become progressively deeper.

At 1444 Stuart, Shingle Style was the order of the day on the second and third
stories, with masonry at street level; shingles again were a major factor in the
design of 1389 Stuart. And 1390 Stuart exhibits characteristics more common in
Queen Anne design, with an emphasis on towers that emerge from the steep roof.

In the decades since, other homes have grown up around the five beauties, which are a landmark in the area.
National Register, Denver Landmark

5 Belmar

South Wadsworth Boulevard and West Alameda Avenue, Lakewood
Master plan and architecture, Elkus / Manfredi Architects Ltd. (Boston);
landscape architecture, Civitas Inc.; graphic design, Sussman / Prejza and
Company, Inc. (Los Angeles); 2004

Once upon a time, what passed for Lakewood's downtown was a shopping center called Villa Italia. As interest in that aging mall dwindled, the city of Lakewood teamed up in 2003 with the real estate development firm Continuum to demolish Villa Italia and develop a new "downtown" and civic core for this city to the west of Denver.

The resulting 100-plus-acre development in reality is predominantly a shopping mall set off by the introduction of municipal streets. Belmar has grown to include numerous stores and restaurants, residential buildings, parking structures, and an area devoted to arts-related enterprises. Among those was the much-vaunted (though short-lived) Lab, which opened in 2004 and in 2006 debuted a clean and organic interior design by California-based architect Hagy Belzberg. The Lab closed less than three years later, when its director was named chief animator of the Museum of Contemporary Art / Denver. MCA Denver sits on land donated by Continuum's managing director Mark Falcone – who also developed Belmar. The Lab's space at Belmar has been incorporated into other uses.

Belmar's look is standard 21st-century clean-cut contemporary for residential areas pushed to the outside boundaries, but more bland in terms of the numerous shops and restaurants that are the heart of the development. With construction of a nearby Lakewood Civic Center and Lakewood Cultural Center, Lakewood may now have a "downtown," but it has not grown organically or with any particular sense of place or regional identity.

6 Lakewood Public Safety Center / Lakewood Municipal Center

445 S. Allison Way
Muchow and Partners, 1983

What a difference 15 or so years can make in a growing city. When the Lakewood Municipal Center opened in the early 1980s, it was a building that stood on its own, a low-slung, angular structure notable for its use of glass and its Modern mastery of the site. (AIA Colorado Design Award, 1984.)

Now, the municipal center has become the Lakewood Public Safety Center. It has been blocked from view by a parking structure, and most municipal functions have been shifted into a new Lakewood Civic Center and Lakewood Cultural Center across South Allison Way. Both those somewhat anonymous buildings opened in 2000, and the entire complex is tied to a shopping center next door – giving new meaning to the term "public-private partnership."

Added to the mix is a place that promises new life for old buildings, in the Lakewood Heritage Center growing behind the civic and cultural complex. The Heritage Center has offered shelter to its first structure: Ethel's & Gil's Her/His Beauty/Barber Shop. The 1942 vernacular Deco building was moved from 3043 W. Alameda Avenue when a state road-widening project threatened demolition. So now Ethel's & Gil's joins an old farmhouse and an odd outdoor "tent" (the Bonfils-Stanton Foundation Amphitheater) in the equivalent of a building zoo.

7 National Renewable Energy Laboratory (NREL) / Solar Energy Research Institute (SERI)

1617 Cole Street, Golden
Original SERI Building, joint venture of Anderson DiBartolo Ponds, 1974; new Research Support Facility (RSF), RNL Design, 2010, along with Science and Technology Facility and New Energy Systems Integration Facility (both SmithGroup)

When the 1973 OPEC energy embargo caused gas and oil prices to zoom, Americans reacted as if they had been slapped in the face. Lawmakers began to formulate policies to push for energy independence, and research into energy-conserving methods and technology (like solar energy and more fuel-efficient vehicles) became popular. But then the crisis passed, and life went on as before. But SERI didn't go away–it just became a different agency in the early 1990s: the National Renewable Energy Laboratory, under the auspices of the U.S. Department of Energy.

So it was natural that as NREL gained steam, it would expand near the original SERI Building, a place close to the foothills but still adjacent to civic amenities. The original building features a dramatic sloped roof and displays a sense of being one with nature. The newer, and highly energy efficient buildings, look like office buildings with a brain. And they are.

The Research Support Facility was designed and constructed to achieve LEED Platinum certification, with the goal of being a net-zero energy facility. Two buildings housing offices, a data center and conference center, are connected by an entrance lobby, creating a project that through its siting, materials selection, and energy-saving features became a demonstration project for other developers, architects, and contractors. Along with the inclusion of high-megawatt generating photovoltaics, the RSF includes sunshades, glazing that responds to the power of the sun's rays to address solar gain, solar collectors, and a mechanical system that stores passively cooled and heated air. Sustainable practices were used as well in terms of the complex's landscaping and how it addresses the reduction of water use.

Materials include brick and metal panels, but also interior walls of beetle-kill pine and the use of examples of recycled materials. Rocks discovered during site excavation were not discarded; instead, they were inserted in wire baskets to create gabion walls used as retaining walls and site walls. Practical can be beautiful, as illustrated by a building that offers more than its share of teachable moments. *Research Support Facility, AIA Colorado Citation Award, 2009; AIA Denver Citation Award, 2011*

8   6th Avenue Bridge
Crosses U.S. 6 to near the Simms / Union exits
David Evans and Associates (Kip Coulter), 2010

The Regional Transportation District – or RTD – is deep into construction of an ambitious (if slow) light rail system designed to serve the sprawling metro area; the hub for this project will be a refreshed Union Station. But if bridge and station architecture at times have left something to be desired, the design of the 6th Avenue Bridge has made drivers on busy U.S. 6 pay attention.

Called a basket-handled tied arch bridge, the 610-foot-long span features a web of 44 cables and is a main element of RTD's West Rail Line. The bridge is constructed of high-strength weathering steel, which allows it to rust naturally to a deep brownish color and require less maintenance in terms of needing repeated paint jobs. At its highest point, the arch measures 65 feet from the top to the bottom floor beam. The bridge, which opened in January 2013, was rolled into place in 2010 during a weekend when U.S. 6 was closed for several hours. This debut was accomplished to the amazement of all who saw the run-up to its placement.

9   Jefferson County Municipal Center
100 Jefferson County Parkway
C.W. Fentress J.H. Bradburn and Associates, 1993

The building, prominent on its site on a rise off of U.S. Highway 6, features the compassionate forms of curved arms and a dome often found in government buildings. But this complex of more than 530,000 square feet also shimmers with a sense of power. No wonder it picked up the nickname the Taj Mahal even before it opened, although that also had something to do with the use of a financing method that skirted public approval.

The architects worked in buff precast concrete with walls broken up by darker square insets. Windows are plentiful, and the parking structure is tucked to one side. Inside is the more luxurious side of the Municipal Center (except, perhaps, for the four mysterious brass-colored balls that form a ring around the dome). Accents in brass and cherry, colorful terrazzo, and red granite detailing mark the interior, all set off by a 140-foot-high atrium at the center.

10   Jefferson County Justice Center and Detention Facility
200 Jefferson County Parkway
William Muchow and Partners, 1984

After a tangled process of competitions and challenges by communities within the country, Jeffco's jail finally was built. Though some wags have suggested the twin cylinders are supposed to refer to a set of handcuffs, such apparently is not true. Instead, the architects raised the detention towers off the ground, putting monitoring areas at the core. Windows are like ribbons wrapping each tower, although narrow for security reasons. As a show of strength, the concrete walls are supported by crossed metal beams, giving a sense of sweeping the occupants up and away from society. A newer sheriff's facility nearby shows more Postmodern sensibilities.

11 Jefferson County Human Services Building
900 Jefferson County Parkway
C.W. Fentress J.H. Bradburn and Associates, 1990

Honey-colored brick accented by strips of dark rose granite combine to produce a building that is a near circle, another symbol of shelter and warmth. This circle is interrupted at the entry, though a plaza continues the concept of closure. Thoughtful brickwork is evident, and light is abundant thanks to a two-story solarium, colonnade, and a lobby that opens to a courtyard at the entry. Though the interior was designed in a no-nonsense fashion, the exterior of the human services building is restrained, human scale, and welcoming.
AIA Western Mountain Region Honor Award, 1991

12 Marquez Hall / Colorado School of Mines
16th and Arapahoe Streets, Golden
Bohlin Cywinski Jackson in association with AndersonMasonDale Architects, 2012

The Colorado School of Mines campus features an incredibly compact assemblage of buildings, in styles that reach far back in time. But recently space has been found for several new buildings, including residential halls, a student recreation center, and the distinctive Marquez Hall. Designed to house the school's Department of Petroleum Engineering, this building displays the clean lines and ingenious mix of materials that makes this structure a campus standout. The building houses laboratories, classrooms, offices, and spaces for amenities, all wrapped in a glass curtain wall and a terra-cotta and steel rain screen system. Cor-Ten steel panels add solidity to a building that rests lightly on its site. Marquez Hall has achieved LEED Silver certification.

13 Golden Welcome Arch
Washington Street, Golden
Paul Reeves, 1949, with later renovations

This old-timey municipal sign may have changed in appearance over the decades, but it still serves the same purpose: to welcome tourists to Golden's main drag and downtown retail, manufacturing, and restaurants. The neon lettering was removed years ago, and the message tweaked. But a town that for years served as the capital of the Colorado Territory loves to proclaim its status as the place "Where the West Lives."

14 The Sculptured House / Charles Deaton Residence
Genesee Mountain, off Interstate 70, west of Denver
Charles Deaton, 1963

Jutting out over the land like a beached flying saucer – or a partially open clam shell – Deaton's "sculptured" house has been widely exhibited, even featured in a movie (Woody Allen's *Sleeper*).

Deaton, an ingenious inventor/architect / visionary, was entranced with the idea of the curve, and the relationship between the curves of nature and those of the human body. So the Denver-based designer sank his money into construction of the home, though he never lived there.

The home's pedestal is reinforced concrete with precast columns; the upper portion, which appears to float over the hillside and highway, is double-shell sprayed-on and hand-troweled concrete supported by a welded steel frame. Crushed walnut shells mixed into the exterior paint add texture. A glass wall sweeps along the massive curve that extends from the hill.

Deaton, who never finished the interior, was quoted as saying that each carefully placed window opening "was cut into the sculpture as one would cut into a melon." Or, cut into a curved exterior that encloses a world of curves.

In the late 1990s, a wealthy Denver entrepreneur bought the house he had admired from afar, and fixed up a place that had been vandalized and open to the weather over the years. The new owner constructed an addition based on one Deaton had designed, and he furnished the home with mid-century Modernist objects. And moved in. But that only lasted so long; there have been other owners, and the occasional financial blip. Still, Deaton's residence remains a home, and a landmark for those driving by on Interstate 70 below.
AIA Denver 25 Year Award, 2008; National Register

New Stapleton and Northeast

When voters approved construction of a new airport for Denver and the region in the late 1980s, the process began to determine what to do with the land that held the existing Stapleton International Airport. Close to the city, but surrounded by homes (and noise-weary neighbors), Stapleton became the subject of intense study, with the eventual goal of turning the giant area into a planned community in which people could live, work, and play according to the New Urbanist credo.

Forest City Stapleton was selected as the master developer, selling off parcels to home builders who needed to follow design guidelines found in the weighty document, the Green Book. The 4,700-acre mega-project has evolved into what in effect is a suburban development on the eastern edge of the city, with a mix of single-family and multifamily residences.

The Green Book focused on several home styles prevalent in Denver, traditional designs that fill the sections developed early in the game, including alley access to garages and getting those big blind garage door "eyes" off the street. Recent developments have become more contemporary in vision, though the truly distinguished projects in Stapleton tend toward public buildings and a commercial enclave known as the 29th Avenue Town Center.

And though visitors may find it difficult to navigate through an area where streets are interrupted by unbuilt parcels, people have flocked to Stapleton to live, work, and play. It is an easy trip into Denver, out to Denver International Airport, and to numerous shops and restaurants. Stapleton is a magnet for families drawn to the new schools and recreational opportunities provided by Central Park, playgrounds, trails, and a rec center.

Stapleton's impact also has attracted a massive shopping area called Northfield, as well as business development in various commercial and office clusters. A demographic study conducted by the Piton Foundation and drawn from 2010 census figures shows that about 75 percent of Denver's

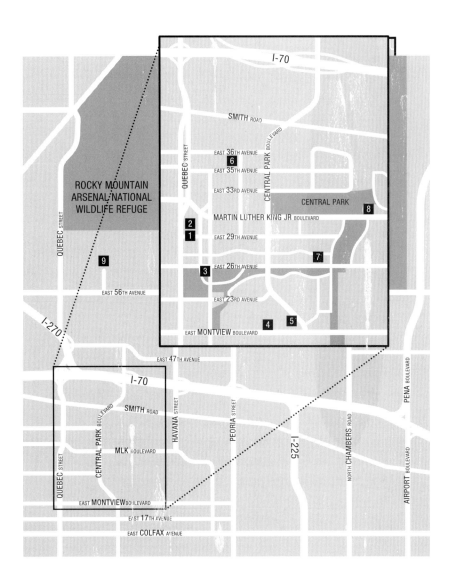

growth has happened in Stapleton and Green Valley Ranch, which is farther to the northwest.

What Stapleton has not done is follow in the Lowry development's footsteps of fully exploiting its history. While Lowry has preserved numerous former base structures as repurposed, living landmarks, Stapleton has taken a different tack. Some buildings have found new uses, but there is still a question of what to do with the former control tower, which has been considered for use as a cultural and community center. Still, several years ago, pressure by preservationists saved – and restored – the distinctive Hanger 61, once used to house the company airplane owned by Ideal Basic Cement Co.

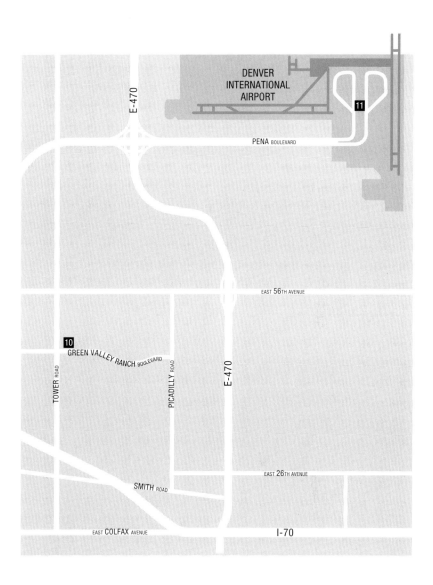

LIST OF BUILDINGS

1 29th Avenue Town Center
2 Sam Gary Branch Library
3 Anchor Center for the Blind
4 Denver School of Science and Technology
5 Hangar 61
6 FBI Denver Field Office
7 Westerly Creek Elementary School
8 Central Park Recreation Center
9 Dick's Sporting Goods Park
10 Green Valley Ranch Library
11 Denver International Airport

1   29th Avenue Town Center
7351 E. 29th Avenue (at Quebec Street)
4240 Architecture, 2004

Stapleton has other town centers and retail areas, but this well-designed mix of retail, office, and residential serves as a gateway and main street for the development. The narrow streets, ample sidewalks, diverse storefronts, and cozy feel are aided by a design that looks to the future through contemporary architecture. A nearby park, a crescent-shaped development at one end, a library, and hidden parking make this a home for pedestrians pulled to a sensitively crafted place that serves myriad needs.
AIA Denver Citation Award, 2004

2   Sam Gary Branch Library
2961 Roslyn Street
OZ Architecture, 2012

Early Stapleton supporter Sam Gary has been honored by this new library, which is tucked into the area behind the 29th Avenue Town Center. In simple materials – the exterior facing the nearest intersection is nearly anonymous – the building opens up to color and detailing toward the entrance. A broad sign and overhang signal that this is a place of welcome, though it faces a jumble of parking and back doors in the town center.

One of the three Denver Public Library's branches funded by the 2007 Better Denver Bond program, this new facility is a busy place, serving a booming population in open and airy quarters designed for both collaborative and individual research and study. The project has received LEED Gold certification.

3   Anchor Center for the Blind
2550 Roslyn Street
Davis Partnership Architects, 2007

The center's Julie McAndrews Mork Building appears playful on the exterior, with its different planes and levels and rambling spaces. But that sense of fun evolves inside into some serious learning, where the building becomes a tool for instruction. The Anchor Center, designed to serve children with vision impairments, incorporates light and color to promote a sense of normalcy and joy in a world of challenge. Spaces such as a sensory garden and a room that displays different acoustics appeal to the development of other senses, while several glowing elements work to use light as an educational element. A cane walk lane incorporates different flooring materials to help children recognize different materials and textures, and outdoor spaces invite exploration through directional aids.

4 **Denver School of Science and Technology**
2000 Valentia Street
klipp architecture, 2004

Klipp's design for the respected Denver School of Science and Technology proves that industrial elements, geometric forms, and a color palette that mixes neutral with bold can give a sexy aura to the study of science and technology. The new emphasis on STEM subjects – Science, Technology, Engineering, and Math – is reflected in architectural elements that combine to make a forward-looking school. A portion of an old airplane wing marks the entry to the rear, facing a hidden parking area, and futuristic touches of metal throughout add rhythm to a building that is LEED for Schools Silver certified.
AIA Denver Citation Award, 2005

5 **Hangar 61**
8695 Montview Boulevard
Fisher and Fisher and Davis, with engineer Milo Ketchum 1959; rebirth in 2009

This rare surviving example of thin-shell concrete construction and engineering features a diamond-shaped domed roof balanced and supported by two immense concrete buttresses. Preservationists and historians – and plenty of others – worried in 2004 that the expansion of Stapleton would be the end of a building that had stood empty for years.

But a persevering artist (David Walters), Colorado Preservation Inc., and a brave developer (Larry Nelson, through his 620 Corp.) took on the job, attracting attention to the structure and eventually repairing loose concrete, digging out a tree that had grown in the cracked dome, fixing the buttresses that hold down the roof, adding caissons to anchor the building, upgrading the electrical system, and replacing pipes and broken windows.

The hangar's unusual sleek form and strong historical ties to Denver make this one of the most important elements of Stapleton, contributing the flair of air travel to a development that can appear more generic than rooted in place. Hangar 61 also demonstrates that adaptive reuse can happen anywhere, if given a chance; the building now houses a church.

6 **FBI Denver Field Office**
8000 E. 36th Avenue
Skidmore, Owings & Merrill, with Anderson Mason Dale Architects, 2010

In a development where the glitz factor is low, as is the case with Stapleton, it's a surprise (and a treat) to round a corner and suddenly see this shimmering cube. Skidmore, Owings & Merrill's design for this four-story FBI field office includes high security and a very strong fence. But the curtain wall – expressed in strips of iridescent glass strips tinged with blue and green – indicates the sense of openness and light existing inside. Simplicity and elegance inform this contemporary, otherwise minimalist office building, which is unexpected in its scale and use of materials. The complex also includes an annex and a parking garage.

7 Westerly Creek Elementary School
8800 E. 28th Avenue
Anderson Mason Dale Architects, 2003

This long, low landscraper of a school presents an assemblage of interesting forms that range from a tower-like section that references the old control tower and a circular section that adds interest to the building. Anderson Mason Dale worked with the Odyssey School to create a project for the Denver Public Schools devoted to exploration and research, all located in a civic campus that serves the community.

8 Central Park Recreation Center
9651 E. Martin Luther King Boulevard
Sink Combs Dethlefs, 2011

The clean lines and notable location make this building stand out as a hub for recreational pursuits. A contemporary design by Sink Combs Dethlefs relies on a mix of unflashy materials, intelligent proportions, and a welcoming white-columned entry to give it a prominent role on the landscape and in the overall community. Certified LEED Gold, the rec center's materials include beetle-kill pine.

9 Dick's Sporting Goods Park
6000 Victory Way, Commerce City
HOK Sports, 2007

Kroenke Sports Enterprises is the owner of this facility and the soccer team, the Colorado Rapids, that calls the place home. This expansive and upscale stadium also marks a big step forward in the area for the sport of soccer, since it is one of the largest soccer complexes in the United States. Stadium architect HOK Sport created a design that gives the facility a place on the skyline, with a series of tilted planes that add interest to a place that is surrounded by parkland (landscape architect is Norris Design) and thousands of parking spaces. Even when this locale is less barren and windswept, the roofline will announce the park's presence.

10 Green Valley Ranch Library
4856 Andes Court
Humphries Poli Architects, 2011

Another branch library funded by the 2007 Better Denver Bond program, Green Valley Ranch serves a large suburban community about eight miles south of Denver International Airport. The design works on two themes: the plains that surround DIA, and the impact of aviation on this part of the metro area. A portion of a cockpit sits in the library's large, open space, where numerous functions coexist side by side. The brick building is accented by areas of metal strips, which promote a high-tech look, though the interior is all about color – bright walls and panes of colored glass set into a collage of windows. In an area that is dominated by homes that share a similar simple style, the library is a civic building that stands out in terms of materials and detail.

11 Denver International Airport
Interstate 70 at Pena Boulevard
Fentress Bradburn Architects (terminal and connectors), after the Perez Group;
with Allred Seracuse Lawler and Partners (concourses), Pouw and Associates
(airport office building, support buildings, curb areas, and parking garage), and
Civitas with BRW and DHM (landscaping master plan), 1995; South Terminal
Redevelopment Program, Gensler, after withdrawal by Santiago Calatrava's
Festina Lente, expected completion 2015

Civic boosters point to the tent-topped terminal at DIA as a signature design for the city, but what the Fentress Bradburn design represents is really more of a symbolic strike. There, out on the prairie, 30 miles from town, sits a big, shining (by day) or gleaming (by night) series of fabric peaks, which the architects say relate as much to the mountains to the west as to any tepees once erected on the plains. And Denver Mayor Michael Hancock has pushed the concept of an aerotropolis at DIA – a true airport city anchored by this massive economic driver.

The airport design went through several incarnations, beginning with a stepped up glass and steel truss "crystal pavilion" roof design by the Perez Group of New Orleans. But when then-mayor Federico Peña pronounced the design "unmemorable," Perez's design was cast aside, and Fentress Bradburn was brought in to design the terminal and connections to the concourses. To cut costs and time as much as to provide a "signature" design, the firm proposed a fabric roof – Teflon-coated fiberglass, to be precise, to rise 126 feet at its peak (or peaks, of which there are 34 in various heights).

By that time, however, Allred Seracuse Lawler and Partners already had designed the concourses in a glass and steel "wedding cake" of rising levels to mesh with the Perez roof design. Veteran architect William Muchow was brought in to coordinate new and old schemes.

And though that helped bridge a gap, the terminal and the concourses still stress different design elements: The terminal is like a grand living room thrown open to the sun, 900 feet long and chockablock with the usual furniture and retail amenities, yet lighted by abundant clerestory windows and glass walls at either end.

Though huge, the terminal works in a more human scale than the concourses, which feel taller and more airy than they are. While the exterior of the terminal is buff block and green glass, the concourses carry a basic white skin, topped by the layered look that was intended to mesh with Perez's mini-mesa.

Of note throughout the airport and its grounds is more than $8 million in public artwork commissioned in a program that began in 1989. Themes touched on the romance of travel, transportation, and the land – with varying degrees of success.

Floors in the terminal and three concourses are among the commissions, as well as large sculptural pieces in the concourses: David Griggs's aerodynamic *Dual Meridian* in A. Alice Adams's loud, neon *Beaded Circle* in B, and Michael Singer's wonderful hanging garden in C. Light-fueled works are installed in both passenger train tunnels – in one, swirling propellors by Antonette Rosato and Bill Maxwell, in the other, a mining-themed trail by Leni Schwendinger. Community-based murals hang at one end of the terminal.

Other pieces commissioned range from directional metal "airplanes" leading from the train to the baggage area (Patty Ortiz) to whimsical constructions and sculptures (from Gary Sweeney and Terry Allen) designed to hold your attention during the inevitable wait for luggage.

As with all public art, controversy has dogged some work installed at DIA.

A few years ago, Doug Hollis's "Mountain Mirage" water feature was turned into a garden area, then restored, then turned off, with plans to remove it so the trains at DIA can be extended. Luis Jimenez's giant blue *Mustang* eventually was installed, and has proved to be perhaps Denver's biggest lightning rod in terms of public art. People either hate or love this rearing horse with the flashing red eyes, which took more than 15 years to reach completion. The sculpture's location was changed, and there was a lawsuit over the artist's delays. Finally, the artist died when a section of the massive sculpture came loose from its scaffolding, killing Jimenez as he worked on it.

Though the saga of *Mustang* continues to fascinate people, an even bigger conversation began when DIA officials selected famed transit architect Santiago Calatrava to design the 500-room Westin Hotel, the train station bringing rail from downtown Denver, and the sinuous bridge that traffic would use to reach the new transit hub. Many loved his designs, while others worried about potential cost overruns. Meanwhile, airport officials, who had wooed Calatrava to the project, cut its budget from $650 million to $500 million, reducing the size of some components.

Sadly, Calatrava withdrew from the project, citing disagreements with project manager Parsons Transportation Group. Calatrava took major aspects of his hotel and transit station design with him, including his signature white architectural elements, and some column designs. The bridge will become a more standard-issue product. And Denver lost another opportunity for an an iconic architectural project as counterpoint to Fentress Bradburn's innovative DIA terminal.
AIA Denver, AIA Colorado, AIA Western Mountain Region Honor Award, 1994

Lowry and Southeast

This vast swath of metro Denver is notable for its diversity, since it includes two repurposed former military installations (Lowry Air Force Base and Fitzsimons Army Medical Center), two of the most contemplative spaces in the region (Babi Yar Park and Fairmount Cemetery), and buildings that have formed a new municipal center in the City of Aurora.

1 Lowry
Bounded by East 11th Avenue, Quebec Street, East Alameda Avenue, and Dayton Street, with a bump out to Havana Street at the south end of the development

A year before Stapleton International Airport closed in 1995, paving the way for redevelopment, the Lowry Air Force Base ceased operation. Built on the site of a former sanatorium in 1937, Lowry became a modern airfield. Its closure, announced in 1991, left another giant parcel – 3.3 square miles of land dotted with buildings and three runways – open for repurposing.

The Lowry Redevelopment Authority was formed that year and set a course that included residential, retail, office, and educational space as well as parks. But Lowry also was able to keep more of its the existing buildings and played off a military theme in terms of aesthetics and branding, mining its heritage in a way Stapleton has not. Although much of the new residential development at Lowry does not feature memorable design, and Lowry's Town Center might look more at home in a suburb, the developed area includes existing buildings recast for another life.

Two historic districts exist in Lowry: the officer's Row Historic District and the Lowry Technical Training Center Historic District. Also, there are scattered designated landmarks throughout the neighborhood. Lowry's historic buildings are clustered around East 4th Avenue, Spruce Street, East Academy Boulevard, and Roslyn Street – a diamond-shaped area just to the east of Quebec Street. In the works is redevelopment of the Buckley Annex area, the last parcel to be transferred to the Lowry Redevelopment Authority when the annex ceased operation and was vacated in 2011.

Several buildings/projects are of note at Lowry, though to get the full effect, it pays to drive through the entire neighborhood.

1.1 – Officer's Row Loft Homes, Roslyn Street from East 1st to East 4th Avenues, Christopher Carvell Architects, 2000: This new development is to the west of the historic old Barracks, bringing a contemporary flair that works well with the structure that became base headquarters in the 1960s.

1.2 – Steam Plant Lofts, East 4th Avenue at Red Cross Way, circa 1940, redevelopment by Jim Hartman, 2006: This massive building with its four shiny cone-like chimneys created heat for dozens of buildings on the Lowry base. It was redeveloped into lofts, with the addition nearby of a townhome complex.

1.3 – Schlessman Family Branch Library, 100 Poplar Street, Brendle APV, 2002:
Although across Quebec Street from the Lowry development, architect Michael Brendle's angular library features a design with significant sections clad in matte aluminum that plays up the concept of flight that runs throughout the old base. Its canted geometric forms give the library a sculptural presence.

1.4 – New Stanley British Primary School, 350 Quebec Court, circa 1939–1942:
This venerable educational facility moved out of its longtime home at East 13th Avenue and Quebec Street in 1994, shifting into buildings that had housed the Officers' Club and Officers' Quarters. More space allowed growth, and gave new life to distinctive buildings rehabilitated as educational spaces.

1.5 – Hangar No. 1 / Wings Over the Rockies Museum, 7731 E. Academy Boulevard, 1940, and Hangar No. 2:
It's not hard to spot Hangar No. 1, and not just because it is a gigantic metal hangar. There is also a real B-52 set on a pedestal on the edge of its parking lot. It's part of the collection of the Wings Over the Rockies Museum, which moved in in 1995 and helps keep alive the military and flight history of Lowry's past. In 2007, Wings officials caused a stir by proposing that Hangar No. 2 next door, which the museum owns, be torn down to save money on maintenance. The museum would sell the land for condos. The neighborhood and preservationists were not happy, and the deal did not work. Instead, Hangar No. 2 is now home to a storage facility, with retail and a developing dining center.

1.6 – The Eisenhower Chapel, 293 Roslyn Street, 1941:
This small chapel with the lines of a Prairie church earned its name because President and Mrs. Dwight Eisenhower worshipped there when they were in Denver. It is located on the east side of Lowry's Town Center.
Denver Landmark

LIST OF BUILDINGS

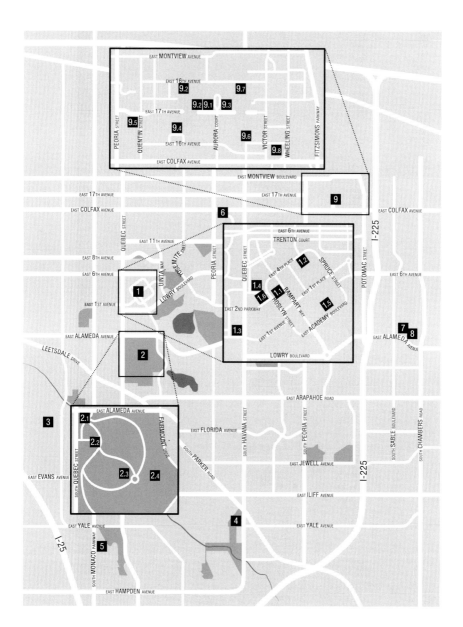

9.3 The Nighthorse Campbell Native
Health Building

9.4 University of Colorado Hospital

9.5 Center for Dependency, Addiction,
and Recovery

9.6 Children's Hospital Colorado

9.7 Fulginity Pavilion

9.8 The Denver VA Hospital, or
Replacement Medical Center Facility

2 Fairmount Cemetery
Entered from East Alameda Avenue at Quebec Street

From family plot and then churchyard, the American style and place for burial grew into an ever more public setting. In the 1830s, spurred on by the growth on the Continent of park-like cemeteries, the first American "garden" cemetery was developed in Massachusetts.

It was an idea ripe for dissemination across the country. And as Denver's relationship evolved in regard to prevailing urban design tenets – culminating in full-fledged allegiance to the City Beautiful movement – the desire for manicured yet park-like cemeteries grew here, too.

The first city cemetery – an 1859 field later cleared to create Congress and Cheesman Parks and new neighborhoods – was nothing so grand. But as the city's big three cemeteries were developed – Riverside in 1876, Fairmount in 1890, and Mount Olivet in 1892 – the idea of a burial site as destination for the living began to take hold.

With landscape design by Reinhard Schuetze, who was instrumental in early Denver parks planning, Fairmount became a social center complete with a special trolley line and fine architecture. Though Fairmount was not alone in the growth of elaborate mausoleums and headstones, many of the region's top designers and civic leaders – Frank Edbrooke and Temple Buell in the first category, Schleiers and Bonfils in the second – found rest in a sleeping city that still garners admiration today for its peaceful atmosphere and beautiful design.
Denver Landmark

2.1 – Fairmount Gate Lodge, East Alameda at Quebec Street, Harry T.E. Wendell, 1890: Architect Harry Wendell's elaborate entry into Fairmount interprets the Gothic arch with Richardsonian stonework and elaborate corbelling. Though intricately decorated and imposing, the Gate Lodge is neither overwhelming nor oppressive in signaling a sense of arrival.

2.2 – The Ivy Chapel, East Alameda at Quebec Street, Harry T.E. Wendell, 1890: If architect Harry Wendell wanted the entry to Fairmount to radiate strength, he strove for delicacy in the accompanying chapel. Finely proportioned and extensively detailed – including deep corbelling at the entry that recalls the Gate Lodge – the late Gothic Revival Ivy Chapel features quatrefoil accents, stained glass windows, and mini-spires at the corners.

2.3 – Memorial Terrace, East Alameda at Quebec Street, Alfred Watts Grant, 1964: Alfred Watts Grant worked in rosy Georgia marble to face a concrete wall designed as an open mausoleum. Long and low, the terrace stretches behind an arcade-type walkway.

2.4 – The Mausoleum, East Alameda at Quebec Street, Mountjoy and Frewen, 1930: Though the modern amenity of the Memorial Terrace serves as a worthy addition to Fairmount's Classical structures, the Mausoleum has not fared as well. Designed by Mountjoy and Frewen as a granite-skinned Greek temple, with a Colorado Yule marble entry, later additions to the building are of cheaper, unsympathetic materials.

3 Krisana Park
Bounded by East Louisiana Avenue, South Dahlia Street, East Florida Avenue, and South Holly Street, circa mid-1950s

HB Wolff & Company developed and designed the more than 150 homes in this mid-century Modern neighborhood, with an eye toward the California contemporary aesthetic of developer Joseph Eichler. (Eichler used architects Anshen and Allen, Claude Oakland, and Jones and Emmons for this development.)

Though many of the homes have been altered in an unsympathetic fashion, destroying their horizontal lines, Krisana Park still holds together as a place where homes are designed to meld interior and exterior. All are marked by the copious use of glass and an accent on open interiors.

A sister 1950s development, Lynwood, lies a short distance to the southeast, where about 80 homes survive in various states of architectural integrity. The Lynwood neighborhood is bounded by South Holly Street, East Jewell Avenue, and South Jasmine Street.

4 Babi Yar Park
East Yale Avenue at South Havana Street
Lawrence Halprin Associates (Satoru Nishita and Byron McCulley), 1971; completion and master plan, Mundus Bishop Design Inc., with the Denver Department of Parks and Recreation, 2011

In the 1970s, a group of Denver residents organized to begin work on a park and memorial to the hundreds of thousands of Jews, Ukrainians, Gypsies, and others who died between 1941 and 1943 in Babi Yar, a ravine outside Kiev. The park was designed by principals of Lawrence Halprin Associates, who were familiar with Denver from their work at Skyline Park downtown. By the early 1980s, the park was partially completed, but attention shifted elsewhere in terms of creating a place that could serve as a commemorative space recalling all people who had suffered from oppression and genocide.

In the first decade of the 21st century, the Babi Yar Park Foundation, the Denver Parks and Recreation Department, and numerous private citizens and organizations began the push to raise money to complete the park's interior. At the entry, two huge black granite monoliths serve as imposing entry markers. Inside the park, various elements summon up the memory of Babi Yar, from a bridge over a ravine to a central space called the People Place, a grove of remembrance, and a path system in the shape of a Star of David. All are set against mainly natural plantings appropriate to Denver's semi-arid climate and a simple landscape aesthetic. The recent work by Mundus Bishop Design has given the existing architectural elements a heightened importance.

As Babi Yar Park evolves – there are plans to place a large sculpture in the park – it has become one of Denver's key spots for introspection, where people today can recall horrific events of the past and vow to never let them happen again.
ASLA Merit Award, 2011

5   Church of the Risen Christ
3060 S. Monaco Parkway
James Sudler Associates, 1970

The first contemporary building in the Archdiocese of Denver, the Church of the Risen Christ is constructed in the form of a curved-sided triangle with entrances at apexes to the east and west. The third apex rises 76 feet, soaring over surrounding buildings, securing stained glass windows, and providing a signature element. Between the two entrances is a two-story area with sacristies and a conference room. A cylindrical baptistry is connected to the church at the west.

Architect James Sudler worked in rough-textured white stucco – three-foot-thick walls with slit openings to admit daylight. Skylights provide illumination for the sanctuary. Inside, Sudler used glass test tiles from the Denver Art Museum project to face the altar. (Sudler worked with Gio Ponti on the original DAM building.) A parish center building was constructed nearby in 1974, featuring stucco walls with decorative granite strips.

6   Martin Luther King Library
9898 E. Colfax Avenue, Aurora
Brendle APV, 2004

As part of Aurora's plan to redevelop what it calls Original Aurora, the city selected Brendle APV to design a building to add a contemporary touch. The library design incorporates dark ironspot brick, aluminum, and glass-walled forms that appear to slice through the building on the diagonal. The architect selected pale blue glass, used in generous sheets that lift the building's roofline and include color in a powerful way. This Neomodern design brings light into the library, while providing a welcome contrast to nearby Fletcher Plaza and other developments in the area that have not been as successful in making old and new coexist in harmony.

7   Aurora Municipal Justice Center
14999 E. Alameda Drive (at Sable Boulevard)
Skidmore, Owings & Merrill, 1989

At 65 feet high and 785 feet wide, the justice center's dome when constructed was the largest dome built of precast concrete in the United States. But that does not mean the center is pompous. This three-story complex – courtrooms, a detention center, and police dispatch center – seems low to the ground. The complex is designed around a large central entrance under the dome, which was painted green to evoke the feel of aged copper.

Although the interior is primarily made of the same precast, it is warmed by light woods, brass, and accent points of dark green marble. Under the dome is a terrazzo floor with a starburst design at the center; look up throughout the building and you'll see grids of the same light woods used in furnishings. Niches in the rotunda allow for informational displays and artwork.

8 **Aurora Municipal Center**
  15151 E. Alameda Parkway
  Barber Architecture, 2003

While Skidmore, Owings & Merrill create a justice center that retains a human scale despite its size, the precast concrete municipal center nearby goes for full-blown monumentality. Between the office space and parking structure, this immense complex features two five-story office wings connected to a curved, glass-walled six-story central building that sports a large concrete cornice. This reinterpretation of Neoclassical style for a civic building is understandable, if not entirely successful. Still, the new municipal center allowed the city of Aurora to consolidate numerous departments into one facility. The location of this mega-city hall places it adjacent to other city buildings, giving this municipality a civic core.

9 **Anschutz Medical Campus / Fitzsimons Army Medical Center**
  Bounded by East Montview Boulevard, Wheeling Street, East Colfax Avenue,
  and Peoria Street, Aurora
  Various architects

New medical buildings for clinical care, education, and research have created an instant city on this former military medical center, with buildings that (for the most part) adhere to design guidelines intended to deliver clean, contemporary structures made of brick, stone, metal, and glass. Divided into zones for specific uses, the Anschutz Medical Campus – still called Fitz by many people – serves more than 500,000 people each year and eventually can grow to a projected 6.5 million gross square feet.

When the University of Colorado Denver decided to move its medical education and health-care operation out of Denver to its Aurora campus, it left behind numerous empty buildings at East 9th Avenue and Colorado Boulevard. Substantial gifts from the Anschutz Foundation won naming rights for the new Aurora campus, which housed a sprawling army medical center until it was decommissioned in 1995. In late 2005, the first two privately funded medical buildings opened, beginning the transformation of one square mile of former military outpost and alfalfa fields into a shining mini-city. Construction stalled until the Colorado Supreme Court declined to review a challenge to keep the state from using certificates of participation to fund public facilities on the site.

After that, the new medical campus boomed, with outpatient and inpatient pavilions, two hospitals (including one, Children's Hospital Colorado, that has already built a new East Tower), several research towers, and a VA hospital pushing beyond the campus's boundaries. Clinical buildings are to the south of campus, research facilities to the northwest, and educational centers are to the northeast. Parking is mainly pushed to the outer limits, which creates a true internal campus but also turns parking structures into visual blocks. To the north of the campus, a new bioscience park has taken off.

At the center of it all is Building 500, the old Fitzsimons Hospital, designed by an unknown architect (probably someone with the Army Corps of Engineers), and constructed of buff/blond brick with touches of sandstone and a white marble entry. Building 500, which dates from 1918, is linked to new buildings by quadrangles and commons. The campus's master plan was devised by Perkins & Will.

9.1 – The Barbara Davis Diabetes Center, Anderson Mason Dale Architects:
This privately financed center was among the earliest buildings to open on the Anschutz Medical Campus. It is notable for its prominent and welcoming stair tower, buff-colored brick exterior, clean Modernist lines, varied window heights, and an amoeba-shaped playhouse sited off the front facade.
AIA Denver Merit Award, 2005

9.2 – University of Colorado Research Complex I, Fentress Architects with Kling Stubbins, followed by Research Complex II by the same team: The first research tower designed by the Fentress team is connected to a second complex by pedestrian bridges in order to bring together 20 research departments. These sleek buildings are marked by varying heights and design elements that relate, but do not mimic each other.
AIA Colorado Citation Award, 2007

9.3 – The Nighthorse Campbell Native Health Building, MOA Architecture:
The most expressive building on the medical campus, and one of the first, serves American Indians across the country. Designed by a Native American–owned firm, it seeks to blend new technology with the symbolism and patterns related to Native American traditions and the impact of nature. Thus the main entrance faces to the east and the sun, and circular elements are repeated throughout, including a council ring, a rotunda topped by a tepee-shaped skylight, and an auditorium that suggests a kiva.

9.4 – University of Colorado Hospital, architects involved in its five building components include Perkins + Will, HDR Architecture, Anderson Mason Dale Architects, Davis Partnership Architects, and H+L Architecture: The UCH components – Anschutz Inpatient Pavilion, Cancer Pavilion, and Outpatient Pavilion, Rocky Mountain Lions Eye Institute, and Leprino Office Building – share a similar palette in terms of the use of rosy-colored brick with metal accents. Notable is the contrast of curves that define some facades, set against other buildings' more angular presence, plus the links formed to knit separate structures into a whole.

9.5 – Center for Dependency, Addiction, and Recovery (CeDAR), Anderson Mason Dale Architects: The aptly named CeDAR is a low-slung, predominantly wood complex that looks more like a mountain resort than a residential addiction treatment facility. Its buildings cluster around courtyards and paths that offer clients opportunities for meditation and exercise. CeDAR taps into history by incorporating the old Commander's House, now called the Lori Wolf House.

9.6 – Children's Hospital Colorado, Zimmer Gunsel Frasca in association with H+L Architecture: The designers used a brighter, more-orange brick for Children's than the ruddy material favored by the University of Colorado Hospital. A rhythmic metal canopy marks Children's presence on East 16th Avenue, though one of its two parking structures hides some of that from the road. Children's is designed to appear as a clutch of smaller buildings, with curved metal elements and brick walls that aim for a softer appearance. The interior is colorful, and includes numerous pieces of art. An East Tower Addition, completed in 2012, was designed by the same team.

9.7 – Fulginiti Pavilion, NAC Architecture: On a campus of giants, this gem-like pavilion is designed to serve staff at all facilities by offering programs on medical ethics. The pavilion, named for a former chancellor of CU's School of Medicine, also includes an art gallery.

9.8 – The Denver VA Hospital, or Replacement Medical Center Facility, H+L-SOM-CRA-SAM A Joint Venture: Scheduled for completion in 2016 after delays over funding, this giant facility will include several separate buildings linked by a lengthy concourse. Entry will be from Wheeling Street.

Southwest

1 Loretto Heights University / Teikyo Loretto Heights University / Colorado Heights University
3001 S. Federal Boulevard
F.E. Edbrooke and Co., 1891

Frank Edbrooke was adept at both academic and commercial buildings, and in the "Old Main" for what was then Loretto Heights University he worked in a traditional Richardsonian Romanesque style in vivid sandstone. Religious imagery abounds on the administration building, which brought the concept of the massive all-purpose educational building to this part of Denver. The dormers at the inner edges of the front bays seem especially small compared to the gables with which Edbrooke topped the wings, while the tower seems almost out of scale with the rest of the building.

In 1989, Teikyo University of Japan purchased the Loretto Heights campus from then-Regis College, adding another branch in a worldwide chain of schools. The school changed its name in 2009.
National Register

1.1 – May Bonfils Stanton Center for the Performing Arts,
3001 S. Federal Boulevard, Musick and Musick, 1963: Colorado Heights University's performing arts center sits on a recessed site to the south of the administration building. Musick and Musick crafted the structure of red brick, with walls that play off of angles toward the side and around to the back, which rests at the
bottom of a hill. The dominant feature of this Modern structure is a curved white wall toward the front, signaling a metaphorical arched stage.

2 Fort Logan National Cemetery and Field Officer's Quarters
3698 S. Sheridan Boulevard (cemetery), 3700 and 3800 blocks of
West Princeton Avenue (buildings)
Frank J. Grodavant, 1889

Fort Logan was established in 1887, though the burial spot first used in 1889 did not become a national cemetery until 1950. More than 50,000 veterans and their families lie at rest at Fort Logan, in a stretch of land marked by a simple entry facility. The fort was named for General John Alexander Logan, who served in the Civil War and who later issued the order that established May 30 as a day in which veterans' graves were to be decorated – Decoration Day, the precursor to Memorial Day.

A few historic buildings – officer's row – have survived, and these former homes are used by several social service and health agencies.
Denver Landmark, National Register

3 **Mile Hi Church campus**
7077 W. Alameda Avenue, Lakewood
Thomas William Hite (spider building), 1973; Brendle APV (administration building), 1998; Fentress Architects (sanctuary), 2008

The universal symbol of the dome conveys a message of welcome, unity, and inclusiveness, whether it tops a civic building or a religious structure. At Mile Hi Church, an inclusive congregation west of Denver, two domes help spread the word.

The first is the unusual original building – Thomas Hite's bright, white creation, which features a shallow dome set upon a frill of slender arched buttresses that serve as legs. All church functions were housed there. Years later, Brendle APV added an administration building built around a series of elliptical shapes; inside are meeting and event rooms. The structure is primarily white, with some accent colors. And years later still, Fentress Architects gave the church the large sanctuary it needed for a growing congregation, again marked by a dome that makes this complex stand out.

For both domed buildings, ingenious construction strategies are as important as the architecture. To construct Hite's thin-shell concrete exterior, workers built a huge, hard-packed mound of earth, then poured the concrete over it; the dirt then was scooped and jack-hammered out. For the Fentress building, workers inflated the fabric roof membrane to a height of 60 feet. The membrane was insulated and reinforced with steel rebar and a concrete coating to form the dome, which is surrounded by a brick structure that includes the entry, prefunction activities, and circulation.

4 **Light of the World Catholic Church**
10306 W. Bowles Avenue, Littleton
Hoover Berg Desmond, 1985

Neomodernism built out of the most ancient of materials is the hallmark of this suburban religious structure. Though sheltered from West Bowles Avenue, Light of the World sports a tower that serves as a beacon to parishioners and neighborhood alike.

This asymmetrical glass-topped spire caps the sanctuary, while areas of serenity – including a building-length colonnade – provide spaces for reflection. Buff brick and honey-colored block join with glass for the exterior, while the simple interior relies on finely crafted wood as decoration. Simplicity and elegance mark this contemporary interpretation of a house of worship.
AIA National Honor Award, 1990; AIA Colorado 25 Year Award, 2011

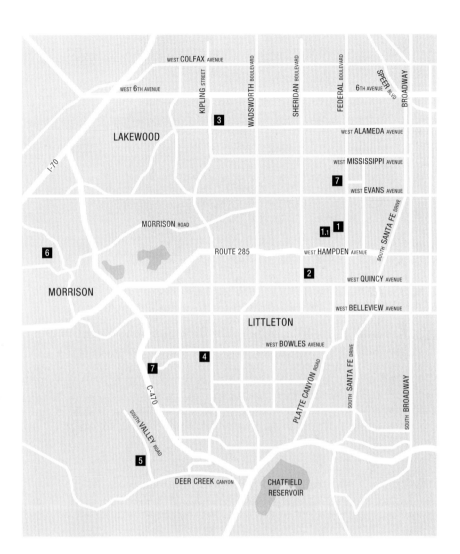

LIST OF BUILDINGS

1 Loretta Heights University / Teikyo Loretta Heights
University / Colorado Heights University
1.1 May Bonfils Stanton Center for Performing Arts
2 Fort Logan Cemetery and Field Officer's Quarters
3 Mile Hi Church campus
4 Light of the World Catholic Church
5 Martin Marietta / Lockheed Martin Space Systems
Company
6 Red Rocks Amphitheatre
7 Dakota Ridge High School

5 **Martin Marietta / Lockheed Martin Space System Company**
12999 Deer Creek Canyon, Littleton
The Architects Collaborative (TAC), 1976

Built as the result of a design competition on a stunning section of the old Ken Caryl Ranch, the headquarters for Johns-Manville was yet another architectural approach to ways in which new technology meet natural beauty.

While I.M. Pei chose to work into Table Mesa in Boulder for his National Center for Atmospheric Research, The Architects Collaborative balanced this long, slender structure atop a ridge near the hogback that is one step away from the Rockies. At one end, the architects did appear to spear the hill, shooting the shaft of aluminum into a portion of the dramatic natural setting.

Ribbon windows run the length of the facade (the halls are about one-quarter mile long), while at one end concrete piers appear to keep the building from tumbling down the mountain. A reflecting pool is designed in two levels to make it seem as if the water is falling off the horizon. As at NCAR, a winding approach is part of the design, allowing the building to appear like a shining gift at the end of the road. Parking is at the rear of the building.

TAC was founded in 1946 by Walter Gropius and a collection of young architects; Gropius died in 1969, and this building is attributed to Joseph Hoskins, with William LeMessurier named as structural engineer.

A decade after the building opened, a sentinel for a vast field of rock formations and wildlife, Johns-Manville's financial demise led to a sale of the structure to Martin Marietta. In 1995, a merger turned that firm into Lockheed Martin.

6 **Red Rocks Amphitheatre**
Red Rocks Park, Jefferson County
Burnham Hoyt, 1941; Sink Combs Dethlefs, 2003

Three decades before Hoyt created his stunning outdoor theater, singers (including Mary Garden and Nelli Melba) had visited the site and commented on the perfect acoustics of the place, set as it was between red-rippled stone outcroppings.

Pushed as a resort development as early as 1904, the parkland (at one point called Garden of the Titans) was not bought by the City and County of Denver until 1928. Parks manager George Cranmer proposed building an open air theater, and through the labor of Works Progress Administration and Civilian Conservation Corps workers, Red Rocks Amphitheatre opened in 1941. Boulders were blown up and the ground cleared to make way for Hoyt's handshake with nature.

Hoyt's genius was to design a theater, orchestra pit, and planter boxes in such a way that the sandstone complex looked as if it had grown on the spot, emerging from the earth just as the stones around it had. Historians say he followed the pattern of the Dionysiac theater at the Acropolis in Athens. Concertgoers need to know only that it is like no place else to see a show.

Over the years, there were additions – mostly bad – including a stage overhang that is just factory-issue metal. Then, in the early 1990s, promoters asked for an expansion.

A few years later, the city sought to make Red Rocks "pay" by allowing corporate logos to be beamed on the rocks. That plan, and a proposal to turn planter boxes into elite seating, went down in flames after an international outcry that the simple beauty of Red Rocks was in danger of obliteration.

A new visitor center (restaurant, gift shop, rental space, and plazas) solved the issue of increased revenue for a venue with a short booking season for concerts and films. The center, first proposed in 1991, basically is hidden from view, built into the side of a hill and topped by a plaza and a circular tower that allows elevator access to facilities below. Construction on that plaza, and that building, follows the lead of the amphitheater, with the same rusticated red sandstone, installed in the same horizontal style and topped by a two-layer cap of stone. Also added were restrooms – lots of restrooms – finished in Cortez slate and red oak. Eroding soil was stabilized and shored up along the south slope. And new seats made of plantation-raised hardwood replaced old splintery wooden planks.

The usual approach to designing an addition to a landmark building is to make the new look distinctly different from the old. In this case, though, allowing the visitors center to follow the dictates of the amphitheatre was the right thing to do. The improvements melt into the background, allowing the beauty of nature – and Hoyt's sure-footed design work – to be the stars of the show.
Denver Landmark, National Register

7
Dakota Ridge High School
13388 W. Coal Mine Avenue, Littleton
Klipp, Colussy, Jenks, Dubois, 1996, with a new wing in 2006 also designed by that firm

Explosive growth in the southwestern part of the metro Denver area prompted construction of mega-high schools designed to accommodate the booming population of outlying areas such as Jefferson County. This included Dakota Ridge High School, a sprawling but well-organized educational complex that offers basic materials, intriguing shapes, and a general sense of spatial well-being. Set against the foothills, Dakota Ridge projects a neutral palette that makes it appear to be part of the land.
AIA Colorado Citation Award, 1997

Southeast and Denver Tech Center

These instant "places" called Edge Cities tend to have catchy names leaning toward the bucolic or the futuristic: Meridian, Greenwood Plaza, Inverness, Interlocken. But what they are is business parks, neither urban nor totally suburban in design.

Pioneering developer George Wallace had a more simple approach toward his project: Just call it what it is. And that was the Denver Technological Center. The Tech Center, split between Greenwood Village and Denver, was an early attempt to put a city – its offices, hotels, and shops, anyway – outside of the traditional urban setting. Broad expanses of green and great looping parkways run through the Tech Center, which began in 1961 with a 40-acre purchase of Arapahoe County farmland and now covers more than 800 acres.

Nine years later, John Madden stepped up to the plate with plans for the Greenwood Plaza Business Park, a 200-acre project that includes copious scattered artwork as well as buildings with an occasional European flair.

Since then, other office park/retail developments have sprung up, offering clean and sterile environments in which to do business. Recently, more residential projects have become part of the mix, allowing workers to live close to work and avoid the daily grind of a highway commute. Trees have matured, giving these business parks a softer look and feel.

The buildings noted here center on the Tech Center and Greenwood Plaza, with the exception of an entry in Inverness.

Along with the introduction of residential opportunities in the area's business parks, another advance has become apparent in this part of the outer metro area: The growth of Denver's ring "cities" along a southeast to southwest band has brought a new maturity that makes an arts center and community hub seem as natural as a sprinkler system. There are two new cultural centers – one in Parker, one in Lone Tree – as well as a museum devoted to wildlife. in an area of "new" cities (Lone Tree, Centennial) and not just edge cities, this is a pleasant, yet not surprising development. Where people go, the arts follow.

LIST OF BUILDINGS

1	4600 S. Syracuse
2	One DTC
3	5555 DTC Parkway / The Kodak Building
4	Great West Life
5	161 Inverness Drive West / ICG
6	Kent Denver School
6.1	The Student Center for the Arts
6.2	Kent Denver School Dining Hall
7	The Blue Cube
8	Littleton Church of Christ
9	Wildlife Experience
10	U.S. Drug Enforcement Agency
11	Parker Arts, Culture, and Events Center
12	Lone Tree Arts Center

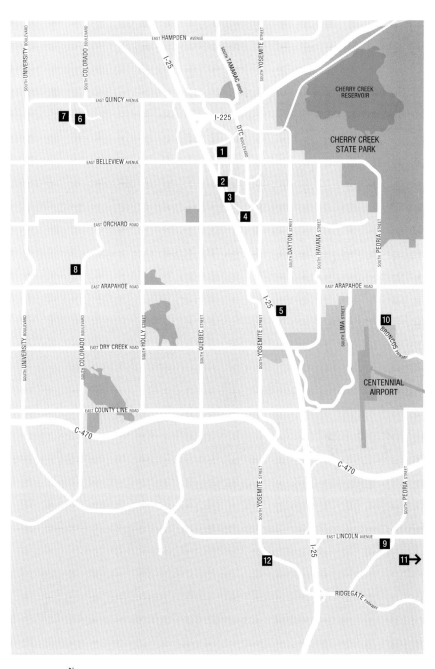

1 **4600 S. Syracuse**
4600 S. Syracuse Street
Jon Pickard Architects, with C.W. Fentress J.H. Bradburn Associates, 1999

Among the more recent Tech Center buildings is a project in which a square tower merges with a seemingly protective (and taller) curved structure – and the curve triumphs.

Jon Pickard Architects worked in finely detailed metal and glass for this sculptural design, although glass appears to predominate. The 13-story building tops out with a clerestory level atop the curved edge, giving a distinctive look to a building that stands out for its clean lines and contemporary materials.

2 **One DTC**
5231 DTC Parkway
C.W. Fentress and Associates, 1985

Subtlety in the Tech Center? In the 1980s? It happened with One DTC, an office building defined by the artful use of two colors of granite to delineate a structure rounded at one end and carved into a series of setbacks at the other. The rhythmic stack of ribbon windows is interrupted only at the elevated base and toward the top, where indentations appear to form a circle for two floors. It's as if a giant hand had squeezed this building, then released it so the windows could flow again.
AIA Western Mountain Region Merit Award, 1986

3 **5555 DTC Parkway / The Kodak Building**
5555 DTC Parkway
Carl Worthington, with Lusk and Wallace, 1969

Architect Carl Worthington was there at the beginning, from 1961, as George Wallace developed his alternative to the evils of doing business downtown. Worthington planned the Denver Tech Center site, as well as designing landscaping and many of its buildings.

Among them is the structure first known as the Kodak Building, though Kodak is long gone as a tenant. Unlike many of the Tech Center's glitzy mega-buildings, DTC 5 is a low-slung structure of exposed aggregate and precast concrete. The design stresses horizontality broken in strategic places by banks of windows and the occasional tower.

Worthington tucked parking under the building, which sits on recessed piers – a first for the suburbs, he has said. Since the design also appeared to nestle the back of the building into the site, the structure does not appear to be sitting on stilts.

4 **Great West Life**
8505, 8515, and 8525 E. Orchard Road
WZMH, first two components in 1985; third tower, Anderson Mason Dale Architects, 1999

For years, Great West Life was the matched set of shimmering silvery semicirculartowers – great bands of reflective glass and aluminum sited along Interstate 25.

Though a third tower long had been planned, the economy was not yet right. Developers, however, did work to make the complex a little less chilly when encountered close up. In 1993, landscape architects Civitas and artist Larry Kirkland reworked the plaza between the first two buildings to add humanizing elements. When the effects of the late 1980s oil bust wore off, the third tower finally went up, creating an impressive sight when driving along a stretch of territory rich with flashy buildings. Great West's composition sets the towers slightly canted on the site, yet allows them to work together as an ensemble.

5 **161 Inverness Drive West / ICG**
161 Inverness Drive West, Englewood
W. Stephen Wood, with C.W. Fentress J.H. Bradburn and Associates, 1998

When the steel on the ICG headquarters began to shoot from the ground, eyebrows shot up: The skeleton looked as if were going to support a building that would tilt over the highway. Was this the Leaning Tower of I-25?

That is exactly the effect the architects were striving for: a dramatic presence along Interstate 25 that would afford fabulous views for those inside and command attention from those traveling by. Add to that the impact of bands of black glass, which made it appear as if cars' reflections were traveling up and over the building, and the building years later still has a certain impact.

The building is another example of a structure in which separate forms appear to pass through each other, in this case a rectangle in textured black granite moving through a bowed-out semicircle in polished black granite. An unbroken facade addresses the highway, with an entry plaza and parking at the back.

6 **Kent Denver School**
4000 E. Quincy Avenue, Englewood

Kent Denver was formed in 1974 when two earlier private schools – Kent School for Girls and Denver Country Day School – united in buildings on former farmland in Englewood. The campus aesthetic centers on red brick on two levels or clusters, including two distinctive new buildings, both designed by Semple Brown Design:

6.1 – The Student Center for the Arts, 2006: Long and low and seeming to take over its site, the center for the arts features curved elements and a glass-lined lobby that showcases activity inside the building.
AIA Denver Merit Award, 2008; AIA Colorado Merit Award, 2009

6.2 – Dining Hall, 2011: Across campus, this light-filled LEED Platinum certified building sports peaked roofs supported by large clerestories and glass doors that sweep open to link to the exterior. An interior green wall adds to the sense of modernity in this structure, which is both school cafeteria and the site of meeting rooms.

7 **The Blue Cube**
14 Random Road, Cherry Hills Village
Michael Brendle APV, 2004

Turn onto Random Road, a winding lane off of East Quincy Avenue, and you are in high-end rural America, with imposing Colonials, important mid-century Modern homes, and newer villas. But then you are stopped in your tracks by a futuristic contemporary residence clad in aluminum panels and dark brick, with the addition of blue-colored glass. This assemblage of geometric forms has become known as the Blue Cube, and for good reason. An unusual addition to the neighborhood, this home is all about volume and massing, arranged one-room deep to optimize light and views in all directions – especially in the more public areas located on the upper level. The overall form resolves in an area that is a blue glass cube, a statement that combines a traditional geometric object with a forward-thinking interpretation.
AIA Denver Citation Award, 2003

8 **Littleton Church of Christ**
6495 S. Colorado Boulevard, Centennial
Semple Brown Design, 2006

Semple Brown's sizable addition to the church did more than expand the sanctuary and other facilities. The project also pushed most parking to behind the building, capitalized on views of the mountains, added intriguing randomly placed windows, and created a smart interplay of materials (wood, concrete, glass) and well-proportioned geometric forms and planes. A curved concrete wall to the north helps point congregants to the rear of the building for parking and for a large children's play area.

9 **Wildlife Experience**
10035 S. Peoria Street, Parker
Klipp Colussy Jenks Dubois, with Overland Partners of San Antonio, Texas, 2002; addition, klipp architecture, 2007

The design for this privately funded museum plays off the rolling prairie around it, stressing as much as possible a sense of the horizontal – especially in the shape and treatment of the sandstone used in exterior and interior walls.

From East Lincoln Avenue, the exterior appears to turn its back on the street; precast walls, in a color that matches the Douglas County soil, are accented by touches of copper on curved roofs and towers.

The museum exterior gives little clue of what waits around the corner, so to speak, except for sloping rooflines that signify a theater and an events hall. That is, until a visitor goes around back and enters through two dusky concrete walls off the parking lot; beyond that is a courtyard nestled between arms of the horseshoe-shaped building. Broad expanses of glass allow a view of the interior through an impressive, soaring wall. Bronze sculptures of wildlife dot the campus. An addition to the museum, designed by the same Denver firm, houses new installations that stress topography, geography, and climate.

10 U.S. Drug Enforcement Agency
12154 E. Easter Avenue, Centennial
Gensler, 2009

This new four-story office building presents two personalities. Buff brick facades appear to be wrapped in a steel and glass envelope, which adds a touch of Neomodern flair not only to the project but also to an office park filled with forgettable buildings. The project – developed as a GSA design-build lease-back competition – earned LEED Silver certification. This building is an unexpected pleasure to encounter, in the same vein as the FBI Denver Field Office in Stapleton. It also has the same level of high-security fencing.

11 Parker Arts, Culture and Events Center
20000 Pikes Peak Avenue, Parker
Semple Brown Design, 2012

Parker has been around for decades, but growth has created a part of downtown that is stunningly new. Still, buildings there try very hard to look historic, with faux-Victorian facades and lots of elaborate trim. Into this semi-imaginary land has sprung a building with strong contemporary lines, an arts center that is new and happy to appear that way.

Semple Brown Design's concept for the Parker Arts, Culture, and Events Center, or PACE, relies on sleek forms and honest materials. These include reddish brick (shades of historic structures in the area) and rusted and weathered metal panels – many of them perforated – that contribute character and richness. This building was the focus of community planning for more than a decade, and that care and concern is evident in the PACE's choice of site and its relationship to the key nearby road called Mainstreet. Generous windows and an amphitheater link the center to its surroundings, making it seem at home with both old and new Parker.

12 Lone Tree Arts Center
10075 Commons Street, Lone Tree
Westlake Reed Leskosky of Cleveland, Ohio, in association with
Tryba Architects, 2011

Lone Tree chose a site for its new arts center that is quite different from that in Parker. The Lone Tree Arts Center is tucked into a shopping center that is at one end of the growing RidgeGate development (RidgeGate Investments contributed the land).

If location makes this arts center a little hard to find, it has one element that sets it apart: a massive metal roof that envelops the building, a mix of gambrel and folded plate that makes it seem as if the roof is going to swallow the center. Built of stone and stucco and featuring sweeping windows, the center is attractive in an anonymous kind of way – until you focus on the giant roof that reaches down and out into forms shaped like prows. It is an eye-catching element that gives the project some personality, stuck, as it is, in a commercial setting. The center also establishes connections to the outdoors through a folding glass wall that opens onto an outdoor terrace theater.

Boulder and North

1 The University of Colorado
Boulder, 1876–present
Architects: various

Like many universities, CU began as a one-building institution, and like many schools of the era, CU's first building was a Victorian pile that housed classrooms, administration offices, and everything else. The state legislature founded CU in 1861, parceling out to Boulder one of the major institutions in Colorado.

Boulder architect E.H. Dimick designed Old Main, which opened in 1876, with a sandstone base, red brick walls, a hipped roof, and twin towers. Buildings added after that, in stop-and-go fashion, included the president's residence (1880, Ernest P. Varian), Woodbury Hall (now Woodbury Arts and Sciences, F.A. Hale, 1890), and Gove and Walsh's magnificent Collegiate Gothic Macky Auditorium, where ground was broken in 1907 but, because of a wrangle over a bequest, the building was not completed until 1922. (Other architects represented during this era were Jacques J.B. Benedict and James Murdock.)

But the eclectic look of the growing campus (everything from Neoclassical to Richardsonian Romanesque) did not please George Norlin, professor-turned-university, president. In 1919, Norlin hired Charles Z. Klauder, of the Philadelphia firm Day & Klauder, to create a master plan and design guidelines for the burgeoning school.

Klauder at first proposed Collegiate Gothic, a campus style that had found favor around the United States. But as memories of travel in Italy's northern hill country formed an overlay on the realities of Boulder's topography, Klauder instead devised a type of Tuscan vernacular for the CU campus: rose and buff sandstone and limestone buildings (drawing heavily on the Lyons sandstone and Ingersoll sandstone quarried nearby), built to conform to a low, human scale with a sense of basic symmetry.

"Klauder style" sandstone was laid horizontally with broken edges emerging from the mortar, carefully crafted to have a natural look. The roof of choice throughout was red tile. Black forged iron provided accents, as did Indiana limestone (now, often precast concrete). Distances between buildings could vary, making some intimate and creating public spaces between others.

As explained by former campus architect William Deno, Klauder wanted his buildings to be aligned along the edges of open spaces, forming an architectural wall enclosing the space. Klauder, in effect, built his own little hill town right by the Flatirons.

Before Klauder died in 1938, he designed 15 buildings; they include the liberal arts building, now Hellems Arts and Sciences, 1921; a wing on the library now known as University Theatre, 1924; the Natural History Museum, now Henderson Museum, 1937; what is now Ketchum Arts and Sciences, 1938; Norlin Library, 1939 (unsympathetically renovated in 1977, when its east facade was enclosed); the University Faculty Club, now the University Club, 1939 plus residence halls and additions.

When the firm Trautwein and Howard took over design for CU, the Klauder "look" began to deteriorate (buildings by Trautwein and Howard range from the 1940s' Aden, Bracket, Cockerell, Reed, Crosman, and Farrand Halls, all in association with Temple H. Buell, to the 1960 Astro-Geophysics Building).

Soon the varied array of styles was again reined in. In 1960, the school commissioned Sasaki, Walker, and Associates of Watertown, Massachusetts, with consulting architect Pietro Belluschi, to create a new master plan. After that, many different architects would be brought in to build projects that had to be approved by a design review committee established in 1964. That committee, the second-oldest campus design oversight body in the country, has urged modern architects to work within the Tuscan vernacular realm while maintaining a contemporary vision.

The newer buildings on campus include structures that range from distinctive to surprisingly conservative:

1.1 – The Engineering Sciences Center, 1965, Architectural Associates of Colorado, W.C. Muchow, partner-in-charge, with Fisher and Davis, Haller and Larson: This reinforced concrete structure pulls together many parts, a Historicist single-pitch roof in red tile, a dramatic reference to the state's mineshaft heritage, all accented with stone to match the exteriors of older buildings. (In 1992, C.W. Fentress J.H. Bradburn contributed the nearby University of Colorado Mathematics Building and Gemmill Engineering Library, which emphasized the Tuscan aspects of campus while adding a quadrangle that replaced a parking lot.) *Engineering Sciences Center: AIA Award Recipient*

1.2 – The Joint Institute for Laboratory Astrophysics (JILA), Harry Weese, 1966, tower by Harry Weese (Weese, working in concrete and sandstone, also designed the 1965 Laboratory for Atmospheric and Space Physics, and the 1971 Duane Physics Building and Muenzinger Psychology Building): Weese's Modernist masterpiece was expanded through the 1989 addition and brick-paved plaza designed by Anderson Mason Dale – an overhaul that produces the initial impact of a stone temple. Underground oil storage tanks are camouflaged by a plaza, and a pumping station hidden – a design, in effect, that pulls together the entire complex.

1.3 – Visual Arts Complex, OZ Architecture (Denver) with Kalmann McKinnell & Wood (Boston), 2010: For years, CU's art students and faculty labored in the nondescript Sibell-Wolle Building, which had been overhauled from an old engineering building into the home of art and art history instruction and the university's art museum. Now the CUAM (CU Art Museum) and the departments of art and art history are housed in a new two-building complex connected by a bridge, the replacement for the demolished Sibell-Wolle Building. This new complex is a surprisingly conservative structure, considering that it serves as home for pursuits that tend to be a bit more free-form in thought and intent. But OZ Architecture and Kalmann McKinnell & Wood took the safe route, managing to follow the dictates of CU's preferred materials and yet erase much of the Tuscan aura without stepping into modernity. The plus side: The CU Art Museum now has wonderful gallery space, generously proportioned and well organized in terms of flow. It's an actual museum, which CU, with its large and diverse collection, has never had before. The complex is LEED Gold certified.

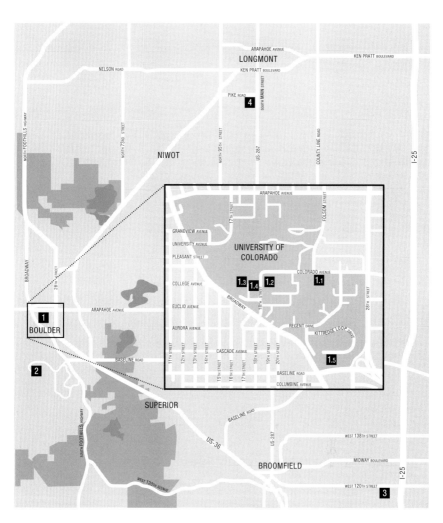

LIST OF BUILDINGS

1   The University of Colorado
1.1 The Engineering Sciences Center
1.2 The Joint Institute for Laboratory Astrophysics (JILA)
1.3 Visual Arts Complex
1.4 ATLAS (Alliance for Teaching, Learning, and Society)
1.5 Wolf Law Building
2   The National Center for Atmospheric Research
3   Avaya Inc.
4   Prospect New Town

1.4 – ATLAS (Alliance for Teaching, Learning, and Society), Downing Thorpe James (DTJ Design), in association with CommArts, Inc., Sparling, WSDG, JVA, and the RMH Group, 2006: This building adjacent to the Visual Arts Complex exhibits a bit more contemporary flair than its neighbor while keeping within the overall campus aesthetic. Perhaps it's because ATLAS includes more rich red sandstone used as panels and surrounds. Or perhaps it's because ATLAS has a tower intended to serve as both beacon and broadcaster. But this hub for information technology seems to be a better fit for its purpose of campus-wide teaching and learning. ATLAS also is LEED Gold certified – the first certification for a CU project. Both the Visual Arts Complex and ATLAS are next to the Euclid Street parking structure.

1.5 – Wolf Law Building, Davis Partnership with Centerbrook Architects (Connecticut), on the Kittredge Road loop, 2006: This imposing (some might say magisterial) building keeps to the basic materials that define this campus. But its placement across the street from the old Fleming Law Building instantly demonstrates a big drawback: Fleming has that low-rise, human-scale massing that ties CU together, while the Wolf Law Building is all about verticality, despite its many setbacks in an attempt to minimize its bulk. It's as if the University of Denver's mission to look like the University of Oxford had suddenly wafted north to CU, turning welcoming residence halls and classroom buildings into mega-blocks. The Wolf project has achieved LEED Gold certification.

2 The National Center for Atmospheric Research
Table Mesa Road, Boulder
I.M. Pei & Partners, 1961–67

Carter Wiseman's book *I.M. Pei: A Profile in American Architecture* sums up the designer's goal with this complex: to make the building appear part of the site. As Pei said: "When you're confronted with nature – such power and beauty – you just don't try to compete with it. You try to join with it, and this is exactly what we tried to do."

A search committee of deans from the architecture schools at institutions represented by the University Committee for Atmospheric Research chose Pei to fulfill the dream of committee director Walter Orr Roberts: build a laboratory space deep in the heart of nature. (NCAR is managed by the University Corporation for Atmospheric Research – UCAR – a nonprofit consortium of more than 100 North American university members and affiliates.)

Pei, the modernist, turned to ancient design forms to comply. (Apparently he had visited Mesa Verde before launching the NCAR project.) His center is a bit cliff dwelling, a bit Stonehenge, a bit any building that forms itself to the earth or from the earth. Rather than fight the Flatirons, Pei worked with them.

The center rises on a mesa overlooking Boulder. Two five-story tower complexes are connected by a two-story center section. Blank walls are given life by a play of verticality against horizontal shelves and lids (Roberts and the other scientists wanted a lot of book and blackboard space, thus few windows). A few curves punctuate what is overall a building of angles and stark sculptural shapes.

The reinforced concrete used in construction is made from stone aggregate from Lyons, concrete "bush-hammered" to expose the stones through grooves made by a pneumatically powered tool. If the material was chosen to make NCAR appear part of the site, the approach was designed to add pure drama: NCAR sits alone on Table Mesa, approached by a long and winding road that builds suspense and anticipation.
AIA Colorado 25 Year Award, 1997

 ### 3 Avaya Inc.
1300 W. 120th Avenue., Westminster
Kevin Roche John Dinkeloo Associates (KRJDA), 2001

This Avaya research and development facility is notable for two reasons: This spin-off from Lucent Technologies is housed in a glass and metal building whose atrium rises like a truncated cylinder with a convex roof that looks like a satellite dish. And it is notable because in an area filled with small-scale retail and residential, Avaya looks as if it had descended from another planet. But, no: It was just the firm's attempt to give this R&D facility a look unlike anywhere else.

Avaya for years was located in a concrete building behind the glass palace (the older building was sold in late 2012 for warehouse, office, and light industrial uses). But management wanted innovative, high-tech work designing new communications tools to be done in a building that reflected what was going on inside. The result is a soaring glass atrium from which two, four-story glass wings emerge to link to parking structures. The building's glass exterior curtain wall and skylights use a clear anodized aluminum frame and gray-tinted, ceramic-fritted glass, although apparently a dozen types of glass are used throughout the facade to address insulation and other solar issues.

KRJDA designed several all-glass buildings for Lucent during this period, stressing openness, flexibility, and views, which in the case of Avaya in Westminster, is the Rocky Mountains to the west.

4 Prospect New Town
Pike Road at U.S. Highway 287, south of Longmont
Development planned by Andres Duany and Elizabeth Plater-Zyberk, 2004

The Denver metro area is awash in new infill developments, from Lowry to Stapleton to Belmar. But while most of these New Urbanist–influenced projects carry a paint box filled with various shades of beige, Prospect is awash in color.

From 80 acres of farmland, John (Kiki) Wallace has developed a high-density "new town" that reflects New Urbanism with a sense of humor. It's Pee-Wee's playhouse turned neighborhood, a place filled with quirks in what seems like the middle of nowhere. The streets have funny names: Tenacity Drive, Neon Forest Circle, Confidence Drive, 100 Year Party Court. The homes may rest on Victorian roots, and sport large front porches and alley access for garages, but architectural features often are exaggerated, and the color palette is bold and bright. Homes are near a "downtown" edge of commercial enterprises, but homes are the most important thing in Prospect, a small-scale flash of color on the plains.

Colorado Springs

1 Air Force Academy Campus and Chapel

Entrances off of Interstate 25, Colorado Springs
Walter Netsch, Skidmore, Owings & Merrill, built 1956–62, first occupied in 1958

When the air force wanted to show its independence from its army air corps past, officials sought to establish a high-profile academy. The location would be away from the Eastern Seaboard, and the style would not be drawn from the Romantic Historicism of the past; the look would be modern and the materials heady with high technology and the magic of flight.

That was no small burden for one school to carry, but the result was startling and, eventually, timeless. Through a competitive process that produced bitter tangles with conservative military and legislative leadership, the academy supporters finally settled on Skidmore, Owings & Merrill (SOM) and designer Walter Netsch. (Among those vying for the commission: Frank Lloyd Wright.)

The solution was to create a campus of buildings that accentuated the low-slung, clean lines of the International Style – structures that held their own against a mountain backdrop but that surely did not fight it. They were constructed on several levels, with the administration building, chapel, and social center grouped around a Court of Honor, cadet quarters, and classrooms below, with parking at the base.

In their quest for a visionary project, the architects drew on the prevailing design ideas of the day, bringing in Walter Dorwin Teague Associates, for instance, to add industrial design finesse to furnishings and interiors, and film great (and showman) Cecil B. DeMille to whip up uniforms.

The centerpiece of the 17,000-plus-acre campus is the standout academy chapel: an aluminum-clad structure topped by a series of 17, 150-foot spires composed of more than 100 tetrahedron planes. Metal and stained glass stand in for stone in this 20th-century interpretation of a cathedral, a soaring testament to might, Modernism, and humanity's growing reliance on technology.

In 2012, work began on a new building that marks SOM's return to the academy campus: The Center for Character and Leadership development will feature that same low-slung concrete base, keeping in scale with the firm's designs of half a century ago. The center will be topped with a soaring glass element that is trained on Polaris, the North Star, and the academy's symbol of the characteristics inherent in future leaders.
Air Force Academy Chapel: AIA 25 Year Award, 1995

LIST OF BUILDINGS

1   Air Force Academy and Chapel
2   Colorado Springs Fine Arts Center
3   Edith Kinney Gaylord Cornerstone Arts Center
4   The Broadmoor

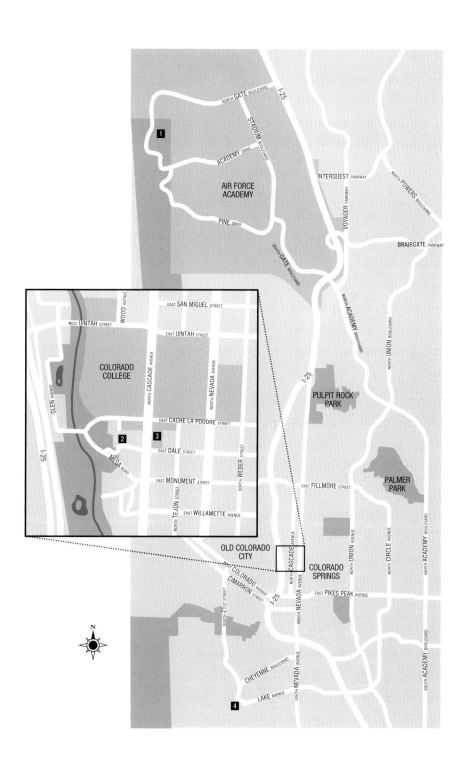

2 Colorado Springs Fine Arts Center
30 W. Dale Street, Colorado Springs
Original building, John Gaw Meem, 1936; addition by David Owen Tryba
Architects, 2007

John Gaw Meem gave the Colorado Springs arts community – and dedicated donors – a complicated building that mixes Moderne and Pueblo influences so that the result shares both Modernist and traditional traits. The Colorado Springs Fine Arts Center's calm yet impressive appearance was almost lost, though, when a thoughtless board and a badly informed director wanted to expand the center by putting an addition right in front, obscuring what made the center so elegant – in effect, to kill it in order to cure the problem of not enough space.

There was great hue and cry, and the project was changed, but the price tag grew. It became apparent that anything this despised was not a design that would prompt big donations. The Fine Arts Center hired David Owen Tryba Architects to create an addition that would indeed provide more space but through a design that complemented Meem's beautiful building. And officials brought in a new director, who arrived in 2003 and began to focus on the collection, while raising money for an addition.

The Tryba team reorganized the place (theater functions at one end, visual art at the other), extended the long corridor that runs from east to west as a major connector, and placed the bulk of the new art space far enough back on the property that the stucco-covered mass is only quietly apparent when viewed from the front. A new glass and metal corridor supports Meem's formed concrete building with its exuberant aluminum trim, and leads to a grand staircase that connects two levels of gallery space. The new building neither dominates nor defers to Meem's design.

A 1970s addition was lost, as were some mature trees; the space for outdoor sculpture was reduced. But more exhibition space was provided that also could inlcude revenue-producing events. In the end, by expending as much time and thought on a project as money, the solution was an addition that in some ways looks as if it had always been there.
AIA Denver Honor Award, 2007

3 Edith Kinney Gaylord Cornerstone Arts Center
825 N. Cascade Avenue, Colorado Springs
Antoine Predock of New Mexico, with AndersonMasonDale Architects, 2008

A decade before this arts center opened, Colorado College hired architect Antoine Predock to fill a prime location near arts-related sites such as Packard Hall, the Worner Center, and, a mere block away, the Colorado Springs Fine Arts Center. Planning had begun even earlier, as the school cited the need for a place that could house interdisciplinary education as well as performance spaces. The hiring of a new president slowed things down, since he wanted to study planning for the entire campus. The Cornerstone Arts Center was put on hold. Three years later, the project was a go, though the design had changed somewhat.

Still, the arts center has the free-form feel of a Predock project: a rambling, multidimensional complex comprising an assemblage of forms in cast block, stucco, and glass at the north end, and an elongated, almost sloping woven-copper-covered extension at the south. The building is unified by a copper prow that grows out of the metal-clad section and appears to shoot out over the rest of the structure. Inside, the feeling is one of openness, and circulation comes via catwalks, which lead a visitor up and around what seems like a giant atrium. The overall impact is a sense of airiness contained in an industrial building – a fitting stage for the creation of art.

  The Broadmoor
1 Lake Avenue, Colorado Springs
Warren and Wetmore, 1918; later additions by Carlisle B. Guy and Associates (Broadmoor West, 1976), Carlisle B. Guy and Edwin Francis (the International Center, home of the imported English pub The Golden Bee,1961), and A.G. Jan Ruhtenberg (the Carriage House Museum, 1936)

How to define the Broadmoor? The height of quiet, old-money luxury? A hub of numerous recreational activities? A microcosm of Colorado Springs' history? All three will do. Built to replace an earlier resort, the Broadmoor was the dream (and investment) of Colorado Springs magnate Spencer Penrose, who moved to Colorado from Philadelphia and left a huge impression on the state. Spencer Penrose founded the El Pomar Foundation, among other civic and investment activities, and his wife, Julie, was a cofounder of the Colorado Springs Fine Arts Center.

But the Broadmoor, which has grown substantially over the years, is also a beautiful soft pink stucco cocoon, a place that hews to an Italian style, sited on a human-made lake, and set against the mountains. To create this place of understated grandeur, with its numerous levels of red tile roofs and delicate decorative elements, Penrose hired architects Whitney Warren and Charles D. Wetmore, who had designed the elegant Grand Central Station and the Ritz-Carlton and Biltmore Hotels in New York. What they produced – which has been expanded and upgraded many times over the years – is a place that reflects a different time, a European style that meets modern expectations. The main building retains its quiet sensibilities and its historic grace, even as its architectural vocabulary has been extended to newer areas.

Rest in Peace

Boom.

Not that it's ever quite that short and sweet, but the noise and dust of an imploded building or the aftermath of the wrecking ball holds a certain fascination for the human psyche. It also can leave a hole in the physical manifestation of a city's aesthetic evolution.

Unfortunately, many wonderful buildings in Denver have been razed for little reason at all. Oh, there always was a reason given at the time, and to many people it seemed a simple matter in terms of the advancement of commerce.

Higher and better use. Progress. Botched business deal. Fads in what is considered a good building and an eyesore. Occasionally, a structure would be so compromised physically that it would be put down before it could hurt someone. In that category was the 1865 Constitution Hall, mortally wounded by fire in 1977. Or maybe, something was just old, or in the way. The 27 square blocks flattened during the Skyline Urban Renewal Project in Denver, which got rolling in 1968, were considered blighted and in need of cleansing and rebuilding. A mere 30 years later, the initial Skyline project – Lawrence Halprin's Skyline Park – was "reconfigured" into a flat piece of ground that still attracted the "wrong" kind of people, the same people that led Denver's business and political leaders to basically bastardize the park.

The Tabor Opera House, a huge step forward for Denver in 1881, came down in 1964, as the city began to reinvent itself. Fancy downtown picture palaces have been lost, along with structures as diverse as the showy mansions on Grant Street and the gritty viaducts in lower downtown.

But Denver, like other western cities, often has not known what to do about historic buildings and the concept of preservation. King of the prairie. Man's home is his castle. Property rights über alles. All are certainly stout tenets of the lingering scent of Manifest Destiny, embodied in continued resistance to the city's landmark ordinance. But in this city, the real bêtes noires have been benign neglect and silly schemes.

A sampler:

– Cause of death: The tangled business deal.

1 Central Bank
15th and Arapahoe Streets

If a Neoclassical gem such as Jacques J.B. Benedict's 1911 Central Bank could come down, what did that mean for less beloved structures? A lot, actually. In the case of Central Bank, the institution, the owner, the lender, and an insurance company were in a knot over loans related to the building (most of the parties were based out of state). The issue wound up in court, when the city and the Denver Urban Renewal Authority sued to stop demolition. Denver mayor Federico Peña tried to stop it, too, but nothing worked – not even the clamor of demonstrators who formed a ring around the building.

In 1990, Central Bank was gone – leaving a plot of land still empty (it's a parking lot). The one bright spot: Talks between property owners and preservationists commenced shortly afterward – primed with a grant from Central Bank. This effort culminated at the end of 2000 with the formation of a uniquely constructed Downtown Denver Historic District.

– Cause of death: Inability to appreciate an architectural period, with symptoms of greed and fuzzy logic.

Mid-century Modernism in Denver has taken more than its share of hits, as structures such as the hyperbolic paraboloid and Boettcher School fell to make way for blemishes upon the civic landscape. One was replaced by a glitzy hotel lobby – financed with public money, thank you – the second by a parking lot and then a medical building.

2 Wallbank House
825 S. Adams Street

Why, you might ask, would someone tear down a masterpiece, and replace it with something of much less architectural value? Because they can. Tician Papachristou and Daniel Havekost designed the Wallbank House in 1958, and it exhibited all the best aspects of Usonian Style: generous windows, a sense of openness, and horizontal lines that made it seem one with the earth. But Belcaro, a neighborhood filled with Modern treasures, has attracted home buyers who want things that are, well, more modern. When it came to the community's attention that the new owner of 825 Adams was going to raze the home and replace it, an area resident applied for historic designation. Legal issues mounted; a Denver city councilman wailed about private property. Eventually, the applicant withdrew the request, and in 2011, the residence was demolished, to be replaced by a very large and very undistinguished house.

3 Skyline Park
Arapahoe Street between 15th and 18th Streets

Lawrence Halprin's plan for a park involved constructing a sophisticated urban canyon, with terraced interior walls and block-built fountains, all protected by side berms and generous landscaping. (The plan was created in conjunction with the overall Skyline Urban Renewal Project program developed by Marvin Hatami of Baum, Polivnik, and Hatami, and Floyd Tanaka of Tanaka and Associates.)

Over the years, a once-loved open space became a much-hated area, blamed for attracting the homeless and scaring visitors with the perception of crime. Downtown business interests and the city of Denver in 2001 held a competition to rework Skyline. A partial reconstruction by Thomas Balsley Associates opened in 2003; Skyline was brought up to grade, a fountain removed, and the result is neither fish nor fowl. Gone was the city park that looked like a park in the city. And though then-mayor John Hickenlooper said at the "new" park's opening that funding would be found to finish the part, that (no surprise) has not happened.

4 Zeckendorf Plaza / Hyperbolic Paraboloid
16th Street at Court Place

Before there was an Adam's Mark Hotel (now a Sheraton), there was a four-part complex called Courthouse Square. Constructed between 1954 and 1958, it included a Hilton Hotel (the slab), a May D&F store (the box), a skating rink (the plaza), and a glass-walled entry structure with a thin-shell curved concrete "floating" roof (the hyperbolic paraboloid). The slab and the box remain, though the metal panels on the box's gridded exterior have been replaced by glass.

The plaza and the hyperbolic paraboloid were lost in the mid-1990s, when an out-of-town hotel architect came to Denver with a plan and a hand out for urban renewal money. Fred Kummer got his money, and the city of Denver lost the paraboloid to a showy, could-be-anywhere hotel lobby fronted by a sculptural grouping of very thin ballerinas. The paraboloid's unusual roof shape reportedly

was the widest-spanning paraboloid in the country when constructed. Developer William Zeckendorf had asked architect I.M. Pei to design the geometrically intricate project. Pei biographer Carter Wiseman credits the plan to Pei, the box and unusual entryway to Henry Cobb, and the slab to Araldo Cossutta.

When the store closed, development pressures increased to create something flashy at the upper end of the 16th Street Mall. Though ideas came forward to use the paraboloid as a nightclub or a hotel lobby, the complex's new owner decided that would not do. It was not big enough. The hotel needed something new. Efforts to landmark the project failed. Though Mayor Wellington Webb had promised to support the city's landmark commission in that process, that zeal evaporated and the Denver City Council turned thumbs down on protecting the plaza and paraboloid. The structure was demolished in 1996, a slow process that left many marveling at the paraboloid's sleek skeleton – too little, too late.

5   Boettcher Elementary School
1900 Downing Street

Denver residents in 1938 had turned down a bond issue to building a school for "crippled children." But philanthropist Charles Boettcher contributed money for a structure that has been called the first U.S. school specifically designed for students with disabilities. Burnham Hoyt designed his 1940 International Style school with a green-and-white concrete exterior of sleek lines and low silhouettes. Inside, terrazzo was plentiful, and ramping systems were made to look streamlined and organically related to the design. Other noteworthy features included an exterior Art Deco clock.

The school had been built near Denver's Children's Hospital so that medical resources were close at hand, via a basement tunnel. But years later, Boettcher School fell victim to the old idea of "kill the messenger": The Denver Public Schools sold Boettcher – mainstreaming of special-needs students was the educational mode by the 1980s – to Children's Hospital. A move to designate the building a landmark failed. Worse, those who had been students there turned out in force to urge the building's demise. Hate the education, hate the school. Boettcher was demolished in 1992, replaced by a parking lot and then another medical building.

6   Denver Motor Hotel
1420 Stout Street

Cities under the sway of the automobile found different ways to approach the concept of parking. In Denver, one of the first of the downtown parking garages went the Art Deco route, in a six-story structure of gray brick with terra-cotta trim. The facade of G. Meredith Musick's 1928 Denver Motor Hotel sported a sunburst frieze with wings at both corners of the roof. The spirited decoration was lost when the building was demolished to make way for a new hotel close to the Colorado Convention Center.

7 Currigan Exhibition Hall
1324 Champa Street

Many buildings were lost because of construction of an expanded Colorado Convention Center, which opened in 2004. Foremost among them was the 1969 Currigan Exhibition Hall, designed by the team of Muchow Associates (administration); James Ream and Associates Architects (design); Haller and Larson (production and supervision); with Karl Berg, George Hoover, Edward Tower (development); Ketchum, Konkel, Barrett, Nichol and Austin (structural engineer); and space trusses by Burkhardt Steel Co.

This elegantly simple building was clad in Cor-Ten steel, and sported the world's largest rigid space frame at the time of construction. Currigan Hall was an engineering pioneer, and brought together a stellar team of architects and designers to produce a building that reveled in the exploration of new technology. Currigan was built through a design competition, and early computers were used to check calculations made during the design and engineering process.

But when the original Colorado Convention Center was built in the late 1990s, Currigan's fate was pretty much cast in stone. The convention center's planned expansion would wipe out Currigan, and the city and convention center architect said Currigan could not be incorporated into the new project.

The interior offered exhibitors 100,000 square feet of airy column-free space, with pyramidal canopy lights that could be raised and lowered to define displays. The exterior was another matter. It mixed the solidity of steel designed to achieve a rusted, protective patina and a big concrete base, with a lacy roofline that opened up to reveal a space frame composed of about 24,000 steel members. Slit windows and metal panels emphasized the hall's vertical strength, while that floating cornice gave the hall a sense of dominance of its site. That was not enough to save it, and it came down.
Western Mountain Region Honor Award, 1969; AIA Denver 25 Year Award, 1998; awards from the American Institute of Steel Construction for design and engineering, and the American Consulting Engineers Council for design

– Cause of death: Progress, or new beats old.

8 Judicial Heritage Center
between East 14th Avenue and East 13th Avenue on Broadway

Denver does not have many quirky buildings, and we lost two of the best when state officials cleared a site for the new Ralph L. Carr Justice Center. What a shame. Where a huge complex now sits, threatening to dominate Civic Center, Rogers Nagal Langhart's 1977 buildings were low, gray, and in shapes that encouraged nicknames. (The firm is now RNL Design.)

The two gray buildings that made up the Judicial Heritage Center were dubbed "the toaster" and "the typewriter" because of their striking shapes and stark

contrast to the other more Classical civic buildings in the district. "The toaster" was home to the state's supreme court and legal staff, a building that rose out of the surrounding plaza to form a narrow three-sided structure open at the center. "The typewriter" was the Colorado Historical Society and museum-boxy building that led to a plaza on East 13th Avenue.

Also lost was an important mural by Angelo di Benedetto, which told the history of justice across the globe and was installed on the ceiling of the void area of the toaster. Those building the new Carr Center said there was asbestos in the mural's panels, and it had to be destroyed.

9 Daly Insurance Building
1576 Sherman Street

Into the nearby sea of limestone government buildings, a dash of modernity proved welcome with the 1959 completion of the Daly Insurance Building. Designed by the preeminent Denver firm of James Sudler Associates as a loft office of three stories with a capacity for eight, the Daly had as its most notable feature a sunscreen made of precast concrete discs on a screen of aluminum rods. Aside from adding shade to the building, the screen provided decoration somewhere between whimsical and stunning, as it appeared to float over the recessed ground floor. But in 2002, the building received a disc-ectomy, when more than 1,400 concrete circles were plucked off the building. The building had been sold to an engineering firm, and the new residents said the discs were intrusive in terms of light. The architect on the project was Blue Sky Studio.

10 Public Welfare Building
Cherokee Street at West 8th Avenue

What began as a city structure eventually became part of the Denver General Hospital campus, now the Denver Health and Hospital Authorities. Architect Victor Hornbein had accentuated technology in this 1947 project, a concrete and brick building in which intermediate floors were suspended from the top by cables, giving a cantilevered look. But Denver Health is always expanding, and Hornbein's structure was demolished and replaced by a forgettable building less than 60 years later.

– Cause of death: Not seeing the forest for the trees, or, what were they thinking? Nothing good.

11 Bosler House
3209 W. Fairview Place

Landmarked in 1984, this home was built in 1875 (in some reports) by one of the founders of the town of Highlands, Ambrose Bosler. The home's imposing Italianate style and rich red brick make it stand out on a site at the end of

Highland Park. Over the years, it has watched over the neighborhood, with several uses. Until a few years ago. An owner who had worked on restoring the home took off the roof and didn't provide protection for the open spaces below. Work stopped. He came to the Denver Landmark Preservation Commission asking for permission to demolish the home because of economic hardship in continuing repairs and maintenance. The commission, not surprisingly, said no. So there it sits now, rotting, deteriorating, and looking very lost. There is a remedy, but it has not been taken: The city of Denver has the authority to enforce appropriate care of a landmarked building, and notes that neglect is not a reason for demolition. What happens next is the question.

12 Harlequin Plaza
7600 E. Orchard Road, Greenwood Village

Among the projects John Madden promoted in Greenwood Plaza was a 1983 building by Gensler and Associates that became a frame for a work of art. Harlequin Plaza not only housed a museum, its dramatically angled gray reflective glass sides wrapped around a spectacular plaza painted in the traditional Harlequin pattern of black-and-white diamonds.

But the plaza, created by the SWA Group of Sausalito, California, lost out to a business deal; new owners preferred a traditional rustic grove of trees and standard pavers, and installed such in 1998. Since then the Museum of Outdoor Arts has moved to civic offices in Englewood, though Gensler's now Harlequin-less Harlequin Plaza still shines up from its slightly recessed location.
AIA Colorado Design Award, 1984

13 Boettcher Center for Science, Engineering, and Research
2050 E. Iliff Avenue

This 1962 Modernist complex (designed by the noted architectural firm of Perkins & Will, with the Denver firm of Fuller, Fuller, and Fuller) for years sat proudly on the University of Denver campus. It announced the school's (and the state's) interest in being a leader in research and development. Its three finely detailed precast concrete units contained classrooms, a library, offices, and an auditorium – all linked by arcades and set around a courtyard/plaza. When an application was made to designate this assemblage of buildings a Denver landmark, DU pushed back and applied for a Certificate of Non-Historic Status for the East Building so it could demolish that part of a distinguished architectural composition that remained timeless in style. Despite fervent opposition by the preservation community, the designation went nowhere, and the east building fell in 2010 – demonstrating that sometimes campuses might be better off if they did not have a campus architect. A compromise between the school and the preservation contingent led to the site of the former East Building becoming campus open space.

*– Cause of death: Lack of vision and no sense
of the value of adaptive reuse.*

14 University of Colorado Medical Center / Health Sciences Center
4200 E. 9th Avenue
1925 through early 1990s, various architects

This former beehive of medical activity has evolved over three quarters of a
century, after horse-trading and fund-raising brought it to its east Denver location.
At the turn of the 19th century, four rival medical schools in Boulder and Denver
sought funding and respectability. The eventual winner was the University of Colorado, which to consolidate its clinical and academic resources settled at East 9th
Avenue at Colorado Boulevard.

But as the center grew, it bumped into the boundaries formed by the surrounding
neighborhood and other medical institutions. With growth impossible, the decision
was made to move the university's medical center to the former Fitzsimons Army
Base in Aurora, which had been closed during a sweeping series of changes
during the Base Realignment and Closure movement of the mid-1990s. As the
medical and support facilities moved to a shiny new campus, the buildings and
land left behind became eyed for development purposes.

Shea Homes proposed one scheme that would have added a town center,
numerous residences, and the introduction of a street grid to align with the
neighborhoods around the medical center. That fell through, a victim of the
economy, and another firm took up the challenge, then saw its backer break
off on his own to propose a major multi-use development. Along the way, it
became apparent that few of the historic buildings or distinctive Modernist
structures were going to survive for adaptive reuse, leading to a major civic
brawl over the fate of two buildings. As with everything at the now-quiet
medical center, things have been in flux as the deterioration continues.
No vision has emerged to repurpose buildings that have years of life in them.
What a waste.

Among the buildings affected are:

**14.1 – Skaggs School of Pharmacy, Colorado Boulevard at East 8th Avenue,
JH/P, 1994:** When the University of Colorado consolidated the offices of its
School of Pharmacy, it commissioned JH/P to design a place that would incorporate labs and classrooms with public spaces open to the environment
and amenable to artwork. The designers responded by saving a grove of trees at
one corner of the property, which had sheltered Carl A. Reed's stone, concrete,
and bronze *Arch of Cosmos and Damian*. The building proper seems to float over
the site, set up on corner concrete piers and lightened even further by the generous use of glass for walls; lower corners are recessed, while the upper edges
strive for a seamless mesh of glass panels.

14.2 – University of Colorado Hospital and Research Wing, 4200 E. 9th Avenue, Schmidt, Garden, and Erikson, 1965: The Chicago architects found a way to add movement and visual appeal to this complex of buildings, which includes an imposing six-story building on the north side of East 9th Avenue as well as a five-story bridge building over that street. The solution: horizontal louvered panels, which form a skin for the bridge building and accent the former hospital. The lower level of the main building is unprepossessing brick, allowing a broad overhang and canopy – dotted with bubble-style skylights – to create a strong sense of arrival.

The Hornbein and White Buildings

Targeted for demolition during the years of the first campus redevelopment plan, these Modernist structures failed to achieve landmark status despite a push by supporters. They have been vacant since the Health Sciences Center moved to a new home in Aurora.

14.3 – University of Colorado Medical Center Division of Child Psychiatry Day Care Center, East 8th Avenue at Birch Street, Victor Hornbein and Edward D. White Jr., 1962: A standout in the welter of massive medical facilities is Hornbein and White's supremely human-scale building. Along with sophisticated Modernist lines and ample, thrusting overhangs in concrete that set off the defining brick material, the architects also included a bit of whimsy, in the form of a vaguely floral stylized motif incised around the concrete cornice. Even the gates are wonderfully detailed, in an irregular sort of checkerboard pattern.

14.4 – JFK Child Development Center / JFK Center for Development Disabilities, 4399 E. 8th Ave., Victor Hornbein and Edward D. White Jr., 1968: Home to a series of health-related organizations, this six-story tower reads as a series of stacked horizontal forms, with extended levels built of custom oversize bricks to remain compatible with the nearby Child Psychiatry Day Care Center. Rooted in the Usonian Style, the building brings distinction to a campus that is an eclectic medley of architectural approaches.

Photography Credits

Photographs in this guidebook are by Charles J. Cordina AIA, except for those on the pages listed below, which were taken by or provided by the noted architectural firms. All images are reproduced by permission.

Cover photography:
Doug Pensinger/Getty Images, Martin Plaza (front cover), Alan G. Gass, FAIA, Denver City & County Building (back cover)

Interior photography:
Stuart Alden: p. 2, p. 88, p. 98, p. 150, p. 180, p. 198, p. 220, p. 231 (#1.1), p. 254, p. 280, p. 296
Marek Zamdmer/I.M. Pei & Partners: p. 8 (#1)
Guy Burgess: p. 9 (#3)
Alan G. Gass, FAIA: p. 9 (#4), p. 17 (#21), p. 26 (#38), p. 34 (#53), p. 50 (#19), p. 61 (#4), p. 64 (#11), p. 65 (#14), p. 68, p. 72 (#1, #2), p. 73 (#4), p. 76 (#10), p. 78 (#13), p. 82 (#21), p. 83 (#23), p. 84 (#27), p. 86 (#33), p. 102 (#1.3), p. 118 (#9, #10), p. 121 (#21), p. 122 (#23, #24, #25), p. 123 (#26, #27), p. 128 (#3), p. 132 (#9), p. 141 (13), p. 147 (#32), p. 154 (#4), p. 156 (#9), p. 157 (#12), p. 166 (#4), p.167 (#11), p. 177 (#6), p. 186 (#6.3), p. 196 (#14, #16), p. 197 (#19), p. 202 (#1), p. 205 (#10), p. 206 (#13), p. 213 (#5, #6, #7), p. 214 (#8), p. 219 (#14.10, 14.11), p. 225 (#3.2, #3.6), p. 232 (#2), p. 235 (#9, #10), p. 242 (#9), p. 251 (#13), p. 259 (#5), p. 269 (#3, #4), p. 276 (#2), p. 301 (#4), p. 305 (#2), p. 306 (#6), p. 307 (#7), p. 308 (#11), p. 309 (#13)
Ron Pollard: p. 10 (#7), p. 62 (#8), p. 105 (#5), p. 141 (#12), p. 216 (#13), p. 266 (#1.3), p. 285 (#6). p. 286 (#7, #8), p.287 (#11)
Frank Ooms: p. 11(#8), p. 27 (#40), p. 35 (#55), p. 48 (#15), p. 74 (#5, #6), p. 75 (# #7, #8), p. 82 (#19), p. 86 (#34), p. 94 (#6), p. 96 (#9), p. 97 (#11), p. 107 (#9), p. 142 (#17), p. 156 (#10), p. 203 (#5), p. 204 (#6), p. 249, p. 258 (#1), p. 259 (#6), p. 260 (#7), p. 300 (#2)
Ron Johnson: p. 10 (#5), p. 285 (#5)
Jim Bershof: p. 14 (#15), p. 33 (#52), p. 43 (#3), p. 46 (#11.3), p. 48 (#16), p. 50 (#21), p. 61 (#5), p. 63 (#10), p. 64 (#12), p. 66 (#16), p. 67 (#18), p. 78 (#14), p. 82 (#20, #21), p. 92 (#1), p. 93 (#3, #4), p. 104 (#3.2), p. 111 (#18), p. 116 (#1), p. 120 (#18), p. 121 (#22), p. 139 (#6), p. 155 (#8), p. 158 (#15), p. 165 (#3), p. 167 (#6), p. 170 (#13), p. 176 (#3), p. 177 (#4), p. 184 (#1), p. 185 (#3), p. 186 (#6.1, #6.2, #7), p. 192 (#1, #3), p. 193 (#5), p. 194 (#6, #8, #9), p. 212 (#1, #4), p. 233 (#5), p. 242 (#8), p. 243 (#12), p. 268 (#2.1)
W.C. Muchow & Partners: p. 15 (#17)
Jack Pottle/Esto: p. 16 (#19)
Robb Williamson: p. 26 (#39)
Nick Merrick/Hedrich-Blessing: p. 28 (#42), p. 250 (#9, #11), p. 286 (#9)
Thorney Lieberman: p. 31 (#46), p. 247 (#3)
Jackie Shumaker: p. 32 (#50), p. 110 (#17)
Andrew Browning: p. 48 (#14)
Richard Canfield: p. 49 (#18)
Elizabeth Gill Lui: p. 52 (#27), p. 204 (#9)
KWAL Photography: p. 61 (#6)

Garen Chucovich: p. 62 (#7)
Steve Chucovich: p. 197 (#17)
David Lynn Wise: p. 62 (#9)
HOK Sport/Thorney Lieberman: p. 65 (#15), p. 109 (#15)
Fred Fuhrmeister: p. 67 (#17)
LaCasse Photography: p. 76 (#9), p. 85 (#30), p. 86 (#32), p. 106 (#6, #7), p. 107 (#11), p. 170 (#14)
Paul Brokering: p. 77 (#12), p. 260 (#10)
Nic Lehoux: p. 79 (#15.2), p. 251 (#12)
Craig Rouse: p. 79 (#16), p. 202 (#3.1), p. 217 (#14.2)
Raul J. Garcia: p. 80, p. 204 (#7)
Jason Knowles/Fentress Architects: p. 81, p. 272 (#9.2)
Greg Sprenger: p. 95 (#8)
Mortenson Construction: p. 96 (#10)
Peter Grimes: P. 105 (#4)
Sergio B: p. 108 (#12)
T. S. Gordon: p. 109 (#16)
Brendan Herrington: p. 111 (#20)
SA+R staff: p. 111 (#20)
Dennis Humphries: p. 117 (#6), p. 240 (#1), p. 242 (#10)
Greg Hursley: p. 119 (#13), p. 197 (#18), p. 205 (#12), p. 206 (#14) p. 276 (#4), p. 300 (#3)
AndersonMasonDale: p. 120 (#16), p. 272 (#9.1)
Brian Sendler: p. 129 (#5)
Root Rosenman Architects: p. 155 (#5)
Ken Paul: p. 156 (#11), p. 271 (#8)
The Denver Zoo: p. 158 (#14)
Dana Miller: 196 (#15)
Mayra Galvez: p. 205 (#11)
D.A. Horchner/Design Workshop: p. 204 (#8)
Michael Brendle Associates: p. 216 (#13)
Continuum: p. 248 (#5)
RTD: p. 250 (#8)
Jeff Sheppard: p. 250 (#10)
James Ray Spahn: p. 258 (#2)
Jim Berchert: p. 259 (#4)
Fred Coester: p. 260 (#8)
Jeff Butler: p. 276 (#3)
Robert Schmid: p. 278 (#5), p. 284 (#2), p. 309 (#12)
Gensler: p. 287 (#10)
Kevin Reeves: p. 288 (#12)
H+L Architecture: p. 292 (#1.1)
Robert Benson: p. 292 (#1.3)
Casey Cass: p. 294 (#1.4)
Jeff Goldberg/Esto: p. 294 (#1.5)
I.M. Pei & Partners: p. 305 (#4)

Index